Bertolt Brecht

Titles in the series Critical Lives present the work of leading cultural figures of the modern period. Each book explores the life of the artist, writer, philosopher or architect in question and relates it to their major works.

In the same series

Bertolt Brecht

Philip Glahn

REAKTION BOOKS

To Nell

Published by Reaktion Books Ltd
33 Great Sutton Street
London EC1V 0DX, UK

www.reaktionbooks.co.uk

First published 2014

Printed and bound in Great Britain by Bell & Bain, Glasgow

A catalogue record for this book is available from the British Library

ISBN 978 1 78023 262 1

Contents

Brecht in Berlin, 1927.

Introduction

Throughout his life and work, Bertolt Brecht demanded that all artistic action, especially his own, be useful: not only practical and applicable for the people who make up its public, but also relevant to them in their respective times. Brecht's own ongoing actuality and usefulness lie in his continuing struggle with history as an evolving, emancipatory immersion in the processes of producing narratives and experiences, images and fantasies. This book is an account of Brecht's work and life pursued from the core of his belief that theory and practice, the ideal and the real, art and life, need to be understood in their interdependent relationality, a position of tension and movement from which to see and act, learn and teach. Brecht historian Hans Mayer observed, 'One still writes about the epic theatre without having studied its dialectics.'[1] The task of this book is to apply Brecht's practice to its own historicization, not in order to add another or tell a more 'real' or 'true' story, but to assess the contemporary relevance of Brecht's work through a close study of the dialogue between the writer and playwright and his time, and how this dialogue can be extended to the concerns and tasks of our own. To look at Brecht's plays and stories, poems and political essays in history is to trace a lifelong attempt at forging productive relations to specific social, economic and political circumstances. These circumstances, framed by two world wars, the Weimar Republic and a global depression, Nazism and exile and the East German version of socialist reality, made for a project that sought to shed light on and at the same time intervene in the ongoing crisis of modern life shaped by capitalist economics, nationalist visions and social utopias.

Brecht is mainly known for his experimental, modernist Epic Theatre and its *Verfremdungseffekt*, the 'alienation effect' or strategy of estrangement. He wrote in 1927 that 'the essential point of the Epic Theater is perhaps that it appeals less to the feelings than to the spectator's reason. Instead of sharing an experience, the spectator must come to grips with things.'[2] At its core, Brecht's approach constitutes an attempt to show the viewer the relations of power and the mechanisms of reality, to lay bare the device. His method aims to situate both artist and viewer within and in conscious relation to the historical present in order to illuminate a position of active, critical involvement in the knowing and making of the world. Exposing social norms and 'truths' as historically determined and culturally produced shows them to be malleable and thus sheds an emancipatory light on the viewer's own agency.

As Jan Knopf and other historians have pointed out, Brecht was far from the staunch Communist or doctrinaire Marxist that much post-war scholarship made him out to be. Rather, he struggled mightily with his role, and with the analytic and productive tools he sought to apply and distribute. He was concerned with access to the various ways and arenas in which common sense and ideas, attitudes and perspectives are made and communicated. Thus his work included songs and poems, essays and letters, speeches and editorials, short stories and novels, radio broadcasts and films. Rather than tell his audience what to think, he asked them to sing and speak and act along with and against the conventions of making histories and identities. For Brecht, the public sphere, that hallowed ground of bourgeois society, was a space of class contestation, a site where instead of preserving social values and communal ideals, coalitions were to be formed. Brecht took pleasure in finding ways to intervene in, turn around and use as weapons the images, languages and gestures of philosophers and beggars, bureaucrats and thieves, priests and workers, to cleverly pit expectations and customs against one another in order to show the limits of communicative and experiential structure and to subsequently articulate the possibilities of their transformation. The results are scenes, chapters, declarations, rhymes and questions that are at once funny and tragic, technical and moving, popular and complex, always sharp, accessible and full of pleasure for the contradictions of being an active part in the very production of history.

Although most Brecht scholarship is limited to theatre studies, his widespread influence – and, often, the misinterpretation of his methods – can be traced in Europe and the u.s. through art and theatre to film and social theory. In the late 1930s, the seminal u.s. critic Clement Greenberg praised Brecht's poetry and politics for its formal innovation, 'despite' its author's ideological leanings. In the 1950s, Brecht's Berliner Ensemble troupe took post-war Paris by storm with productions of *Mother Courage* and *The Caucasian Chalk Circle*. Under Roland Barthes' tutelage, the journal *Théâtre Populaire* devoted its entire January–February 1955 issue to 'The Brechtian Revolution'. Barthes was himself very much influenced by the German playwright's work, and went on to pen multiple essays on him and credit him as a decisive element in his own intellectual formation and the birth of semiology.[3] In the socially and politically engaged counter-cultural climate of the 1960s, Brecht's dissolution of canonical ideas concerning the place of stage and audience, performance and reception, and his introduction of the 'everyday' as a political and social concept – his attempts to turn 'oil, inflation, war, social struggles, the family, religion, wheat, the meat market [into] subjects for theatrical representation' – enjoyed great popularity.[4] One of the most thorough and critical implementations of Brecht's 'political modernism' is found in the French cinema around Jean-Luc Godard and in 1970s British film and theory, particularly in the pages of the journal *Screen*, which in turn had a great impact on American artists like Yvonne Rainer. Griselda Pollock and Sylvia Harvey have assessed Brecht's considerable influence on the making and study of 1970s British film in general and feminist practice in particular.

In the U.S., Brecht's works and theoretical writings were published in translation, and his plays were frequently performed as off- and on-Broadway productions, influencing artists from the San Francisco Mime Troupe to Bob Dylan. Brecht was discussed in *Studies on the Left*, *Partisan Review*, *Aspen*, *Evergreen Review*, *Studio International* and *Artforum*, among other publications. His name was equally ubiquitous (if usually as a passing reference) in art journals and artists' interviews, and his theoretical writings and dramatic strategies were debated by artists and writers including Andy Warhol, Michael Fried, Dan Graham and Lee Baxandall. Meanwhile, Herbert Marcuse and Louis Althusser discussed Brecht as a timely facilitator of an art that, as Marcuse advocated, 'spark[s] action, practice . . . break[ing] through this universe of mental and physical pollution in which we live'.[5]

In her 1982 'critical recovery' of Brecht, entitled 'Whose Brecht? Memories for the Eighties', Sylvia Harvey points out that as history's contexts change, undertaking the Brechtian task of 'knowing the world' as a step towards critical intervention and transformation means first acknowledging the contingency of both the world and the task.[6] The 'questions that enable actions', as Brecht put it, are always asked from positions specific to their circumstances of formation, so the enquiry must begin with 'Who is asking, and when?' Similarly, in the 1990s, Fredric Jameson and Terry Eagleton argued for the ongoing validity of Brechtian methods. In *Brecht and Method* (1998), Jameson introduced the term 'actuality', referring as much to the material praxis of Brecht's theories as to their timeliness (*Aktualität*).[7] As an extension of Brecht's dialectical approach to viewing the world, a contemporary critical assessment of his life and work has to take into account today's specific historical

PARIS APPLAUDIT BRECHT

context, because it is only with our current set of sociopolitical and cultural circumstances and potentials that Brecht can be judged as relevant, as *aktuell*.

This book is arranged chronologically, tracing Brecht's engagement with the thought and politics of his time, with a modern world passing through several waves of upheaval and various permutations of psychosocial order and disorder. In his major dramas as well as lesser-known poems and prose, letters and diary entries, Brecht confronted war and the wheat market, folk culture and mass communication, the pleasures of learning and sports as a dramatic model; he collaborated with Erwin Piscator and Kurt Weill, studied Karl Korsch and Chinese theatre, joined forces with Walter Benjamin and Ruth Berlau and argued with Theodor Adorno and Thomas Mann. But this book is also informed by

Brecht's focus on *das Werdende* – an understanding of the world as in a constant state of becoming. Though the focus of this book is on Brecht's life, work and times, its methodology expands the scope of enquiry to points of historical continuity and rupture, exposing Brecht's work as a set of possibilities rather than old standards; it takes into account what Brecht was, has been and is or can be today.

Scholars of Brecht's work, and of the avant-garde in general, have identified a triad of commitments that historical events have rendered all but inapplicable in the post-war period: there is Brecht's commitment to socialism, a commitment ostensibly difficult to recover at the height of the cold war; then there is the emphasis on science that marks much of Brecht's writings, and his belief in the transformation of social reality through the emancipatory powers offered by scientific thought and technology; finally, there is the issue of the avant-garde and Brecht's reliance on the working class as an agent of revolutionary change and the artist's role as facilitator of an organized, left-wing, popular consciousness.

Yet today these commitments are no longer 'difficulties'. On the contrary, they have become opportunities. Questions of socialism, technological progress and class have become urgent topics in contemporary discourse and culture and serve as leitmotifs throughout this book. The post-Soviet supremacy of free-market capitalism no longer goes unchallenged, as the system is tested by its own neoliberalist logic as well as by digital technologies and information networks that provide sites of exchange and labour, enabling the formation of new social bodies and public spheres where 'extreme sharing' and 'gift economies' transcend the limits of for-profit production and interaction. Brecht's anti-foundationalism, his warnings about techno-euphoria and the naturalization of history and his emphasis on a political working class are pointedly relevant in this context, two decades after the end of the totalitarian experiment in socialist and communist life and well into the age of the global information network. While avoiding the ever-present pitfall of the uncritical resuscitation of the avant-garde, this book will emphasize the trajectories of socialism, technology and class, as well as related topics of communication, participation, labour, pedagogy, the avant-garde and audience as issues that not only drove Brecht's project but are radically altering our understanding of the twenty-first century as a moment of legacy and transformation.

To today's participants in the debate around the possibilities of emancipatory and progressive sociopolitical, economic and cultural production – ranging from J. K. Gibson-Graham and Jacques Rancière to Luc Boltanski and Eve Chiapello to Peter Sloterdijk and Oskar Negt – questions of new social configurations, evolving means of information exchange and the making of knowledge, subject to questions of ownership and participation, constitute the heritage and the horizon of this debate. In some areas this book will serve as a clarifying lens through which to evaluate Brecht's contribution. For example, the issue of pedagogy has recently resurfaced in the discourses surrounding contemporary visual arts in particular, and Brecht is periodically invoked as an example of the artist and intellectual as teacher or leader, but not always as one to follow. To the French philosopher Jacques Rancière, 'the Brechtian paradigm' reproduces binaries of active and passive, those who know and those who are ignorant, instead of, as Rancière advocates, allowing for an 'equality of intelligences'.[8] But Brecht's stipulation of an inequality of knowledge distinguishes between those who know and those who have not been given the chance to know. The *Verfremdungseffekt* is more dialectical 'auto-referentiality', as Jameson put it, than simply pulling the proverbial wool from the masses' eyes.[9] This modernist self-reference has as its subject the work itself, the audience *and* the very notion of self. Emancipation, to Brecht, is the ownership of the mediation between self, idea and reality. There is no equality as such, no one truth to know or be taught. The 'notes' accompanying the distribution of *The Baden-Baden Teaching Play on Agreement* (1929) in 1930 caution against a simplistic translation of the stage as an experimental arena in collective subjectivity into everyday life: even if the *Lehrstück* did achieve certain social and intellectual 'congruences', such 'artificial and shallow harmony would never be able to provide on a broad and vital basis even for minutes a counterbalance to the type of collective formations that tear apart the people of our time with a very different type of violence'.[10] The passivity that Brecht abhors is not the passivity of inaction but the refusal or inability to act politically, to engage in actions of emancipatory consequence.

This book charts Brecht's lifelong commitment to 'act humanly [*menschlich*]', which, according to Friedrich Dürrenmatt, meant to 'side with a revolution'.[11] Brecht's work in theatre, art and literature and his uncompromising character drive us to take a side as well.

1

Poet of Crisis, 1898–1923

Born two years before the end of the nineteenth century, Bertolt Brecht belonged to what Hannah Arendt called the first of three lost generations: a generation shaped by the horrors and suffering of the First World War and the demise of the Wilhelmine Empire that this war brought about.[1] Though Brecht's experiences of the front lines were limited to a brief stint as a nurse in a military hospital, he was deeply affected by the psychological, emotional, social and physical struggles on the home front. Brecht's coming of age as a person and an artist was characterized by a complicated and profoundly conflicted participation in his generation's search for a national identity, for history and tradition and for a way into the twentieth century. In Germany, as elsewhere, the war had been greeted with enthusiasm as it not only promised a new beginning, the hope for a spiritual cleansing and renewal, but provided a sense of unity and purpose for a country that had come late to nationhood and suffered from the upheaval of a comparatively belated and rapid modernization. Looking back after the war, Brecht retrospectively articulates his own sense of placelessness in the opening lines of the poem 'Of Poor B. B.' (1921):

> I, Bertolt Brecht, came out of the black forests,
> My mother moved me into the cities as I lay
> Inside her body. And the coldness of the forests
> Will be inside me till my dying day.

In the asphalt city I am at home. From the very start
Provided with every last sacrament:
With newspapers. And tobacco. And brandy
To the end mistrustful, lazy and content.[2]

Unlike many of his contemporaries, who reacted to experiences of modern mobility and transformation with bitterness and a nostalgic *Flucht nach hinten*, or flight backwards, Brecht used the chaos of the times as a chance to observe and comment, to experiment and explore. While he himself was not totally spared from the general mood of confusion and melancholia, Brecht took pleasure in denying himself and those around him the feeling of stability offered by aesthetic order and tradition, instead embracing the crisis as an opportunity to interrupt the reproduction of known positions and perspectives and create new ones.

During his precocious youth in Augsburg and Munich, before he moved permanently to Berlin in 1924, Brecht was already toying with the conventions of class. Brought up in a family of comfortable social and material status, and educated in the canons of German culture and Prussian attitudes, he wrote poetry, prose, songs and plays that waded deep into the crisis of bourgeois subjectivity – a subjectivity marred by the apocalyptic *Endzeitpsychose* of the *fin de siècle*, by warmongering and national defeat, and by the uneasy transition into parliamentary democracy and liberal capitalism of the Weimar Republic. In the face of the prevailing responses of traditionalist revivals, the Expressionist cult of flow and apocalyptic transcendence, Brecht practised strategic reversal and subversion in many of his early works, turning the bourgeois public sphere inside out by infusing it with forms and tales that make for uneasy social self-reflection. Even in this early period one gets a first glimpse of the power of Brechtian defamiliarization: heroic folk songs of perseverance are turned into bitterly humorous ballads of decay (as in 'Legend of the Dead Soldier', 1918) and the comforting familiarity of psalmic instruction into manuals of everyday defiance (as in 'Liturgy of the Breeze', 1924). Similarly, in his essays and reviews, some published in the local papers, Brecht parodies the already-deflated nationalist soul and toys with the party-line rhetoric of the early republic (including the anti-Bolshevik 'Song of the Red Army Soldier', 1919). His early plays, such as *Baal* (1918) and *Drums in the Night* (1922), made the much-heralded common man that much *more* common. Lawless and beyond any moral and ideological programme, prone to excess and regress, his characters are a long way from spiritual or social salvation but, for Brecht, in a sense that is their saving grace.

Collaborating with friends and strategically appropriating from genres high and low, Brecht always sought to convey a truly alternative perspective. Rather than presenting an arena where the privileged preside over universal matters, the stage, the poem and the editorial are seized and shaken by a cacophony of the banal and unsavoury, facilitating a new outlook set apart from those established by artistic and experiential conventions.

Tradition

Eugen Berthold Friedrich Brecht was born on 10 February 1898 in Augsburg as the first child of Berthold and Sophie Brecht. Once an important trade city between Italy and Northern Europe, Augsburg had become home to a growing infrastructure of industrial conglomerates, and by the time the war broke out in 1914, it was one of the centres of the German war industry. Brecht's father, from a middle- and working-class lineage that included fishermen and labourers as well as teachers and doctors, benefited from the town's pre-war prosperity, rising from clerk to general manager in the Haindlsche paper company in 1900. Spurred by increasing industrialization, the working-class movement gained a foothold in

Brecht's home town, and Augsburg was the site of the Allgemeine Sozialdemokratische Arbeiterkongreß (General Congress of Social-Democratic Workers) of 1870 and the resulting Augsburg Workers organization. Social-Democratic newspapers, including the *Proletarier* and *Volkswille*, were published in Augsburg, the latter soon to give voice to the young theatre critic's lauding observations and searing judgements.

Augsburg was home to a number of theatres and various respected cultural institutions, and it lay in close proximity to the creative and social life of Munich, with its cabarets and Prinzregententheater, the satirical journal *Simplicissimus* and the *Blaue Reiter*. Yet Augsburg provided distance from and perspective onto the more radical developments and upheavals taking place in the larger urban centres in Germany. Brecht scholar Hans Mayer has ascribed Augsburg a crucial function in Brecht's early life and work, arguing that the young poet used the town as a site of separation where he could choose the questions he deemed important enough to consider. Yet Augsburg was not a place 'from which romantic outsiders stare and long for the new man and the new spirit'.[3] Brecht's home town was largely governed by a military and civil servant apparatus, complete with its norms and attitudes. Threatened from below by the working-class movement and shaken by the increasing massification of bourgeois values and ideals, the German *Bürgertum*, or bourgeoisie, sought solace in an esoteric high culture and patriotic myths of communal identity, the administrative structures of the state and the representational sphere of military order and discipline. Brecht found this fertile ground on which to explore conformism and resistance and the individual's relation to his or her environment.[4] Brecht's struggle was less Oedipal than institutional; unlike the Expressionists, he did not storm the ramparts to kill the fathers in a melancholic-existentialist affirmation of the human spirit. While Brecht sought to abandon his own milieu as well, it was not in order to conform elsewhere, but to resist conformity itself.

In a public speech in 1892, two years after Bismarck's dismissal, Emperor Wilhelm II declared, 'Germany is slowly growing out of its child-size shoes in order to begin its adolescence.'[5] Gaining substantial momentum towards the end of the nineteenth century, Germany had been rapidly transforming from an agrarian into an industrial society, its population exploding and mobilizing both geographically and socially. The success of this speedy modernization has been attributed to a powerful but volatile mixture of tradition and progress. The artisanal trades and their emphasis on apprenticeship and skill were complemented by the rigorous scientific research methods at the reformed universities. Bismarck's social welfare policy and a newly organized labour force found their correlate in the almost absolutist power of the constitutional monarchy. A work ethic instilled by an authoritarian (effectively Prussian) state and an education system emphasizing diligence and frugality met a surging mass culture that sought to entertain those now endowed with a little leisure time and money to spend. But post-Bismarckian Germany lacked confidence. Modern German identity was, and is, according to historian James Sheehan, marked by 'diversity and discontinuity, richness and fragmentation, fecundity and fluidity' and a profound psychosocial insecurity rooted in the colliding ideals of economic prosperity and independence, nationalism and *Volk* (the people), cultural and technological modernity, liberalism, socialism and conservatism.[6] Ruined during the Thirty Years War and unsuccessful in the failed revolution of 1848, the bourgeoisie could not accommodate the growing social and economic appetite of the new masses. The middle class consisted mostly of the notorious German *Beamten*, powerful civil servants embedded in the state's bureaucratic machine. The state itself under Bismarck and Wilhelm II was ostensibly the keeper of German virtues, of order and discipline, and offered security complete with pseudo-feudal symbols like titles and insignia, uniforms and medals. Fearing the labour movement as much as the vulgarity of technocratic progress and mass culture, the bourgeoisie fled into the arms of the omnipresent father figure that Thomas Mann so aptly characterized as 'General Dr von Staat'.[7]

But this class desertion, or *Renegatentum*, as historian Christian Graf von Krockow called it, proceeded in several related, though often ambiguous, directions. De facto, the bourgeoisie abandoned the public sphere as an arena for the articulation and affirmation of liberal ideals. Yet it continued to maintain its facade in an act of denial and ideological consolation. In addition to the military and administrative apparatuses, an increasingly esoteric high culture was sought, as well as a growing mass-market literature catering to escapist fantasies of past and exotic adventures, and a romantic and often bitter anti-modernist populism steeped in Germanic myths and a Francophobia that valued community over society and hierarchy over equality.[8] Any of these offered respite from social and ideological drift, yet their competition to anchor the German soul resulted in perturbing dissonance. The function of culture was judged accordingly. The German bourgeois public sphere at the end of the nineteenth century was, as discussed in great detail by sociologist and philosopher Jürgen Habermas, refeudalized as much as privatized. Culture, once, ideally, reserved for the autonomous critical exchange of what was actually or ostensibly relevant to all members of society, was now increasingly coming under ownership – by commercial, private interest, by the sanctity of classic German tradition and *Geistesgeschichte* (intellectual history) or by an equally untouchable Germanic spirituality.[9] The crucial aspect of this transformation was that the bourgeois public sphere – its language, its channels of communication, its emphasis on a tradition of critical disinterest – was not disbanded but repurposed.

As critical *raisonnement* was replaced by a sphere of *Handlungsersatz*, of substitute action, Brecht and his peers found themselves in the midst of a romantic exploration of the past. Yet Brecht wanted nothing to do with the popular quests for 'natural' forms of belonging, part of the German *Seelensuche*, or soul-searching, that haunted the Wilhelmine Empire. Beginning around 1913, Brecht began writing on an almost daily basis, jotting down poems and fragments in his journal and publishing several in the school newspaper *Die Ernte* (The harvest), composing verses for war postcards (sold to benefit the local Red Cross) and writing lyrical letters to his younger brother and only sibling, Walter. By 1914 he was already contributing poems and essays to the *Augsburger Neuesten Nachrichten*. Brecht was critical of his own early attempts. A diary entry from 21 May 1913 comments on a preceding exercise: 'This is the rehearsal of a ballad. I have not mastered the form yet!'[10] But he pressed on: more than 100 poems and fragments have been preserved, and many more are presumed lost. Despite a lack of literary confidence, the writings of the fifteen-year-old are impressive in their variety of forms and styles, contents and perspectives. Rather than the emotional narcissism typical of adolescence, Brecht's early writings evince his interest in trying out different voices. The poem 'Sacrifice!' (1913), in a reversal of the prevailing chauvinist call for individual self-sacrifice, rallies the *Volk* to aid those slighted by the circumstances of life. Only four days later, Brecht composed the 'Banner Song' (1913), singing of brotherly, heroic death in duty to the fatherland.

The lesson plans of the schools Brecht attended indicate a conventional, albeit expansive, curriculum ranging from Greek mythology and Renaissance history to Latin and religious studies to Goethe, Kleist and Schiller, Shakespeare and Molière. Brecht's friends and peers considered him a *Literaturexperte* and recall that he read not only what was assigned in class but also crime stories and Karl May's Wild West fantasies, Gerhardt Hauptmann, Arthur Rimbaud and François Villon. One fellow student recalls that in 1914 Brecht's father gave him Frank Wedekind's collected works.[11] According to Brecht's friend Hans Otto Münsterer, what defined this early period of creative production until the early 1920s was 'the liveliness and spontaneity of youth, which can afford to admire almost simultaneously Cesare Borgia and Saint Francis'.[12] Throughout the ongoing development and transformation of Brecht's work, as it keeps pace with the unfolding of historical events and circumstances, it is culled from various sources and influences as well as an astutely critical observation, manifest in the earliest of his writings.

Brecht's early poetic career unfolded in the form of songwriting. He and his friends spent hours on end in his attic room composing ballads and other oratory intonations for public presentation. The earliest collection of poems is called *Songs for Guitar by Bert Brecht and His Friends* and, led by Brecht and his guitar, the 'Brecht clique' was known to roam Augsburg, carrying lanterns while singing songs of lust and adventure, alcoholism and decay. The collection is dated 1918 but includes earlier pieces. The title emphasizes Brecht's status as a leader among his creative companions along with his reliance on collaboration, a combination that would shape his method of working throughout his lifetime; it also betrays what would later crystallize as Brecht's attitude towards the role of authorship and art in a larger cultural, social and political framework of production. Collective improvisation, discussion and exchange, whether in the sanctity of Brecht's home or as spontaneous acts on adventurous excursions through town or in the back room of Gabler's Tavern, were key to forming and performing acts of engaging with the authority of social lore and working through personal experiences. During his time in Augsburg, Brecht forged friendships and creative bonds that would endure for years to come, providing characters and behaviours for stories and plays or resulting in ongoing collaborative partnerships, such as that with artist and set designer Caspar Neher.

Brecht presented himself as an antidote to the notion of the contemplative, solitary genius-artist. In the tradition of Goethe and Wedekind as well as Rimbaud and Villon, Brecht's poetic works

Brecht, left, with friends, roaming the countryside, 1918.

amounted to what Goethe had called *Gelegenheitsgedichte* (poems of occasion), based on and inspired by reality.[13] 'Workers' from 1913 is a fascinating testament to the young Brecht's powers of critical observation. He begins by describing the trek of tired and exhausted labourers walking home after work, worn down by the lack of blue skies, self-determination and hope in their lives. Then he writes:

> If not in the many years
> Once in anger violently rise
> And with a rattle
> While wildly cursing
> Yet shake off their shackles?
>
> But at home! There are wife and tot
> They need the father dearly
> When he sees *them* in his mind's sway
> His curses die away

And it is hard to think clearly
And revenge and freedom are forgot![14]

Long before developing a political consciousness and a dialectical
method of enquiry based on his exposure to Marxist theory,
Brecht, at the tender age of fifteen, relates what he perceives
first-hand as the reality of everyday working-class life, its routines,
demands and necessities, to the potential and possibilities of
transformation caused by alienation. As his father was the general
manager of the Haindlsche paper company, Brecht and his family
lived among the working people in the company housing project,
or *Sozialbauwohnung*, which his father supervised. There is no
hurrah to the defiant survivalism of the human spirit, no appeal
to proletarian solidarity – art here remains wedded to its circumstances. The poem articulates a tension between public and
private, between perceptions of political and personal reality as
exclusive arenas of action. Responsibility to and ownership over
agency, the ability to take charge of one's fate, is compartmentalized;
solidarity confined to a notion of community based on kin rather
than class and labour.

The presentation of his works was as important to Brecht as
their production, their real-world application to complement the
Gelegenheit (occasion) of their origins. In the traditions of folk
songs, ballads and the *Moritat* (publicly sung stories of crimes and
titillating events), Brecht found a timely, yet familiar and popular
way of telling his stories. During and after the war, Brecht and his
friends visited the *Plärrer*, a fair and folk festival taking place in
Augsburg every spring and autumn. According to his friend Max
Knoblach, Brecht claimed that at the *Plärrer* one could 'experience
the world the way it really is'.[15] Brecht, Knoblach recalls, was
attracted by the fairground workers' uninhibited ways and unconventional lives. The singing bard, or *Bänkelsänger*, stood on top of
a wooden box and relayed colourful and, in the case of the *Moritat*,

gruesome stories of events and incidents near and far, accompanied by a lute or a hand organ, or sometimes an illuminating tableau or canvas.

Brecht was fascinated by these 'common man's newspapers' as much as by what his brother Walter remembers as the 'unforgettable songs of the servants' he heard at his parents' house, telling of scary robbers and desperate loves.[16] The directness of the ballads' content and form and their lack of sentimentality, the spectacular effect of their undisguised simplicity, impressed Brecht greatly and he concluded that he, too, wanted to tell stories that would 'knock their listeners' teeth out'.[17]

Similarly, the young poet welcomed the concrete reality and immediacy of some of his favoured authors' artistic forms. For instance, he admired Wedekind's stage presence and the quality of his performance, the distanced and playful lightness with which he told of dark times and the accessibility of his language. On the occasion of Wedekind's death in 1918, Brecht wrote admiringly of his appearance: 'There he stood, ugly, brutal, dangerous . . . singing his songs in a brittle voice, a little monotonous and very unschooled: Never has a singer impressed and shaken me this much.'[18] Villon he held in great esteem because of his refusal to conform to socially acceptable behaviour and because of his unconventional methods of canonical verse. Brecht saw in him a 'rich people's terror, a thug and panderer, *Bänkelsänger*, rascal' whose workshop was the 'forest and the tavern' and who sang out of pleasure and without regret in the voice and language of the people.[19]

Brecht fashioned his own presentations, whether strategically or because of a lack of melodic abilities, in similarly disharmonious ways, reciting more than singing. Brecht's first wife, the opera singer Marianne Zoff, recalls that his metallic voice sent shivers down her spine, while the novelist and playwright Lion Feuchtwanger describes the musicality of the Brecht-based character in his novel *Erfolg* (*Success*) as:

bright, cheeky, with a shrill voice, ugly, unmistakably vernacular
. . . These ballads contained events of the everyday and the
everyman, seen with a big-city folksiness, never seen like this
before, thin and angry, with a rascal scent, unconcernedly
spirited, never heard like this before.[20]

Brecht's emphasis on the unromantic and unapologetic
presentation of his stories stems from his abiding determination
to deal in objective findings rather than morals or worldviews.
He was beginning to get into trouble at school for his irreverence
towards sacrifice and patriotism, and he wanted nothing to do
with the nostalgic camaraderie of the famous *Wandervögel*, a youth
organization that was part of the populist middle-class condemnation
of and flight from urban life, even though some of his friends and
his brother were members. The singing hikers drew upon the
legacy of German folk music in their opposition to the urbanization
of society and their desire to rediscover a lost relationship to the
natural environment and to each other. A similar naturalism,
deeply tied to pre-modern, somewhat aristocratic ideals of
community and dwelling, prevailed among the German youth
movement in general, an attempt to escape the stringent
conservatism of their fathers. The bitterness and *Kulturpessimismus*
of, for instance, Julius Langbehn and Oswald Spengler stood next
to Ferdinand Tönnies's celebration of organic communal life and
Stefan George's fantastic resurrection of the heroic, male European
youth led by the arbitrariness of a spirit liberated from material
needs and rationalization. Neither the *Aufbruch* (radical departure)
heralded by Expressionism and Jugendstil, on the one hand, nor
the high culture of the refeudalized bourgeoisie, on the other, had
much room for notions of progressive social change.

Brecht himself had ambitions of deserting his own class, but
not to move upward. Written in 1938, with hindsight and, undeni-
ably, a good measure of autobiographical calculation, the poem

'Driven Out for Good Reason' describes his discomfort with the
inheritance of social constraints:

> I grew up as the son
> Of well-to-do people. My parents put
> A collar around my neck and raised me
> In the habit of being waited on
> And schooled me in the art of giving orders. But
> When I was grown up and looked around me
> I did not like the people of my own class
> Nor giving orders, nor being waited on
> And I left my own class and joined
> The low people.[21]

Like his countrymen, the young Brecht was swept up in the
prevalent atmosphere of restlessness and transition. Yet he was
not seduced by the comfort of status prescribed by education and
socialization. On the contrary, his explorations and experimentations
with new and old forms of cultural comforts led to an unmasking of
the *Doppelmoral*, the duplicit morality of the bourgeoisie. He began
to take great pleasure in reappropriating the forms and narratives
of virtuous heroes and pious deeds, the purity of love and
immutable grandeur of nature. His love songs often verge on
the harsh and vulgar: 'A Bitter Love Song' (1918), for example,
exchanges the sanctity of everlasting devotion for a lust that sub-
sides as physical beauty fades. Brecht advises its recitation to be
'mournful and clangorous'.[22] As with Wedekind and Villon, this type
of presentation as well as the use of vulgar language clash with the
form's indication of romance. In other works, the body is celebrated
as a site not of private intimacy but a carnivalesque celebration of
breaking moral taboos. In many cases, marriage is exposed as an
institution that hides everyday transgressions under a mantle of
moral codes. In the 'Ballad of the Love Death' (1921), the medieval,

Shakespearean motif is distorted as love is reduced to fornication and the idealization of the immortal romance is replaced by the process of physical decay. Brecht describes the death *through* love as much as the death *of* love and the poetic conventions that perpetuate it.

Brecht's works of the early 1920s add a more direct socially critical perspective. 'Of the Child Murderer Marie Farrar' (1922) tells the story of a woman accused of murder after unsuccessfully trying to abort her pregnancy, then killing her newborn son. The poem is part of the *Bittgesänge* (songs of supplication) section of the *Manual of Piety* (1927), Brecht's second collection of poems. Rather than have her repent, for her pregnancy out of wedlock or for the desperate measures to which she resorts, Brecht accuses the society that has failed her, a communal structure unable and unwilling to support behaviour outside what is commonly acceptable.[23]

In Brecht's songs and poems, the natural environment is often the site of indecent frolicking: characters roll around in meadows and have raucous picnics along riverbanks and in forests. Nature is a reminder of a paradise that never was, the province of death and destruction as well as a practical platform for dubious adventures. In 'Spring' (1915), the joyful expectations of the season are foiled by the cruelties of war; in 'The Song of the Railway Workers of Fort Donald' (1916), nature appears as man's enemy, the winner in a battle between willpower and environmental forces; in 'Of Swimming in Rivers and Lakes' (1919), the potential for self-abandonment in nature is juxtaposed with the how-to mechanics and doctrinaire tone of the back-to-nature movements. In 'A Liturgy of Breath' (1924), Brecht constructs a parallel between nature and classical poetic form. Comprising seven stanzas, each followed by a refrain borrowed from Goethe's 'Wandrers Nachtlied' ('Wanderer's Nightsong', 1778–80), the poem both in form and narrative challenges naturalized social structures and the

cultural traditions used to perpetuate them.[24] While Goethe's
poem, which foregrounds the calm and quiet of nature, was a
cornerstone of German edification, Brecht's poem describes a
struggle between competing forms of order and the language with
which these are ascertained. The story of an old woman tormented
by sociopolitical forces and the brutal repression of those who
come to her aid is told in an everyday language reminiscent of a
classical folk tale or song; nature as established by lyrical tradition
not only averts its eyes from injustices committed but covers them
with a veil of serenity. For Brecht, death had become a social rather
than a natural matter. At the end of the poem, as solidarity and a
new political consciousness eventually manage to stand up to
mounting oppression, the protagonists attack not the henchmen
of the authoritarian state but Goethe's silent birds, sleeping peacefully
in the treetops.

'A Liturgy of Breath' remained unpublished until 1927, when
it appeared as part of the *Bittgesänge*, emphasizing the work's use-
value as a tool for critical reflection on inherited views and attitudes.
Writings like 'Spring', 'The Song of the Railway Workers of Fort
Donald' and 'Of Swimming in Rivers and Lakes' attained a similar
function due to their distribution in publications of bourgeois
conviction that, in addition to the *Augsburger Neueste Nachrichten*
and *Der Neue Merkur*, later included the *Berliner Börsen-Courier*
and *Die Weltbühne*, among others. Refusing to preach to the choir,
Brecht was giving voice to the confusion and dissonance of his
time, and rather than try to replace one worldview with another, he
dissected and connected traditions and attitudes in the face of those
clamouring for a sense of purpose and continuity.

This dialectic of tradition and realism also determined much
of Brecht's prolific work as a theatre critic. He wrote most of his
reviews of plays staged at the Augsburger Stadttheater between
1919 and 1921 for the daily newspaper *Der Volkswille*, the organ of
the United Social-Democratic Party (USPD) until December 1920,

then briefly of the German Communist Party (KPD) until its prohibition in January 1921 because of 'seditious tendencies'. The texts evince little reverence for the enthralling power of the classics, be they old or recent, Schiller's *Don Carlos* or Ibsen's *Ghosts*. Brecht was more interested in the performances themselves – the actors, the stages, the audience – parts of which he described in minute detail. His assessments stood out for their lack of respect for and provocation of established writers, dramas and actors, resulting in the Stadttheater's revocation of complimentary tickets for the critic and, on one occasion, an actress's attempt to sue Brecht for insulting her. Whether strategic or not, Brecht's use of crude language and description rather than a privileged discourse of expertise yielded a powerful combination of entertainment and critique that addressed the theatre as a cultural institution as much as the individual plays. He deplored, for example, the 'pretentious rhetoric' of Georg Kaiser's dramas, concluding, 'To write in such a fashion that as few as possible dare to say that they understood you is not a work of art.'[25] On the other hand, someone like the cabaretist Karl Valentin, sitting in a beerhall in front of an audience that is smoking and drinking, presents the 'dry, inner humour' of the 'inadequacies of all things, including ourselves'.[26] And like Charlie Chaplin, according to Brecht, Valentin rejects 'virtually all mimic and cheap psychologism' when he demonstrates the pathetic yet hilarious everyday entanglements of individuals with their surroundings, each other and themselves.[27]

This early emphasis on pleasure, popularity (in the sense of *Volkstümlichkeit* or common culture) and concern with the audience's quotidian experiences provided a crucial platform for Brecht's development of an aesthetic or theatrical theory.[28] He began to draw parallels between theatre and sports, advocating the latter's palpable connection with reality, the absence of the so-called fourth wall at the front of a stage and the viewers' physical and psychological proximity to the event, protagonists and the language of its presentation. Brecht also extended his critique to include the Augsburger Stadttheater and its lack of commitment to the arts: following the war, the institution lost much of its regular middle-class audience and, as a consequence, the governing cultural body invested heavily in the opera house, which almost exclusively staged light operettas. In several articles and an open letter, Brecht assailed the administration's choices, insisting that theatre is more than business or spectacle and needs to put the 'art's interest' before any individual interest, be it that of the director, the actor or the institution.[29]

At that point, what exactly 'art's interest' is remains unspecified. But read within the context of Brecht's other writings at the time, his comment is a call for an art in proximity to social reality and the way in which that reality is experienced as a social and mediated act. It is the responsibility of the theatre to acknowledge and make perceptible that reality and art as a form of its mediation, a language in which experiences are not only transmitted but also produced. This early emphasis on participation extends to Brecht's demands of criticism, its self-conscious use of language and positioning vis-à-vis work and audience. Barthes will later call this the 'state of complicity with the world' which he counts among 'The Tasks of Brechtian Criticism', a practice that is 'by definition extensive with the problematics of our time'. He proclaims, 'Brechtian criticism will . . . be written by the spectator, the reader, the consumer, and not the exegete: it is a criticism of a *concerned* man.'[30] It is to become a tradition in the way Brecht put to use the traditions of his time: collective actions of critical performance, persistently renewed.

War

Death is the protagonist in many of Brecht's poems from just before until after the First World War, whether nature reveals itself as a site of destruction and decay, as in 'The Burning Tree' (1913) and 'Vulture Tree' (1917); cavalier fervour drives a fiddler beyond the brink of life, as in 'Passion' (1913); or the dutiful pursuit of workshop labour takes its inhuman toll, as in 'July 1913' (1913). The texts have a strangely captivating melodramatic force, a sometimes quasi-erotic, spontaneous and immediate sensuality. But Brecht is interested less in metaphor and symbolism than in a poetic factuality. The red colour of the sky, the blaze of the flames, the blood on the ground are as real as life and death, though this does not preclude a certain Nietzschean tone of heroic, almost majestic triumph: there is something lustful about living in the face of death's imminence, and about dying despite a passion for living. The texts written prior to and at the beginning of the war in particular share in a general atmosphere of grand fatalism and euphoric renewal that appropriated Nietzsche's existentialism as an affirmation of patriotic fantasies of virtuous superiority. But where his peers' celebration of catastrophic devastation resounds with individual sacrifice for the sake of a greater, more perfect and fulfilling good, Brecht's works have the curious quality of reportage: he takes on various voices and perspectives, using a language that rapidly shifts between the poetic and the descriptive, the tragic and the comic.

The young writer found himself in plentiful company as poets rushed to greet the war. In August 1918 alone, 1.5 million war poems were reportedly penned in Germany.[31] As in much of the rest of Europe, in Germany the prospect of chauvinist unity and patriotic nonpartisanship brought jubilation. Capturing and amplifying the feelings of a nation, writers like Rudolf Alexander Schröder, Ernst Stadler and even Rainer Maria Rilke sang of altruistic camaraderie, higher duties and the eternal glory of the German *Volk*. The old French ideals from 1789, freedom, equality and brotherhood, were replaced by Germanic notions of duty, order and justice. The explicitly anti-modern rhetoric around community and natural order by politicians and cultural leaders alike veiled the reality of a war that was driven by a rationalist quest for economic gain and the expansion of military and technological power. As appointed nemesis, France was cast as the example of an artificial social structure, dividing a people for materialist gain, thereby effectively designating class struggle as un-German.

Scholars are divided over the extent to which Brecht's writings – his poems, his war 'letters' and 'postcards' – reveal an affinity with the rejection of Enlightenment ideals in favour of an essentially anti-democratic and joyfully subservient attitude. Ronald Speirs points out that the young poet suffered from a heart condition which, as he recorded in his diaries, troubled him and occasionally caused anxiety. Combined with a youthful appetite for rebellion, Brecht, according to Speirs, may have been particularly susceptible to poetic bouts of contemplating death and its defiance.[32] Reinhold Grimm, on the other hand, argues that Brecht's early enthusiasm for the war was a calculated manoeuvre intended to establish him as a published writer.[33] It is true that neither Brecht's written correspondence at the time nor his diary entries reflect the kind of nationalism and battle bravado of the pieces that he submitted for publication, or jotted in his notebooks as exercises in literary competition.

In addition to publishing a few poems and collaborating on some postcards for the war effort sold by the Red Cross, Brecht wrote the *Augsburg War Letters*, his response to the *Deutsche Kriegsbriefe* (German war letters) that appeared regularly in the *Augsburger Neuesten Nachrichten*. In just two months, August and September 1914, the *München-Augsburger Abendzeitung* printed no fewer than seven of Brecht's *War Letters*. Brecht himself avoided combat, using his heart condition, his father's influence and later his enrolment in medical school at the university in Munich. While newspapers at the time printed reports from the front lines, telling of heroic deeds and military triumphs, interspersed with a bit of humour and anecdotes, some allegedly written by the soldiers themselves, Brecht's *War Letters* covered the home front. He immodestly put himself on the same level as the soldiers and the professional war reporters, but shared his readers' perspective on the era's historical events.

The letters describe the general euphoria with which the city of Augsburg sent its sons to fight the enemy and the erupting cheers over publicly read telegrams from the trenches. The overall tone is one of affirmative necessity, the sacrifice of individual needs in service of the fatherland. But even the first *War Letter*, dated 14 August 1914, cautions the reader by portraying the sadness and anxiety of those who watch their loved ones go: 'Much misery can be seen.'[34] Other observations seem to carry a hint of irony, as when the mention of the kaiser's overnight military stardom ends with the remark that the conversations about him, avidly conducted at the beerhall regulars' tables, 'are not at all ridiculous'.[35] The next letter puts the 'happy' war in quotation marks, and the emotional toll on those who get news about their fallen husbands, brothers and sons gains in presence.[36] Brecht also refrains from celebratory declarations of heroism and derogatory remarks about the enemy. His view is more and more fixed on the victims and the price of war, on both sides, and in their juxtaposition of rhetoric and report; his texts build relationships between the beguiling ideals directing the Great War and the cold reality of the calculating, mechanizing war apparatus.

In 1918, the year he himself began to serve (he was a nurse in Augsburg's auxiliary military hospital from October 1918 until January 1919), Brecht wrote one of his best-known war poems, 'The Legend of the Dead Soldier'.[37] Like many other texts Brecht wrote at the time, and especially those later collected in the *Manual of Piety*, the 'Legend' was meant to be sung. When it was performed, the audience's reactions ranged from standing ovations to fist fights, owing in part to Brecht's provocative delivery. In 1921 he presented the song in a Berlin cabaret and was subsequently banned from further engagements there. And in 1923 the national-ist daily *Berliner Lokalanzeiger* accused the Deutsches Theater of 'crude tactlessness' for printing the text in one of its pamphlets.[38] Kurt Tucholsky later wrote admiringly: 'Some people have stuck it to the Prussians, but none like this! . . . This is a poetic achievement of great calibre.'[39] Looking back in the mid-1930s, Brecht recalls the context of the poem's production, describing the army's attempt to find all remaining 'human material' for a final offensive: 'The seventeen- and fifteen-year-olds were dressed and sent to the front. The word "k.v.," which means "*kriegsverwendungsfähig*" [fit for active service], once again frightened millions of families. The dead are being dug up for active service.'[40]

'Legend' tells the story of a nameless soldier who opts to die a hero's death as he realizes that the war offers no prospect of peace. But the war is not yet over, and the emperor decides to have the deceased fighter exhumed. In a scene reminiscent of George Grosz's famous drawing *KV*, published in the Dada journal *Die Pleite* in 1919, a commission determines that the man is fit for service. What follows is a grotesque parade, led by a *Bürger* with his German sense of duty, that with 'oompah' and bare-bosomed ladies, schnapps and much hurrah drags the corpse across the fields and through the villages back into battle. Incense masks the stench of decay while the colours of the empire cloak a faeces-stained shroud. The soldier himself disappears among all the hubbub. Here Brecht cunningly points out the instrumentalization of the individual by an overarching apparatus that transcends the institutions of church, state and military to manifest itself in all facets of everyday life. The poem has a musical lightness and outright funny passages, but it also offers simple, moving moments:

And they took the soldier with them
The night was blue and clear
If it weren't for your helmet,
You could see the stars of home.[41]

In this text, nature takes on a human and humane character, while the people are exposed as barbaric. The heavens offer only stars, and the red of dawn provides a glimmer of hope. The resurrection has religious overtones, but there is no salvation: the soldier dies twice. Brecht takes on the myth of the hero's death as made popular in best-selling books like Rainer Maria Rilke's *Die Weise von Liebe und Tod des Cornets Christoph Rilke* (*The Lay of the Love and Death of Cornet Christopher Rilke*), which was published in 1912, immediately sold out and supposedly could be found in every young soldier's backpack; and Walter Flex's *Der Wanderer zwischen beiden Welten* (The wanderer between two worlds, 1918). Yet Brecht also confronts the powerful and ideological fusion of patriotic and religious form and tradition at a time of secularized, functionalized faith.

Brecht repeatedly appropriated the familiar forms of pious instruction in an attempt not to restore but to expose the role of religion in a culture that exchanged promises of salvation for blind obedience. His early poems and ballads employ the familiar language and dialect of *Lutherdeutsch*, while their easily memorable structure, rhythm and repetition recall the rituals of church service and recitation of biblical passages. But Brecht aims literally to dis-illusion his audience: 'The Heaven of the Disappointed' (1917) describes a space of eternal suspension between dark and light where 'sullen souls . . . sit tearless, mute, and very alone'.[42] And 'The Legend of the Harlot Evelyn Roe' (1918) reverses the story of Maria of Egypt, who through a miracle is turned from whore into saint, transforming a tale of mercy and forgiveness into a ballad where a repeatedly exploited and abused but penitent girl is awarded eternal condemnation instead of reprieve.[43]

Beginning in 1920, Brecht wrote a number of 'Psalms'. The open structure and irregular verse of the biblical originals perfectly fit the haggard writer's attempts to work through a number of personal experiences: his mother had died in May of that year and he was constantly travelling between Augsburg, Munich (where he was enrolled at the university for medical studies) and Berlin, where he sought fortune and fame. Having attended the obligatory confirmation classes as an adolescent, Brecht was well aware that the classical psalms were intended to provide an often musically enacted dialogue between God and his people, giving concrete shape to God's transcendence and omnipresence and emphasizing the form's applicability to everyday concerns and even sociopolitical dilemmas. Yet Brecht seemed less interested in the subversive potential of these texts than in their open form. A diary entry dated 31 August 1920, reads, 'I have to write psalms again. Rhyming takes too much time.'[44] Brecht's psalms retain the themes of death and caducity, while love serves neither compassion nor forgiveness but the pragmatic satisfaction of physical needs.

The search for a new subjectivity and an expansion of the notion of 'God' was common during the years following the war. Expressionist writers were experimenting with non-classical lyrical forms and looking for a new understanding of selfhood, while a new religiosity signalled a turn away from war and militarism. Brecht's psalms stand out in their profane content and intentionally uncontrived language. In the chaos of post-war struggles to fill vacuums of power and meaning, Brecht found himself experimenting with strategies of resistance that opposed both old *and* new forms of complacent artistic and intellectual attitudes, even if the latter came in the guise of progress and innovation.

Resistance

Between April and July 1918, Brecht wrote *Baal*, his first full-length play and his first serious attempt to break into the world of theatre, which, as a critic, he deemed broken beyond repair:

The German drama is sinking, apparently, fast, fain, compliant.
... But we want to make ourselves at home, spread our legs
against the planks, and see how we can move the ship forward.
Maybe we will guzzle the water swelling through the leak,
maybe we will drape our last shirts from the mast as sails and
blow against it, that is the wind, and fart against it, that is
the storm. And go under singing, so that the ship has some
contents when it hits bottom.[45]

As with his poems, Brecht set out not to renovate an art form but
to resist its repeated reconstruction as an institution that peddled
lofty ideas far removed from contemporary reality.

The play tells the story of Baal, a present-day poet who, with his
eccentric and amoral lifestyle as well as his verses, challenges the
social norms and values surrounding him. He drinks, brawls, lazes
and fornicates to his heart's content, sacrificing not only his friend
and his friend's lover but, ultimately, himself. Baal's life and his art
are one, and like Brecht in his rendering, he forgoes all aestheticization and, in the tradition of the *Moritat*, sings candid songs
of violent deeds and attitudes. Rather than a site for reflection or
engagement, the world is a material playground, used and abused
with indifference. After grazing the fields empty with smacking
lips, the protagonist leaves the audience to ponder: 'What else is
the world for Baal? Baal is full.'[46] Baal dies lonely, in the woods,
among the loggers who have come to fell nature and bring *civilis* –
Brecht's neologism for civilization and syphilis.

The play, on a methodological level, has both biographical and
historical dimensions. It bespeaks the author's war and post-war
experiences, his rejection of prevailing worldviews offered to make
sense of the war's destruction, which left men and spirits maimed.
And it is a testament to Brecht's defiant embrace of life. He himself
appeared to treat the world as a set of tools, wielded according to
one's own desire. The young playwright continued to oscillate

between Augsburg, Munich and, increasingly, Berlin. As a medical student he selected whatever courses fitted his creative needs rather than curricular demands, attending more classes in the history of literature and drama than in chemistry and anatomy. As a medical orderly during the war he wore yellow shoes, carried a riding crop and addressed the doctors as 'fellow colleagues'. He playfully, if at times reluctantly, continued to change his attitudes towards life and his role in it. A diary entry from the time attests, 'I keep forgetting my points of view, can't resolve to memorize them.'[47] He also conducted a number of amorous relationships. Between 1919 and 1924 Brecht fathered three children – Frank, Hanne and Stefan – with three women: Paula Bannholzer, whose parents refused to entertain the thought of the unkempt poet as their son-in-law; the singer Marianne Zoff, whom he married in anticipation of their daughter's birth; and the actress Helene Weigel, who would remain his wife, collaborator and most ardent supporter throughout his life. (Another daughter with Weigel, Barbara, would be born in October 1930.) The emerging play-wright's infamous statement 'Let them grow, the little Brechts' underlines a rather cavalier attitude towards partnership and par-enting. He was always on the move, fickle in his commitments to ideas, causes and people, and like his protagonists' recklessness, his was as adventurous as it was melancholic. He lived the life of a vagabond, with little money or food, while his letters and journal entries express a constant concern about the well-being of his children and their mothers.[48] Alcohol was easier to obtain than food in those days, and in early 1921 Brecht was admitted to the Berlin Charité hospital, where he was treated for severe under-nourishment.

In the context of the post-war chaos, *Baal* affirmed the wreckage of the country's war, a failed attempt to prove to the German people and the rest of the world that pre-modern virtues and values would reign supreme. Though not published until 1922, after many revisions and additions over the preceding years, and first staged in 1923, *Baal* hit the nation where it hurt. In the autumn of 1918, faced with deadlocked fronts and unprecedented calamities, General Ludendorff and the army command had chosen to spare the last lives left and called for a truce, while navy generals decided to mount a final, desperate assault. Mutinying sailors in Kiel and Berlin were able to avert this *Nibelungen* finale. Ironically, the Wilhelmine Empire then declared its own end and proclaimed the republic, as Prince Max von Baden – chosen by Ludendorff and the infamous Field Marshall Paul von Hindenburg to negotiate an armistice with the Allied forces – on his own authority declared the kaiser's abdication and made Friedrich Ebert chancellor. This turn of events led to a historical assessment of this *Novemberrevolution* as a revolution-from-above.

The coalition government under Ebert offered a hopeful and important glimpse at the possibility of a parliamentary democracy, but any fundamental change in political attitudes and outlook was precluded by a lack of national self-reflection – a lack diligently mplemented by an intricate bureaucratic and military apparatus that maintained its pre-1918 structure and personnel. Inconsequential compromise disguised as the liberal virtue of tolerance and conciliatoriness, as Kurt Tucholsky pointed out, was the order of the day:

> Since November, we're dancing minuets where we ought to slash, burn, topple. Happily the *Bürger* lies in his bed, the government purrs oh so comely. . . . Let us make a compromise, for it causes no distress.[49]

At least 9 million people had died in the First World War and 30 million had been wounded, captured or were still missing. To many, the end of the war came as a surprise, as authorities and newspapers had continuously promised that the soldiers and the

George Grosz, *Post-war Idyll*, 1921, drawing.

people's perseverance would be rewarded with victory in the end. Marching through ravaged landscapes, the soldiers returned to a homeland riven by power struggles, factional uprisings and competing narratives over how the war was lost and what was to come next.

The decision against the military's doomed grand finale and for the affirmation of life over blind principle could have served as the fledgling republic's founding myth. But the state's new *Bürger* clung to tales of betrayal instead. Interior and exterior enemies, be they Bolshevists or the French, were blamed for the downfall of the empire, conveniently circumventing any critical examination of national beliefs or the motives of those who profited from those beliefs during and after the war. Whether in theatre, literature or other forms of culture, the general trend was towards entertaining spirituality, to distract from hunger, inflation and the humiliation of the Versailles Treaty, while fulfilling a desire for existential meaning transcending the petty and contingent burdens of everyday reality.

In contrast, Brecht demanded that art be 'Simple joyfulness. Truthfulness . . . Soldier against the metaphysical', a fighting against culture that was like 'masturbating with a rubber on', that is, merely self-gratifying, yet afraid of lust and sensuality.[50] In *Baal*, all protection comes off: 'Baal feeds! Baal dances!! Baal transfigures himself!!!'[51] The play offers no anti-hero, no romance, no solution – nothing but crippling self-awareness. The inspiration for the play is said to come from various places: Baal is the dark pagan God of the Old Testament, ecstatic celebrant of the here and now (*Diesseits*); other sources maintain that Brecht was inspired by a failed, bedraggled Augsburg poet by the name of Johann Baal, who roamed the bars and beerhalls; and there is the story that *Baal* was originally a response to Hanns Johst's Expressionist play *Der Einsame* (The lonely, 1917), which Brecht criticized as removed from reality and unwilling to grapple with the individual's experience of social dissonance and alienation. Brecht himself aimed to emphasize his play's constructedness. Its overall form is 'open', presenting not a logical, coherent, progressing whole but a collage-like interchangeability of individual scenes and elements. Furthermore, Baal is *asozial* or anti-bourgeois not only in his amoral behaviour and his denial of a sensible totality, but in the ways in which he turns his art into life and his life into his art. Addressing Baal's cunning, his performance, his misleading of others within the play, Brecht points to art's use-value and, ultimately, its function as commodity – a reification of ideas and images, sold under the guise of Kantian 'disinterestedness', thereby affirming the social impossibility of such aesthetic autonomy.

Yet audiences longed for artistic remove. The nineteenth-century transformation of the German theatre from an arena of aristocratic self-representation to a bourgeois *Bildungs*-institution turned the stage into a 'school of the moral world', as explored most thoroughly by Enlightenment philosopher and writer Gotthold Ephraim Lessing, who declared that the goal of drama was to 'enlighten and improve the mass and not to confirm them in their ignoble mode of thought'.[52] Actors were to lead by example, and complete psychological and emotional immersion was essential to the success of virtuous instruction. Lessing continued, 'The tragedian should avoid everything that can remind the audience of their illusion, for as soon as they are reminded of it, the illusion is gone.'[53] Similarly, Goethe demanded of the drama that it present complete harmony and wholeness of all parts. In Wilhelmine Germany, the director was required not to please the public but rather to act as its spiritual leader. And when the Deutsches Theater was founded in Berlin in 1883, a number of new principles were officially implemented: the audience was no longer allowed to interrupt performances by applauding their favourite actors or asking them to repeat scenes; actors were not to accept flowers or step out of character; and the house was to be darkened during the performance so that members of the audience could no longer see one another as before, thereby literally leaving the public in the dark. Max Reinhardt, arguably the greatest presence in German theatre between 1903 and 1920, saw the stage as a second, separate world, one owned by the artist and released from life. As the director of the Deutsches Theater, Reinhardt produced over 100 plays on national and international stages. He insisted on the actors' total identification with their characters, not reproducing nature but creating it, appealing primarily to the mood of his audience rather than their intellect.

Interestingly enough, this kind of art greatly appealed to the established Left, even after the war. Following the events of the *Novemberrevolution*, the Social Democrats were heading a middle-of-the-road government, appealing to the *Bürger* and civil servants, the German middle class and all who fancied themselves as such – a normalizing refuge for those who had seen the spectre of the proletariat and feared political extremism. Recalling Mann's observation of the unpolitical man, Karl Vossler, rector of the University of Munich, remarked about his fellow Weimar citizens: 'Always in new forms the old stupidity: a metaphysical, speculative, romantic, fanatical, abstract and mystical kind of politicking . . . People who lament this way are presuming they are too elevated, too spiritual for politics.'[54]

Meanwhile, attempts to politicize artistic production and reception met stiff resistance, particularly from the Social Democrats, who argued that political theatre would distract from important union and party duties and that the drama troupes should strive for 'higher' forms of culture, emulating the *Bildungsgut*, or bourgeois traditions of cultural heritage, in an attempt to ward off the damaging massification of art and the loss of moral mission it entailed. With a choice of words that surely would have pleased Brecht, the party's secretary for cultural affairs declared his fears that *Afterkunst*, literally, 'anus art', could lead to the 'flattening of workers' brains'.[55] It was not until about 1925, the beginning of a relatively stable economic and political phase of the Weimar Republic, that a German agitprop theatre and other more class-conscious forms of dramatic performance would flourish.

It was into this climate of transitions and remanifestations that Brecht sought to introduce *Baal* – and in early 1919 he came close. During the short life of the Bavarian *Räterepublik*, also known as the Munich Soviet Republic, the Munich Nationaltheater's newly appointed leadership sought to democratize the institution and, as part of it, issued a call to young artists to participate in the founding of a provisionary stage for new dramatic literature. Brecht offered *Baal*. Brecht's friend Münsterer recalls that the playwright had good contacts with the Nationaltheater's new 'artistic secretary', Jakob Geis, who worked to get *Baal* accepted for production. Following the untimely demise of the *Räterepublik* and under pressure from the city's administrative apparatus and the Right, the theatre's new guard gradually disbanded and the new director, Karl Zeiß, reneged on any promises that were made to Brecht. A journal entry from 16 June 1920 states: 'Zeiß does not want to stage *Baal*, supposedly because he fears a scandal . . . The sensation of the winter collapses.'[56] The play would not be staged until 8 December 1923, in Leipzig, where it caused the expected scandal.

Instead, *Drums in the Night* was Brecht's first work to find its way to public presentation, premiering to great acclaim at the Münchener Kammerspiele theatre on 29 September 1922. Written after *Baal*, the play was originally titled *Spartakus*, as it bore witness to the so-called Spartakus Uprising of January 1919 and its consequences. After the declaration of the republic in November 1918, Brecht, like many others, got involved in local politics and was able to experience first-hand the rise, manipulation and subsequent violent repression of the *Räterepublik* in Munich and elsewhere. Brecht briefly joined the local 'workers and soldiers' council' while working at the military hospital, and acquaintances recall seeing him at a few rallies and assemblies. Both there and as part of the council, the poet kept a low profile, sitting at the back jotting notes. The young republic was a volatile mixture of soviet councils, a freely elected national assembly and powerful paramilitary organizations. Infighting among the various factions over Germany's political course led to a general strike and the Spartakus Uprising, in which the coalition parties of the Ebert government and the newly founded German Communist Party (KPD), labour unions and revolutionary organizations jockeyed for position newspapers were occupied, factories shut down and heavy street fighting broke out. In an attempt to restore law and order, Minister Gustav Noske, who was put in charge of the military in and around Berlin by Ebert, recruited the infamous Freikorps, a paramilitary right-wing organization consisting of former soldiers and mercenaries, backed financially by big business and industry. Marching on Berlin and its vicinity on 10 January, the Freikorps violently and ruthlessly killed hundreds of insurgents, and after several days of open agitation appealing to the public's disdain for disorder, assassinated Karl Liebknecht and Rosa Luxemburg on 15 January. These events in turn sparked tumultuous upheavals all over Germany.

Only a few days later, Brecht wrote a first version of *Spartakus*. By early March, he presented the draft to Lion Feuchtwanger, who maintained good connections to the Münchener Kammerspiele and who, according to Brecht, thought the play was 'genius'.[57] The impetus for the title *Drums in the Night* is said to have come from Feuchtwanger's wife, Marta. Feuchtwanger himself recalls a 'quickly thrown together dramatic ballad' about a returning soldier's struggle to be at home and join the revolution, told in an 'unfashionable, wild, strong, colourful language'.[58] The play's protagonist is the presumed-dead artillerist Kragler, who upon his return to Berlin finds his fiancée Anna pregnant by and engaged to the war profiteer Murk. Murk plans to establish himself securely in the bourgeois milieu by marrying Anna, the daughter of an industrialist. Anna's parents own a factory that made ammunition baskets during the war and, now that procreation is high on the national agenda, changed its production to baby carriages. Both economic and marital arrangements are quickly adjusted to the times' demands. Broken and homeless in more ways than one, Kragler sets off to join the revolution. In the bars and on the streets, he loudly tries to persuade workers to participate in the armed struggle and later leads the storming of the newspapers. But when Anna returns to him, Kragler abandons all political conviction. At the end of the play, as his comrades face death through artillery fire, Kragler walks away, declaring, 'My skin is supposed to rot in the gutter so that your ideas can go to heaven? Are you drunk?'[59] The revolution is as much disillusioned as is love – Kragler returns to Anna out of pure material selfishness: 'Now comes the bed, the big, white, wide bed, come!'[60]

Hannah Arendt has said that, to Brecht, what was more important than the war was the world that emerged from it, that he chronicled a threefold breakdown of tradition stretching over the duration of the Weimar Republic: politically, the decline and downfall of the nation state; socially, the transformation of a class society into a mass society; and spiritually, the rise of nihilism.[61] But as his early work already shows, Brecht was mostly interested in the way in which an array of sometimes successive, often competing belief structures veiled the continuities of oppression and exploitation and how culture as a constitutive part of the public sphere provided the narratives necessary to justify asocial, egotistical behaviour. Thus he found an ongoing transformation of nation and state rather than its abandonment, an affirmation of class structures in mass society and nihilism appropriated for the ratification of capitalist and ultimately fascist agendas. Like much of his early lyrical writings, *Drums in the Night* is as much a contemporary portrait of the relationship between various characters to each other and the world around them as it is a work about how such relationships are mediated by historical circumstances and available value systems. The play shows a world guided by ideals but driven by profiteering and the pursuit of material and spiritual ownership.

And ongoing historical developments made it increasingly pertinent: by the time *Drums in the Night* premiered on 29 September 1922, the German republic and its economy were well on their way to a substantial crisis. The reactionary Kapp Putsch of 1920 and the murder of foreign minister Walther Rathenau deeply shook the fragile republic, while the steep reparations assigned under the Versailles Treaty took a heavy financial and psychological toll on the nation. The government placed the greatest economic and existential burdens on the middle classes and the workers. Inflation was slowly but surely gaining momentum and made those with property very rich very fast, while gains made by the labour movement during 1918–19, such as collective bargaining and the eight-hour day, came under constant attack in the name of national sacrifice. The *Schieber* and *Raffke*, or schemers and grabbers, ruled the black markets, and their spectre tortured the increasingly cynical souls of those who suffered at their expense. With *Drums in the Night* Brecht hit a nerve at a time when one of the most popular songs candidly described the general attitude and outlook in 1922: 'We'll drink away our grandma's little house, her little house, We'll drink away our grandma's little house, the first and the second mortgage too!'[62]

The play's reception shows that not everybody was as willing to face the social and political realities of the time. One of the extras for the Munich performance remembers that in anticipation of his bourgeois audience's dramatic expectations, Brecht had posters hung in the hall reading 'Glotzt nicht so romantisch!' (Don't gawk so romantically!). To Brecht, the premiere was a great success. Karl Valentin was sitting in the audience and the well-known writer

Herbert Ihering had travelled all the way from Berlin. Reviewing *Drums in the Night* for the *Berliner Börsen-Courier*, Ihering emphasized the playwright's social realism:

> Brecht sees the person. But always in his effect on another person. Never are any of his figures isolated. For a long time, there hasn't been a poet in Germany who without presupposition had the tragic necessities: the interconnection of fates, the effect of people on one another. . . . The twenty-four-year-old poet Bert Brecht has changed the poetic face of Germany overnight.[63]

But when staged at the Deutsches Theater in Berlin three months later, on 20 December, critics and audience reacted quite differently, expecting much more enchanting fare, to which they were accustomed from Germany's premier house and Reinhardt's repertoire. The prominent critic Alfred Kerr, who had already rejected *Baal* after Brecht had sent it to him a few years earlier ('No theatre; a chaos with possibilities'), wrote a long review for the *Berliner Tageblatt*, which, like the *Frankfurter Zeitung*, was one of the most important liberal, bourgeois newspapers at the time. Kerr deemed *Drums in the Night* a 'tohubohu', 'shrieking', 'a ragout-chef's grab-bag'.[64] Comparing him unfavourably to the Expressionist playwright Ernst Toller, Kerr wrote, 'Brecht apparently thinks that the times' reflection can be captured through senseless yelling, boozing, and chaos.'[65] Kerr was a proponent of Max Reinhardt's 'magical theatre' and met Brecht's strategies of disillusionment through dramatic form and language with principled opposition. Many of the reviews of the play were primarily concerned with questions of form; few discussed the play's political dimension with regard to its content, a calculated deconstruction of a bourgeois reality based on layered facades of individual integrity and social order. Alexander Abusch was one of the few to mention the play's effect on its viewers' expectations:

The whole coterie of petit bourgeois theatre audience sat stupefied by the content of the Brechtian play. Especially the brains of the vanguard *Bürger* and *Bürgerinnen* malfunctioned upon this unwonted fare.[66]

The publicity made Brecht an overnight sensation. Ihering recommended the young playwright for the prestigious annual Kleist-Preis and pushed for Brecht right up to the prize's bestowal on him in December of 1922. Brecht was officially recognized and honoured by the institutions he set out to offend.

Beside the conscious attention given to the cultural habits of its audience, another important facet of *Drums in the Night* was its concern with constituency. Deliberately or not, Brecht portrayed the problems of winning over soldiers and workers for the revolution in the wake of the First World War. Kragler's disorientated opportunism speaks as much to a perverted survivalism as it does to a loss of faith in past promises and future ideas. Baal's art of nihilist vitality has been replaced by Kragler's negative affirmation of a pathetic materiality. Victories are by necessity small and personal; neither bride nor community nor country offers a cause worth self-abandonment. A result of and threat to the sociopolitical order that engulfs him, Kragler remains a contradictory, volatile figure. Writing in November 1918 for *Die Rote Fahne*, Rosa Luxemburg assessed the spectre of the revolution:

The reactionary state of the civilized world will not become a revolutionary people's state within twenty-four hours. Soldiers who yesterday, as gendarmes of the reaction, were murdering the revolutionary proletariat in Finland, Russia and Ukraine, and workers who calmly allowed this to happen, have not become in twenty-four hours supporters of socialism or clearly aware of their goals.[67]

Historian Eugene Lunn has described the 'defeat of proletarian revolutions in Central Europe (in the years 1918–23), and the victories of fascism thereafter' as bringing 'a crisis upon traditional Marxian orthodoxy', leading to the development of a Western Marxist current that, at odds with both Social-Democratic and Communist doctrine, turned to culture as a 'vital but neglected part of an historical dialectic of society, and as a means of better understanding the stabilizing features of modern capitalism'.[68] Brecht's early poetry, essays, reviews and plays placed him at the centre of this struggle, and his work throughout the Weimar Republic, the Third Reich and the German Democratic Republic would continue to do so. As an artist, he is usually described as developing from a happy anarchist to a Marxist convert; he has been accused of being a staunch supporter of the Communist party line, even of being a Stalinist. Yet the few things Brecht ever held onto were his critical distance, his sceptical humour and his pragmatic commitment to observation. He always resisted the urge to fall in with comfortable social and political mythologies, and his work was persistently driven by the contradictions and complexities of situating himself and his audience in an active and contingent relationship between image and reality, mediation and experience.

2

'Mehr guten Sport': Brecht in Berlin, 1924–8

The Big City – the Machine, the Battlefield

Brecht relocated permanently to Berlin in 1924. He moved in with his future wife, the actress Helene Weigel, whom he had met earlier that year through his friend the playwright and director Arnolt Bronnen. Lured by romance and propelled by his newfound success, Brecht had been travelling to the German metropolis with increasing frequency. *Baal* and *Drums in the Night*, as well making Brecht a Kleist prizewinner, had established him as an up-and-coming playwright. Kiepenheuer Verlag secured the general permission for all of Brecht's plays written between 1920 and 1924, including *Baal*, while Brecht retained the right to offer individual pieces to other publishing houses. Brecht was also offered a temporary position as dramatist at the Deutsches Theater, which he accepted.

Berlin offered a pace very different from Munich – transactions, conversations and attitudes seemed faster, more exciting and more superficial. Berlin embodied the myth of the Golden Twenties, and while the big city was alluring on its own, the end of the Soviet Republic and Hitler's failed Beerhall Putsch in 1923 had turned Munich into one of the most reactionary cities in Germany. Berlin was a place of new beginnings. Yet the city's dazzling urbanism also carried a raw harshness. To Brecht, the loss of self and subjectivity among the masses pushing through the streets and bars was simultaneously threatening and liberating. The urban experience was a *Kampfplatz*, a battlefield in the struggle to come to terms with the new. Brecht was fascinated by the ugly and non-literary, frequenting the cinema, mass sporting events like the *Sechstagerennen* bicycle races at the Sportpalast and car races at the Avus and bars populated by prostitutes and pimps. It was the absence of empathy in the encounter with modernity that attracted Brecht, as well as its ambiguities and the insecurities it triggered in him. He ruminated in his journal, 'How do I, a man from Augsburg with multiple talents for seeing and rendering the world, come to these markets, cafés and funhouses, and among such people?'[1]

In Brecht's factographic works of the mid-1920s, ranging from the plays *In the Jungle of the Cities* and *Man Is Man* and the poetry collection *From a Reader for City Dwellers* to *The Threepenny Opera*, Berlin is a site for the projection of collective fears and desires. Oswald Spengler had summed up the provincial angst of many Germans when he wrote in his book *Der Untergang des Abendlandes* (*The Decline of the West*, 1923):

> Instead of a world, there is a city, wherein the life of faraway countries gathers while the rest withers away; instead of a type-true, soil-grown people, there is a new sort of nomad, the parasitical city dweller, traditionless, cohering formlessly in fluid masses, utterly matter-of-fact, religionless, intelligent, unfruitful, deeply contemptuous of the countryman (and especially that highest form of countryman, the country gentleman), hence a monstrous step toward the inorganic, the end.[2]

The city dweller was a popular protagonist of the era, featured in George Grosz's drawings as collected in *Ecce Homo* (1923) and soon to be the central figure in Alfred Döblin's *Berlin Alexanderplatz* (1929) and Erich Kästner's *Fabian* (1931), presenting not so much an antidote to the provincially moral countryman as an articulation of the contradictions of modernity.

The psychological stability of the mid-1920s republic depended heavily on repression of the disappointment, disillusionment and deception caused by the lost war. The humiliation of the Versailles Treaty and the ongoing burden of stifling reparations sought compensation in a nostalgia for clear discernment of friend and foe. The parliamentary system, with its shifting coalitions among many parties, had blurred Left and Right. Conservative rhetoric focused its attention on the chaos, the lack of unity, the opportunism that had – according to the *Dolchstoßlegende*, the right-wing account of internal betrayal as the fatal stab in Germany's back – caused the fall of the German armies and continued to weaken the national body. To many, the Weimar Republic was an extension of the war, and Berlin was home to its maimed bodies and broken spirits. For those on the Right, the city stood as a reminder of betrayal and cowardice waiting to be rectified. To those on the Left, it presented pluralities and the limits of convictions, the failure of nationalist ideology, maybe even ideology at large and the dawn of a realist era. The writer Heinrich Mann saw in Berlin a place of hope: 'Germany's future is being demonstrated today in Berlin. Whoever wants to have hope ought to look there.'[3] Brecht recalls a similar spirit when first developing ideas for his play *In the Jungle*. A journal entry from the time reads:

> As heroic landscape, I have the city. As a standpoint relativity. As a situation the entry of humanity into the big cities at the beginning of the third millennium, as content the appetites (too big or too small), as practice for the audience the enormous social struggles.[4]

Berlin lacked a long-established class of patricians, and its cultural and intellectual constitution as well as its architecture embodied the Prussian rulers' taste for internationalism. Yet those who found this absence of tradition a welcome ground for experimentation were in the minority. Berlin was home to countless theatres, cabarets and cinemas; it was the capital of music and literature, of journalism and publishing; yet its appeal hardly reached beyond the city limits. Only three best-sellers published over the Weimar Republic's fifteen-year lifespan reflected the 'Weimar perspectives' of its authors (Kästner, Erich Maria Remarque and Thomas Mann); the typical German reader was mostly interested in gripping tales of heroism (often in war) and stoic inwardness as well as adventure and love stories.

Brecht himself interpreted the city-as-jungle as the mechanism of the reliable binaries of old and new, order and chaos, the provincial and the progressive gone awry. The new was not novelty, but the rejection of prevalent ideational simplicity. Looking back from his late-twentieth-century vantage, philosopher Peter Sloterdijk describes the Weimar Republic as 'an age of a universal dawning of reflection, insofar as at that time, such tactics and theories of artfulness and of "simplicity with duplicity" were developed at all levels'.[5] The multiple meanings provided by the encounter, artistic or otherwise, with the psychosocial environment served to complicate the simple or, vice versa, to simplify the complex. For Brecht, art was at its core a struggle over the relationality between experience and knowledge, and not necessarily one that could be won: 'With *In the Jungle* I wanted to improve [Schiller's] *Robbers*, and prove that battle is impossible due to the inadequacy of language.'[6] A new language was needed in order to understand that of which one had no prior knowledge. Art as a renegotiation of relationality was the foundation for social rather than merely technological innovation.

It is important to point out that Brecht's works of the mid-1920s are commonly seen as transitional from an anarchic-nihilist phase to a deep and often vulgar Marxist commitment as he encounters and processes the writings of Marx and Fritz Sternberg. Yet Brecht's Berlin practice is less a matter of progressing (false) consciousness than an example of the playwright's close immersion in and reading of history. Part of the ongoing validity of his work and method is his emphasis on the historical specificity of artistic engagement, of understanding art as a critical practice that changes according to the contingency of context in order to remain viable both as a way of knowing and of changing reality and its mediation. Throughout his career, Brecht consistently took a dialectical approach to the world around him, sometimes more and sometimes less subtle or effective, and though he could be doctrinaire about his convictions, his method of continuous reflective and reflexive interrogation of cultural mechanisms was, due to its own logic, anything but.

Once in Berlin, Brecht rewrote his play *In the Jungle*, begun three years earlier, and renamed it *In the Jungle of the Cities*. It tells the story of a family's fight to survive, literally and spiritually, in the big city. The young protagonist Garga, his parents and his sister are lured by promises of wealth and opportunity, but when these fail to materialize, not even time-honoured morals and familial bonds can prevent their demise. As the father succumbs to alcohol and mother and sister take to the streets, Garga, who dreams of a life as a logger on the South Seas, fuelled by literature, becomes entangled in a prolonged fight with the capitalist lumber merchant Shlink. Shlink demonstrates that the bourgeois ideal of free thought as the basis for a meaningful, ordered social existence and the possibility of changing one's fate is incompatible with the freedom of the market. The merchant seeks intimacy through a shared process of alienation, enacted through the fight between the ideal and the real. No matter how steadfastly Garga and his family hold onto ethical and moral convictions, they are lured deeper and deeper into a game where the only way to assert one's identity is to give it up. To be out for solely one's own advantage is to be just like everyone else, and the loss of all artificial pretences and categories such as right and wrong, good and bad, is at once a liberation and a death sentence. In the end, there are no heroes; neither morals nor instinct prevail. Not even the fight confers meaning.

Looking back in 1952, Brecht writes, 'The play deals with the impossibility of the fight, here taken positively, as sport.'[7] The introduction to the printed version published in 1927 by Propyläen Verlag in Berlin further elaborates on the sports metaphor, describing the work as an 'inexplicable wrestling match between two people' and addressing the reader directly: 'Do not break your head over the motives of this fight, but instead . . . judge impartially the fighting form of the opponents, and train your eyes on the finish.'[8] Language and its limits as a means to signify, symbolize and naturalize experience turn *Jungle* into a site of confusion, so much so that most critics expressed puzzlement over what they saw. Joseph Stolzing wrote about the 1923 Munich premiere for the fascist *Völkischer Beobachter*: 'I could not give a summary [of this play] because I had not the faintest idea of what was happening onstage.'[9] Tellingly, Stolzing panned the performance for its 'Yiddish' jargon and incoherence, implying further that chaos rather than clarity was favoured by the attending 'Jewish community'.[10] Brecht was adamant about finding a way to adequately communicate the experience of modern, urban man as well as the limits of fully comprehending it, and therefore the possibility of transgressing and developing it.

During this period, Upton Sinclair, Rudyard Kipling and Schiller became important touchstones for Brecht. After reading Kipling, Brecht noted:

> Thinking about what Kipling did for the nation that 'civilized' the world, I made the epochal discovery that actually nobody has yet described the big city as jungle. Where are its heroes, its colonizers, its victims? The hostility of the big city, its vicious stony consistency, its Babylonian language confusion; in short: its poetry has not yet been made.[11]

But Brecht knew of Sinclair's novel *The Jungle* (1906, published in Germany the same year), which he discussed as a contemporary alternative to Schiller's *Don Carlos* (1787) and its protagonist's struggle for freedom and conviction, any conviction:

> God knows, I have always loved *Don Carlos*. But these days I am reading in Sinclair's *Jungle* the story of a worker who is starved to death in Chicago's slaughterhouses. It is about simple hunger, coldness, illness that get a man down. . . . This man once has a small vision of freedom, is then beaten down with a baton. His freedom has not the least to do with Carlos's freedom, I know: but I can't really take Carlos's servitude seriously any longer.[12]

What the two works share is their inability to go beyond an aesthetic, an image, of freedom (as Brecht observed, 'With Schiller, freedom is always only demanded.') The review of the *Don Carlos* performance continues: 'One wanted to speak humanly (and didn't quite do it, couldn't in part).'[13] Indeed, in *Jungle*, words and acts of speaking are, like the city itself, cold, distant, monologic. Brecht cultivates this direct manner in order to find a linguistic realism, a reality of form that corresponded to the reality it expressed and produced.

The author shared his contemporaries' fascination with a mythical America – a place all the more real for its wildness. American investment in economic recovery in Germany under the Young and Dawes plans further enshrined the U.S. as the land of progress, prosperity and confidence, of commercialism, exploitation and barbaric ruthlessness. With its Wild West past and cut-throat present, America was an antidote to the German nation's feelings of insufficiency, to the narrow-minded, pastoral *Kleinbürgerlichkeit*, to the desperate and defensive nostalgia for old days and old ways. The 'cult of America' comprised jazz and boxing, American lingo and dress, tales of crime and gangsters; German artists and intellectuals smoked Virginia cigarettes, drank whisky, even changed their names (Bertolt became Bert, Georg Grosz became George Grosz and Helmut Herzfelde had earlier changed his name to John Heartfield in protest against the war).

In letters and journal entries, Brecht likened Berlin to the 'cold Chicago', with its archetypal urbanization and socio-economic rationality.[14] To use Chicago to talk about Berlin allowed for critical distance – the American myth a demystification of the German present, the foreign locale a stage for an allegorical approach to the mechanisms of perception rather than an overt naturalism solely dedicated to the description of circumstances. The matter-of-factness Brecht gleaned from his observations of American life was a way of acknowledging the constructed relation between material and ideological reality. The city as heroic landscape was unnatural, and thus transitory. Regarding the longevity of modernity, its material and historical substance, a journal entry from July 1925 reads, 'But after some consideration I take them [iron-and-cement buildings] generally to be more ephemeral than some farmers' huts.'[15] Brecht's city is subject to historical change, and he specifically avoids its anthropomorphization. The urban environment is an arena for the study of behaviours.

The plot of *In the Jungle of the Cities* appears chaotic at certain points, but the events described therein are neither absurd nor incomprehensible – its author simply refuses to obey dramatic conventions and provide a sound explanation for behaviour. Conventional harbingers and institutions of sense and sensibility, like the family, marriage and the language of the books that are the dwindling sources and bulwarks of Garga's honour, fantasies and ideals, have little or no practical value in his fight with Shlink. Hurling quotes at Shlink in the library, Garga resembles Rimbaud: 'He is essentially a German translation from the French into the American.'[16] He clings to the literary in an attempt to ward off Shlink's blunt and unapologetic facticity. To Brecht, Garga as Rimbaud is the resistance to the bourgeois novel and its concern with verisimilitude.[17] The language is episodic, affirmative of its origins and presence, rather than referential: 'I put together word mixtures like strong drinks.'[18] Language is politicized through the articulation of its historicity, its moment, place and function of speaking and listening.

In 1925 Brecht wrote that most literature stems from 'a shortage of thoughts for *den Hausgebrauch* [domestic, everyday use]. . . . We can only through events get to a few pathetic thoughts. It is easier to invent these events than to get the thoughts into one's head without them.'[19] Focusing on actual events, Brecht embarked on a project of utilitarian literature during the mid-1920s, including the aforementioned *Manual of Piety* as well as the poetry collections *From a Reader for City Dwellers* and *The Three Soldiers: A Children's Book*, illustrated by George Grosz. Many of the poems contained in these collections were published individually throughout the 1920s, many of the *Manual of Piety* texts during the previous decade. But their compilation and dissemination as books was a strategic move. The 'manual of piety', the 'reader' and children's books were popular forms of education and acculturation; appropriating the familiar format, Brecht turns manuals of instruction into tools of learning. Opening the *Manual of Piety* (first published in 1927), one finds a long set of instructions of how and when to handle the book's different sections. Some are '*geistige* exercises', potentially offering one or the other 'insight into life'.[20] Others are to be consulted, while smoking or accompanied by an instrument, in times of 'raw natural disasters (rainfalls, snowstorms, bankruptcies, etc.)', the adventures of bold men and women in far corners of the world supplying cues for action.[21] The first page of *The Three Soldiers* (issued as part of the *Versuche* series in 1932), a dark tale of controversial characters, questionable motivations and atrocities in modern warfare, briefly states that the book is to be read to children and is meant to give them the opportunity to ask questions. The poems of the *Reader* are part of a broader Weimar phenomenon;

several other authors, including Kurt Tucholsky, Walter Mehring and Johannes Becher, wrote critical assessments of the city and its inhabitants. The *Reader* is, in a sense, an extension of the *Jungle*, more direct in its appeal to its audience to engage in the production of images and ideas. Writing in the *Berliner Börsen-Courier* in April 1927, Brecht's critical champion Ihering observed this transition, linking a recently restaged and rewritten version of the play to the revolutionary quality of the poems. He wrote:

> Brecht is not a lofty revolutionary. He fights neither for, nor against. He neither glorifies technology, nor abnegates the mechanization of the times. To him, this is self-evident. He lives in it. To him, this is the basis, matter, material for production. A transformation has already happened. He is a revolutionary because he lives in an already changed world.[22]

Unlike many other authors of urbanity, Brecht was less interested in the city itself than in the attitudes and behaviours of the city dweller. Any sort of urban atmosphere, decor or milieu are overlooked in favour of what Walter Benjamin, with regard to Brecht's poetry of the time, called *Armseligkeit*, or poverty: a lack of sympathy for urban romanticism but a great sensitivity to economic, social and psychological destitution.[23] The city demands and enables a technical, cold and mechanical form of writing, which *takes stock*, and thereby transcends conventions.

Over approximately a dozen pages, the *Reader* offers a number of observations and vantages, of opportunities lost and taken, people met and left behind, expectations defied and standpoints betrayed. Brecht gives advice, then takes it back:

> Separate from your comrades at the station
> Go into the city in the morning with your coat buttoned
> Find a place to stay and when your comrade knocks:

Open, oh, don't open the door.
Instead
Cover your tracks!
. . .
Eat the meat that's there! Don't save!
Go into every house when it rains, and sit on every chair that's
    there
But don't stay! And don't forget your hat!
I tell you:
Cover your tracks!
. . .
(Or so I was told.)[24]

The *Reader* is 'poor' in language and metaphor, yet rich in its offer
to acknowledge speaking and thinking, reading and writing as a
form of urban reality unburdened with the labour of matching the
everyday to myth but instead letting it play out. This is precisely
how the city is a social matter for Brecht: it provides the encounter
of different experiences, all mediated but bare and open in their
heterogeneity, their force, their competition. The possibility then
emerges of enacting a different idea, creating a different reality, one
that comes from the process rather than the result of urban reading.

Public Bodies, Body Politic

In the mid-1920s, German selfhood underwent a number of physical,
psychological and social transformations. Crazes for sports and
fitness took place alongside the presence of war invalids on the
streets of Berlin. The urban crowds and the dwindling of traditional
family structures, the mass production of cultural wares and the
phenomenon of the 'new woman' challenged customary notions
of individuality. To many, new social formations stood for progress

and modernity, but this euphoria was also feared, and the republic turned into an arena of competition over the type and quality of the inevitable progress. Technology and an economy looking beyond the satisfaction of needs towards the production of desires created mega-subjects of consumers and classes, producers and spectators. To famed German politician Walther Rathenau, progress and regress were closely related phenomena, and the former in itself led not to emancipation but dependency, a mechanization of existence.[25] Others, like social scientist Friedrich von Gottl-Ottlilienfeld, revered Henry Ford, 'grand master of technical reason'.[26] Ford's book *My Life and Work* was a best-seller in Germany and praised as an example of Enlightenment thinking: instead of achieving economic and social growth at the expense of the worker, Ford proposed a defeudalization of life under capitalism, where the organized availability of labour and its products guaranteed equal participation in progress and prosperity. Meanwhile, the Dadaists, for their part, famously denounced the perceived myth of bourgeois individualism and celebrated more egalitarian techniques of production, as practised in Russia's revolutionary workshops: 'Long live the machine art of Tatlin!'

But the unease with which the new form of collectivism was greeted did not merely stem from a suspicion of whether or not modernity would keep its promises and rewards. In many ways, post-war progress was an extension of the modern war machine itself, and a continuation of the mutilation of the sovereign male subject and its patriarchal social order. The massive military machine and its mechanization of destruction had made the First World War an unprecedented phenomenon of depersonalization. The steel of the tank and the weapon, the equipment bonding soldiers to one another and to the fighting body, became the artificial limb, the implanted metal plate, the wheelchair. The matter-of-factness of this reassembled human existence forcefully rejected the psycho-corporeal wholeness of bourgeois individualism, just as the physical, erotic and social androgyny of *die neue Frau* (the new woman) affirmed the potential, and to an extent the actual, interchangeability of the subject as a functionalist piece in the new culture of mass production and consumption. Hans Ostwald wrote in his *Sittengeschichte der Inflation* (A moral history of inflation, 1931):

> Everything seemed reversed. . . . Above all it was the women who in many respects completely transformed themselves. They asserted their demands, particularly their sexual demands, much more clearly. . . . If during the war women were forced to take over many male jobs, they did not allow themselves afterward to be pushed quite all the way back into the home.[27]

In this context, Brecht's play *Man Is Man* stood out for its reflection on the different forms of Weimar collectivity. Looking back in 1930, Brecht described the relation between social elements and their totality during the Weimar Republic in his essay 'The Dialectic Dramaturgy':

> The war shows the role that was assigned to the individual in the future. The individual as such attained effective engagement only as representative of the many. But his engagement with the great economic-political processes was restricted to the exploitation of the many.[28]

This observation sheds light on the ideological function of parliamentary democracy at a time when the experiment in political participation effectively served to justify the empowerment of private, mostly industrial, interests and a systematic undoing of workers' rights and social security in the name of the common good. The state strained to disseminate symbols and conduct rituals of unity to conceal opposition among the numerous parliamentary factions and the conflicting pressures from powerful economic agendas. State funerals like those of Rathenau and Ebert, and celebrations following the end of the French Rhineland occupation in 1930, pandered to nostalgic-nationalist desires. Brecht's statement also shows his factual attitude towards what he perceived as the inevitable process of post-war deindividuation and the point at which a critical art and theatre had to engage. A dialectical dramaturgy would not posit a reactionary bourgeois art affirming the myth of a centred, individual subjectivity (as he accused Thomas Mann and others of doing), but rather commit to the empowerment of the revolutionary subject to shape the structure and quality of ineluctable social relationality.

Brecht's journals and notes show that he started developing the idea of the individual's interchangeability in the wake of the war and during his time in Munich.[29] In 1920, he wrote the poem 'This Was the Citizen Galgei': 'The citizen Galgei could be / just as well another one.'[30] Galgei and the transformation of his personality due to outside pressure was a project Brecht developed into a play over the next few years with the help of the writer Elisabeth Hauptmann (who after his move to Berlin became one of his closest collaborators as well as his lover) and, to a lesser extent, friends like Caspar Neher, the author Emil Burri, and the director Bernhard Reich. Engaging thoroughly with Kipling and Döblin, and with certain motifs and narrative structures directly appropriated from their writings, the play debuted as *Man Is Man* in 1926 in Darmstadt. Here, the playwright and Neher, who was responsible for the set, first employed what would become a paradigmatic element of the Epic Theatre: the half-raised curtain, which provides the audience with a literal and metaphorical insight into the workings of the stage. The play tells the story of three colonial soldiers who have lost their fourth man and find the credulous Gay to be a perfect ersatz comrade. Via the rite of a fake execution, Gay is purged of his old self and inducted into his new role in the foursome military body. In the middle of the play, one of the protagonists, flanked by an effigy of the playwright, addresses the viewers directly: 'Herr Bertolt Brecht declares that man is man. . . . Here, tonight, a human being will be reassembled like a car, without losing anything in the process.'[31] *Man Is Man* largely garnered responses of puzzlement and incomprehension with regard to its content, while the 'technical' choices, like Neher's half-raised curtain and the dissolution of the illusionary space through a 'constructivist *Gestänge* [scaffold] *à la russe*', according to the critic Bernhard Diebold met with great enthusiasm. Diebold goes on to link Brecht's efforts to Bolshevik 'uni-formation', though remarking on the playwright's unwillingness to call his collectivism by a programmatic name.[32] Indeed, Brecht struggled to cast his efforts in the correct light. When the work was broadcast as a radio play in 1927, the introduction for the first time describes the *Ummontierung,* or remontage, of Gay as a positive act:

> This Galy Gay is not at all a weakling, quite the opposite, he is the strongest. But he is only the strongest after he has ceased to be a private person; only as part of the mass does he become strong.[33]

With the rise of fascism in the early 1930s, Brecht revised the play again so as to emphasize that not all forms of human materialization are positive, that there are, as he wrote later, 'false, bad collectives' exploiting 'the real social collective of the workers'. Certainly, this insight was part and parcel of the work from the beginning; Brecht was counting on the play's form to let the members of the audience think through which type of collective identity would be the most conducive to its constituency: 'In a good *verfremdeten* [distancing] presentation, this growth into the criminal is certainly demonstrable.'[34]

In 1927, Brecht met the sociologist Fritz Sternberg, who, along with Karl Kraus, offered an important confirmation of the playwright's committed critical analysis and his idea of art as a social practice. Sternberg's 1926 book *Der Imperialismus* contains a passage describing the artist's central role in a successful socialist revolution: the articulator of the proletarian class consciousness. For Sternberg, as for Brecht, a new perception of the world was a matter of making conscious an already-existing reality of social relations. This is why Sternberg describes the decline of the conventional drama as a historical necessity, and refers to already 'living in Marxist times'.[35] It also explains Brecht's fascination with a specific type of facticity he found in the temporal straightforwardness of boxing matches, in the event-language of the police report, even in the banal, corporeal act of sex as an antidote to the commercialization of love. In the *Reader*, one finds the lines, 'I speak to you merely / Like reality itself.'[36] This reality of social relations is at the core of *Man Is Man*, of its motto of *Einer ist keiner* – 'one is no one' or 'one body is nobody'.[37] Only vis-à-vis the collective and one's place in it can the individual understand and determine his own actions. What is destroyed in the process of human reassembly is the commodity of individualism *as well as* that of the consumer. *Man Is Man* is a *Lustspiel*, a parable designed to avoid naturalistic forms of realism in favour of an active demonstration; it is geared towards the collaborative or communal labour of actors and audience.

To Brecht, the individual body is at once personal and social, a site of negotiation between the subject's experience and social knowledge or, as social theorists Oskar Negt and Alexander Kluge describe it, a battleground for social antagonisms.[38] If the body produces and is produced, makes its way through the world, probing, exploring, as much as it is guided and inscribed by its surroundings, then the labour of experience is a question of ownership, of who has the power and the right to wield the tools of history and fantasy. It is, to return to Brecht's occupation as poet and playwright, a matter of enabling production and distribution not only for the artist, but for the actor, the viewer, the reader.

Emancipation is thus what historian Leslie Adelson calls 'moments of freedom, not *from* social constraints but *in* social process'.[39]

This notion of emancipation is especially compelling with regard to Brecht's treatment of women at the time, as it relates to his observation that 'one body is nobody'. In the *Moral History*, Ostwald points out that the assertion of the 'new woman' was in large part physical and sexual:

> In every conceivable way they intensified their claim to the rights of life and a full range of experience. Amorous scandals came much more strongly to light. Some of them served as symbols of the time. Nudism was no longer confined to specific circles and to theatrical revues and cabarets. It permeated fashion throughout society: the pretty leg was discovered and gladly put on display.[40]

Brecht's own relationship to the women in his life, in their roles as wives, lovers and colleagues, was controversial. Within a few months of moving to Berlin, Brecht asked Weigel to find a different apartment for herself and their son Stefan (born in November 1924) so that he could freely pursue his own aims, both creative and erotic. Along with his declaring his right to promiscuity while granting his partners no such freedom, Brecht's multiple liaisons and largely casual fatherhood have dismayed many commentators. On a professional level, some scholars point out the extent to which Brecht's work was in fact the labour of his female collaborators, including Weigel, Hauptmann and, later, Margarete Steffin; critics have accused Brecht of advancing a notion of collectivism that was actually based on opportunism, mechanization and exploitation.[41]

As for the female characters in his plays and poetry, much Brecht scholarship has pointed to the work's inability, in general, to see women, like men, as anything but impersonal cogs in the revolutionary machine. Still, Sara Lennox has argued that despite

Brecht's 'explicit conception of instrumentality in human relation-ships', there are moments where the plays present alternative modes of action and behaviour, 'truths' based in irrational, emotional, private drives, 'though against [Brecht's] intention and interests'.[42] Such contradiction and contestation of the body and of subjectivity, indeed, form the very basis and method of Brecht's work of the time. In *Man Is Man*, the widow Begbick is the only protagonist able to adapt to her circumstances and then shape them. As a widow, Begbick is master of her own fate. She is the proprietress of the canteen where most of the play unfolds, where she offers food and, to some, including Gay, herself. She consciously takes advantage of female clichés, thereby affirming the play's underlying theme of product versus production: the collective of consumerism promises equal access to modern life and identity through its ready availability of reified and pre-made wares, material, emotional, intellectual and otherwise, while only the latter – production as action owned – provides participation in the process of shaping self and society. Begbick is a woman who, according to historian Angelika Führich, 'controls her sexuality rather than falling victim to it'.[43]

The control of sexuality as product and production is again articulated in the then-unpublished poetry collection *Augsburg Sonnets*, written during visits to Augsburg and in Berlin between 1925 and 1927. The poems reflect the Italian tradition of the sonnet (though not all of them are sonnets in the classical sense), presenting vulgar, popular language and pornographic subject-matter in poetic form. Sexuality fares much better than love in these accounts of modern affection; the ephemeral quality of longing and desire has been turned into a commodity, the power of its myth continuously eroded through the artifice of its materiality. Sex, on the other hand, especially sex for sale, presents the object of desire in its most unabashedly blatant form. The *Augsburg Sonnets* portray the prostitute as a woman liberated from the dependency of marriage, which desanctifies the relationship between man and woman, turning it into one of labour and exchange and thus into a site of struggle over ownership. In the poem 'Advice from an Older Whore to a Younger One', the guidance given is factual and calculated: the *Fohse* – which in German means both 'whore' and, crudely speaking, 'vagina', that is, both purveyor of sex and the sex object – is put in charge of her own actions. As a subject, she is what Negt and Kluge call a 'chain of attributes' rather than a coherent, fixed form of ego identity. Being at once 'human' and methodical, authentic in her female eroticism yet adaptable to the customer's needs, emotionless in her lovemaking yet not 'mechanical', the prostitute is a site of identity contestation where the *possibility* for subjectivity resides in the actions and attitudes taken. The body is filtered, processed and pursued, and selfhood is no longer a matter of private concerns such as hopes and feelings.

In 1930, Brecht contributed to a publication against the infamous 'paragraph 218' added to Germany's Civil Code in 1926, which made abortion a crime, punishable by incarceration. Brecht's 'About §218' is concerned less with women's rights than with ownership over the termination of life in general. The text accuses the state of wanting to retain a monopoly over who gets to live, as it is already practising with 'adult, fit-for-work humans'. Besides alluding, intentionally or not, to the wartime notion of 'fit for active service', under which the empire sent thousands of less-than-able soldiers to certain death under the pretext of serving the common good, Brecht implies that the state's implementation of collectivity is geared not towards greater social productivity but towards private, financial interest. The poem argues that as a truly public act, of which the state presents itself as the guarantor, abortion is not a private or economic matter but a social one; the choice of whether or not to raise a child is not a matter of law or principle but depends on the power allotted to the individual to determine and control her subjectivity and abilities as a productive member of society.

Brecht's interest in collectivity and the body was further manifested in his enthusiasm for sport because of both its factual, no-nonsense form of drama and its quality of audience participation. Weary of the passive, introspective consumption of theatrical performance, Brecht and many of his colleagues discerned in the passionate spectators who packed local boxing halls and racetracks a new mode of viewing. Not just any crowd would do. In the unpublished 1929 essay, 'Young Stage – Social Revolutionaries', Brecht bemoaned the audience that populated even the more progressive theatres:

> this whole faddish, helpless, intellectually lazy mass, who came here propelled by some strange, entirely perverse drive for education and a less strange desire for gossip, who, belonging to a perishing class, will never be able to glean anything from our things.[44]

Brecht felt that the new audience, 'demanded by the new drama', did not need to be created: 'He exists, though thus far not in the theatre.'[45]

There was a popular debate among Weimar public intellectuals around sports, fitness and health, as sports were no longer seen as just lower-class amusement but had become accepted as a progressive form of popular entertainment. Compared with the bourgeois ideal of the reasoning public, the audience of sporting events had traditionally been decried as 'herds and mercurial mobs, who appeared incapable of individual thought, easy to provoke, and difficult to pacify'.[46] But different perspectives were emerging as the allegorization of sports became an important ideological tool. The writer Hermann Kasack observed in sports a communal subversion of the individual ego in collective ecstasy, while Hermann Bahr in his article 'Geist und Sport' (Spirit and sport, 1928) emphasized the importance of sports spectatorship as a repudiation of high culture in favour of more objective, sober, more 'real' standards for the engagement with culture. But while many avant-garde artists and writers were caught up in a euphoric embrace of the productive as well as receptive facticity of sportive competition, attracted by its direct, accessible language and the appeal of the unadorned, noted critic and sociologist Siegfried Kracauer provided an insistent voice of dissent. In his 1927 essay 'Sie sporten' (They sport), Kracauer first expressed his concern about sports as a substitute culture where the audience was swept away in a spectacle of 'Ersatz Triumph', a struggle that lacked immanent meaning, removed from its historical moment and place and therefore without relevant political impact.[47] The enthusiastic consumption of athletics exhausted any potentially disruptive energies of the multitude. In the collection of writings *Die Angestellten* (*The Salaried Masses*, 1930), Kracauer criticizes sport's integral role in the production of leisure as an arena actively separated from the work sphere – the mechanical diffusion of revolutionary drives through consumption and entertainment.[48] The substitute function of culture is crucial to the *geistig obdachlos*, or spiritually, intellectually homeless white-collar workers, who differ from the proletariat in their lack of social identity. In their yearning to belong, the *Angestellte* are satisfied with the passive participation provided by consumption and spectatorship, which offers, as Kracauer puts it, 'asylum for the homeless'.[49]

Brecht, for his part, saw in the reception of sports not an ersatz but an alternative mode of experience. His conception relies on a crucial differentiation among forms of collective identity and behaviour: public, mob, consumers, masses. Throughout the second half of the twentieth century, the history of the avant-garde in general and the study of Brecht's work in particular have often been reduced to a trajectory of undifferentiated anti-individualism, which in its reactionary embrace of social equalization paved the way, or even directly led to, fascist and Stalinist totalitarianism.

But Brecht was not the only one to observe that appreciation of athletic events included profound knowledge of the rules and the players' abilities and strategies, as well as a keen ability for critical judgement. The urban crowds assembled around the boxing ring and in the velodrome were the new theatre's dream collective: 'He who has been to the *Sportpalast* knows that the audience is young enough for a sharp and naïve theatre.'[50] In 'More Good Sport', the playwright goes even further, declaring: 'We pin our hopes on the sporting public.' The essay, first published in the *Berliner Börsen-Courier*, describes this public as informed and diverse: '15,000 people of all classes and facial features, the smartest and most fair audience is the world', which, unlike the theatre's, knows exactly what they are in for:

> The *Verderblichkeit* [demoralization] of our theater audiences springs from the fact that neither theater nor audience has the faintest idea what it is that is supposed to be happening. In the sport arenas the people know when they buy their ticket exactly what will transpire, and it does transpire as soon as they take their seats.[51]

Brecht's polemic is directed at the esoteric art appreciation of high-culture connoisseurs; he tightens the screws when he bemoans the lack of 'fun' in the 'old arts'. But his point, as David Bathrick has argued, is ultimately an epistemological one.[52] When the audience *knows*, it is in a position to make demands, to be critical, to judge. It is this interest in material life and its experience that makes the sporting public different from the fascist mob, the passive consumer, the bourgeois public sphere's assembly of private individuals.

> There seems to be nothing to stop the theatre from having its own form of 'sport'. If only someone could take those buildings designed for theatrical purposes which are now standing eating

73

their heads off in interest, and treat them more or less as empty spaces for the successful pursuit of 'sport', then they would be used in a way that might mean something to a contemporary public that earns real contemporary money and eats real contemporary beef.[53]

To Brecht, sport is popular, but not populist. For theatre and art to be like sport would mean not to address the audience directly but to include it as a public whose interests, needs and experiences are subject to debate and reflection but not conflated or subsumed as part of the work itself. Art is to be a real-time event that draws an audience in which everybody is an expert, passionately and knowledgeably immersed in discussions of form and performance.

Sachlichkeit

In his 2007 book *The Century*, the French philosopher Alain Badiou presents Brecht as 'an emblematic figure of the twentieth century', an era whose subjectivity is 'prey to the passion of the real and placed under the paradigm of definite war'.[54] What draws Badiou to Brecht is the playwright's articulation of the antagonism that defines 'Germany's identity crisis': the tension between a romanticism of Wagnerian dimensions – 'This has less to do with Wagner's genius', Badiou remarks, 'than with its appropriation by petit bourgeois *ressentiment*: the bankrupt shopkeeper in rags mistaking himself for Siegfried in a Kaiser helmet' – and a cynical, paralysing nihilism.[55] Brecht's work 'thinks the enigmatic link between destruction and commencement', finding social, political and dramatic innovation not in the unreserved replacement of the outdated with the new but in the old's 'nourishing decomposition'.[56] Brecht's interest in the *Sachlichkeit* or facticity, the facticity of the city and the masses, of technology and sports, of prostitution and crime writing, lies not in their abolition of romantic or bourgeois notions of individuality or existence per se, but in their chronicling of the demise of the old to make room for alienation and discontent to emerge as a critique that is increasingly harder to suppress. What drew Brecht and his peers to sports was not just the audience's engagement but the contest itself as a technical model of reality where, in the end, the outcome was based on unadulterated, unmediated force. This was the upside of Kracauer's lament regarding the depoliticization of sport: ideology could represent physical competition in *völkisch* terms but, as the National Socialists found out for themselves when Jesse Owens repeatedly shattered the myth of Aryan supremacy during the 1936 Olympics in Berlin, the facticity of the contest defied any racist *Überbau*. Boxing in particular offered a violent deconstruction of the stage without its abandonment. The actor on this stage was accountable for his actions, while their presentation challenged the formal and narrative artifice so integral to the concept of entertainment.

Brecht was one of many Weimar artists and intellectuals who were enthralled by boxing. The avant-garde mingled with the heroes of the ring, like Max Schmeling, Paul Samson-Körner, Hans Breitensträter and Erich Brandl, at soirées organized by the art dealer Alfred Flechtheim and on the pages of his journal *Querschnitt: Magazin für Kunst, Literatur und Boxsport*. A number of artists even took up boxing themselves, among them John Heartfield and George Grosz, the actor Fritz Kortner and the opera singer Michael Bohnen. The rejection of theatricality was the shared, decisive appeal, and any tampering with the material 'realness' of boxing was vehemently denounced. Greater specialization and abstraction, as through the increasing attempt by 'experts' to apply 'a whole nomenclature of technical terms' and 'point systems', and the technical TKO rather than a true knock-out, belied, according to Brecht, a tendency toward 'l'art pour l'art'.[57] The *Querschnitt* even presented reports on matches by fighters themselves, in a language as direct and straightforward as their performance in the ring. Brecht's own boxing stories took a similarly factual approach, using reportage and interviews to effect as direct a perspective as possible.

Brecht cultivated a friendship with Samson-Körner; several photographs show the two spending time together. A staged image of 1927 captures Elisabeth Hauptmann at the typewriter, among a few friends and colleagues, with Samson-Körner sitting at a piano at the other end of the room and Brecht standing in the

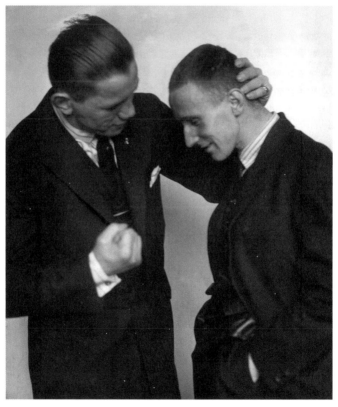

Brecht with Paul Samson-Körner, *Berliner Illustrierte Zeitung*, 1928.

centre, as if connecting the worlds of the fighter and the Weimar intellectuals. Another photograph, published the following year, shows Brecht and the boxer as complementary characters: raising his fist as if to throw an uppercut, Samson-Körner towers over the diminutive writer, who has his hands in his pockets, gaze turned downwards, a sly smile on his face. But the heavyweight champion has placed his other hand gently on the back of the poet's head in a nearly tender embrace. There is something almost homoerotic in this picture, a curious charge of masculinization that suggests the Weimar cult of the strong, male body as the physical and psychological catharsis of a nation's men maimed and humiliated by war and reparations. Brecht's short story 'The Uppercut' (1925) and *The Vita of the Boxer Samson-Körner*, an incomplete serial novel published in *Scherls Magazin* in 1926–7, emphasize the ambiguity of the boxer image: on the one hand the fighter is gruff and uneducated, brutal, the least likely role model for bourgeois sons or those with *bürgerliche* aspirations. On the other hand, he embodies ideals of masculinity, wholeness and individuality. The form of the interview and first-person narrative also affirm the subjective voice of a coherent self, but in the banality of their language and structure, the lack of psychological development found in the more traditional *Bildungsroman* (a type of novel concerned with the spiritual, moral and social education and maturation of a young protagonist), Brecht's texts defy easy consumption. As in the photographs of Brecht and the boxer, the elements do not quite add up, so they come under scrutiny themselves.

In a sense, these texts resemble the works of the Berlin Dadaists, such as Hannah Höch's collages and John Heartfield's montages, in their 'nourishing decomposition'. The emphasis on construction and constructedness not only makes room for an awareness of the production of language but foregrounds the alienation that stems from experiencing the rift between disparate images and ideas, between the possible and the actual, the picture and the thing. In an article published in the *Arbeiter Illustrierten Zeitung* (Workers' illustrated paper) on the occasion of its tenth anniversary, Brecht addresses the type of reportage offered by someone like Heartfield, who was one of the publication's staff artists:

> In the hands of the bourgeoisie, photography has become a terrible weapon *against* the truth. . . . The photographic

Hannah Höch, *Beautiful Girl*, 1920, collage.

apparatus can lie just as much as the typesetting machine. The task of the A-I-Z to serve the truth and reconstruct the real facts is of undeniable importance and, I believe, is being solved brilliantly.[58]

Brecht's contribution to this project of truth-telling was the demystification of art and language. Using a historically specific and determined type of speech, he aimed to denaturalize views, positions and attitudes that had been presented as given, transhistorical, inalterable. To Brecht, the images provided by bourgeois art as well as by the Neue Sachlichkeit (New Objectivity) were what Barthes called 'depoliticized speech', which turned history into nature, robbing events of how they came to be, how they function, how they change. 'Things lose the memory that they were once made.'[59] Instead, Brecht looked to historicize the natural in the affirmation of the production of the present. In Barthes' words:

> This is a political language: it presents nature for me only inasmuch as I am going to transform it. . . . There is therefore one language that is not mythical, it is the language of man as a producer: wherever man speaks in order to transform reality and no longer to preserve it as an image.[60]

It was in this pursuit that Brecht picked a very public fight with Thomas Mann, while ridiculing the Neue Sachlichkeit's *Technikkult* and accusing Erwin Piscator for his merely formal mechanization of the theatrical apparatus.

In 1926, celebrating its one-year anniversary, the journal *Literarische Welt* announced a number of competitions with the goal of helping young artists gain visibility. In the literary category, Brecht was chosen as the juror for poetry, Ihering for drama and Alfred Döblin for fiction. Rejecting all of the several hundred poems submitted, Brecht instead chose a poem he found in a bicycling magazine and declared its author, Hannes Küpper, the winner. In the article accompanying Küpper's 'He, he! The Iron Man!', a poem documenting a victory of Australian cyclist Reggie MacNamara, Brecht explained his decision, arguing that the young poets had failed to write something that was not old, that they rivalled their precursors in 'sentimentality, insincerity and unreality'. Like that of Rilke, Stefan George and Franz Werfel, the works of these young poets had no 'use-value'. Brecht ends with a provocation: 'I recommend to Küpper to produce more songs of this kind, and I recommend the public to encourage him through rejection.'[61] A considerable outrage ensued, with responses in the *Literarische Welt* and many other publications. Some writers objected to the belittlement of German literary accomplishment; others, including Klaus Mann, Thomas Mann's son, defended the rejected poets against the banality of bicycle lyricism. One of the young poets protested publicly against Brecht's decision, whereupon the playwright advised the outraged contestant to 'subscribe to a cycling magazine', where he would learn that 'in uneducated circles far removed from the *Literarische Welt*, it is considered unfair to reject a judge *after* the race'.[62]

After the war, Thomas Mann, the personification of bourgeois literature, had cast himself as a figure of modernist writing, offering aesthetic autonomy and categorical continuity in times of moral chaos and social upheaval. *Geist*, good taste, *Formwillen* and artistic discipline presented, according to Mann, a necessary antidote to the type of naive revolutionary and largely incoherent literature and theatre of the younger generation, including Brecht. Thomas's son Klaus then took it upon himself to explore the topic of the generational divide, addressing the question of how to bridge old and new while avoiding what he saw as the reactionary *Vatermord*, or patricide, that would leave the vulnerable culture rudderless. In 1926, the literary journal *Uhu* published articles by and a conversation between the Manns. Klaus Mann wrote, 'The father's work

Six-day race, Berlin Sportpalast, 1929.

stands before us, and we educate ourselves, learn from it.' Thomas
Mann contends, 'Maybe it is less the parents who changed than the
children, meaning that they have grown older and more reasonable,
seeing their parents in the right light.' The younger generation,
according to the elder Mann, had lived for some time off the myth
of patriarchal tyranny but now, faced with the challenge of warding
off the 'wave of analytic revolution' that had swept Europe from
Russia, the 'tendency towards the immoral, toward a smug disorder'
would no longer suffice. 'The Bolsheviks, they hate the soul', he
wrote, and because American modernism was itself soulless, it was
left to the tradition of nineteenth-century European – German and
French – culture to 'guard the soul'.[63]

This provocation Brecht could not resist. That same month, in
the Berlin weekly *Das Tage-Buch*, Brecht took aim at both father

and son, displaying obvious dissatisfaction with the fact that the younger Mann had been chosen to represent the new as much as with the declaration that the time of revolutionary youth was over. Brecht presented the 'harmony in the literary forest' as yet another act of active depoliticization aimed at concealing the fact that 'boys' like Klaus Mann were tired from merely watching their fathers and had given in. He further elaborated that the notion of the patriarchal tyranny was far from the reason for the *Vatermord* (patricide): 'Truly, we didn't kill those fathers because they were hard and violent! Instead they did not feel it because they were soft and mushy.' Brecht adds, 'To our controversial fame as *Vatermörder* we will have to add the very indisputable as *Kindermörder* [child murderers].'[64]

Brecht had taken aim at Thomas Mann before, accusing him of inventing things in order to then ironically judge them and characterizing the traditional German novel as a counterproductive distraction from reality. Instead, the playwright advocated a return to the crime story and its *Gaunerjargon*, or gangster jargon, a language existing through agreement (*contrat littéraire*) between writer and reader to describe 'all the occurrences of human life, feelings, gestures, viewpoints, entanglements, situations'.[65] The idea was to put forth a truly new attitude to the present, including 'the creation of *Formschlüssel* [formal keys] that can access the new subjects'.[66] This entailed an approach not unlike that of modern science, rejecting harmony and idealism and creating 'chaos' by restoring the complexity of events and ideas through historical specificity. For Brecht, the acknowledgement of the social and political reality at a given moment would enable that reality's transformation. The chaos to be experienced and known was the schism between the real and the ideal and the acknowledgement of their incompatibility – dialectics not as synthesis but as a constant state of becoming. Useful is the type of art that articulates the reality of the relationship between the material and the idea, the given and the possible; useful are the forms and mediums that remain factual in their presentation. The power to report rather than embellish or divert became the new directive for the arts in general and the theatre in particular:

> Practically speaking, *what is desirable is the production of documents.* By that I mean monographs of important men, outlines of social structures, exact and immediately applicable information about human nature and heroic presentation of human life, all from typical standpoints and not, regarding its usefulness, neutralized by form.[67]

Sachlichkeit, to Brecht, was thus a form of communication, a technique of representation made possible and indeed necessitated by urban life, sports and technology. Only by maintaining an active and contingent relation between the audience's experience of everyday life and its mediation would this speech remain political. Döblin, in his own assessment regarding the state of fiction writing in the Weimar Republic, put it this way: 'Short stories, as well as short novels, require not only a special technique but the special willingness to establish a modern, close contact with the reader.'[68]

During the mid-1920s Brecht published dozens of stories and essays in a wide variety of newspapers and magazines, ranging from the yellow press like *bz am Mittag* and liberal dailies like the *Berliner Börsen-Courier* to more specialized papers such as the literary section of the *Frankfurter Zeitung* and the theatre journal *Die Scene*. Poems like 'The Cities' appeared in the magazine *Der Simplicissimus* in 1926, presenting the big city as empty and meaningless without its inhabitants and thus emphasizing the role of the urban dweller in producing modernity. An untitled poem published in the *Berliner Börsen-Courier* in early 1927, on the other hand, advises the reader to forget everything they have ever heard regarding their place and possibilities in the world and their mothers' and society's encouragement to succeed;

it counsels that the world is one's oyster, and to realize instead that to learn the 'ABC' is to learn how oppression works. The readers are told, 'This is not to discourage you!'[69] Brecht asks his audience to accept, to *concur* in order to not be deceived.

The social dimension of Brecht's work at this time was for individuals to see themselves as part of a larger whole. At this point, he did not see the proletariat as a revolutionary force, though he clearly was concerned with a redistribution of the ownership of experience and knowledge. The usefulness of the *Einverständnis*, or social agreement, is manifested in the production of a social consciousness of the given, rather than a class-consciousness of the possible. Brecht belonged to a group called Gruppe 25, which included, along with Döblin, the 'raging reporter' Egon Erwin Kisch, who embodied the art of journalistic writing as a form of social participation. Gruppe 25's interest in reportage, questionnaires, radio broadcasting and filmic ways of direct, collective seeing inspired their use of short texts, self-revelatory narration, multiple perspectives and popular, even banal subject-matter. To Brecht, such forms of communications technology themselves interpellated the individual as a collective subject, exchanging psychology and inwardness for an objective, 'seeing from the outside' cognition. But unlike his Neue Sachlichkeit peers, Brecht never confused the technological apparatus with its applications, and he was wary of an undifferentiated embrace of modern progress. His well-known poem '700 Intellectuals Pray to an Oil Tank', written most likely in 1927 and published in *Der Simplicissimus* (among other places) in 1929, demonstrates his critical attitude:

You ugly one
You are the most beautiful!
Do violence onto us
You factual one.
Erase our individuality!

Make us collective!
Because not how we want:
But how you want!

Brecht directly addresses the schism between the promise of liberation and the renovation of dependent relationships as one god is
enthusiastically exchanged for a new one in the name of progress
and enlightenment. The text ends with an astute analysis of how
technology creates symbolic ownership via commodities rather
than actual ownership of *Geist*, or intellect. The last verse directly
recalls the tone and rhythm of the Lord's Prayer and offers a
neologism of Ford and progress (*Fordschritt*):

Therefore answer our prayers
And deliver us from the evil of the *Geist*.
In the name of electrification
Fordschritt and statistics![70]

To Brecht, technology, mechanization and the accompanying
deindividuation were meant to empower, not lead to new forms
of exploitation and repression. As the capitalist and fascist versions
of collectivity became increasingly apparent, Brecht tried to articulate
more clearly how his idea of the individual vis-à-vis the community
differed from a mass culture of consumption and spectacle ultimately
resulting in what Walter Benjamin denoted the *Volksfest* of fascism.[71]
In an unpublished note from 1929 titled 'Individual and Mass',
Brecht wrote:

Our notion of the mass is derived from the individual. The mass
is therefore a composition. . . . The notion of the 'individual' is
here based not on separation but on allocation. The divisibility
of the individual is to be emphasized (as the belonging to several
collectives).[72]

Brecht aims to overcome the exclusive binary of the subject and the social (as well as the private and the public) by turning the idea of the collective into a strategic and dialectical rather than absorbent form of belonging.

In 1927, Brecht had planned a *Ruhrepos*, an operatic revue about the coal-mining and steel works in the German industries' heartland. The project's audience was supposed to consist of 'all parts of the population' gathered to learn about the realities of production and the production of reality: 'But not only the clearly visible achievements of the human *Geist* are to be presented here, but also the worldview of our time itself. Also the image that our time has of itself is worth recording.'[73] The so-called Ruhrpott or Ruhr Valley was a crucial site of struggle over the nation's independence and politics, as under the Versailles Treaty much of the revenue generated in the region was earmarked for reparation payments, and the Allies kept a close watch on potential arms production. But the mines and factories were also the stage where the drama of capital, labour and control over the Weimar Republic's political future unfolded. Brecht's opera project was foiled by local politics and financial difficulties; the few songs that survive put a face on the 'unknown worker', while the machines get a chance to tell their own tales. Both workers and machines reflect on their roles, their past and future and their relative bond to one another, which is limited to he fact that both are products rather than producers. The crane 'Milchsack Nummer 4' remarks to a worker, 'You are not yet alive, I am still dead.'[74] Both workers and machines are only vital parts of progress when the subject and the apparatus no longer generate and absorb alienation but work according to their potential.

Brecht joined Erwin Piscator's directors' collective in 1927, established as part of the Piscatorbühne, the playwright's own new theatre, after he had been dismissed by the Volksbühne (people's theatre) in 1926. Brecht admired Piscator's productions because of their attempt to bring politics onto the stage and raise the theatre's technical standards. Working with the collective gave Brecht the opportunity to study technological innovation in the use of sound, film and projections, and stage design. Writing in the *Berliner Börsen-Courier* Brecht defended Piscator, dismissing those who had driven him from the Volksbühne as 'lazy and stupid', as unwilling to recognize or intimidated by the revolutionary power of the new drama.[75] Elsewhere he praised Piscator's efforts to 'electrify the theatre and raise its technical standards'.[76] In a retrospective outburst of generous egomania, he declared Piscator 'the only other capable dramatist'.[77] But Brecht remained sceptical of what this electrification of the stage could actually accomplish. Prefiguring Walter Benjamin's famous differentiation between the aestheticization of politics and the politicization of aesthetics, Brecht remarked that what truly counted was the 'current tendency to regard the Piscatorian attempt to renew the theatre as revolutionary', perceiving 'not politics' attempted appropriation of the theatre but theatre's of politics'.[78] According to Brecht, what had to change was not simply what was being staged, but the very relationship between audience and stage. He explained:

The politically laudable translation of the revolutionary spirit through dramatic effects, which solely create an active atmosphere, cannot revolutionize the theatre and is a provisional solution, which cannot be expanded, but only replaced by a truly revolutionary theatre. This [current] theatre is at its core anti-revolutionary, because it is passive, reproductive. It depends on the pure reproduction of already existing, hence, dominant, types, meaning bourgeois types, and has to wait for the political revolution in order to find its models. It is the last form of the bourgeois-naturalistic theatre.[79]

Brecht's idea of a *sachlich* theatre was different. And even though he was just beginning to articulate a new aesthetic for the stage, he succeeded in producing a true Weimar play, reflecting his pre-occupation with providing an insight into the mechanisms of the republic's social and political self-understanding as well as the difficulties in reappropriating the cultural apparatuses and their relationship to the audience.

The Threepenny Opera was Brecht's greatest success and arguably the biggest theatrical achievement of the 1920s. Popular with its audiences (less so with the critics), it ran for almost a year in Berlin, was translated into several languages, put on all over the world and made into a film and a novel. There were several other printed derivations as well as songbooks, concerts and recordings (including the world-famous 'Ballad of Mack the Knife'). Though *The Threepenny Opera* made Brecht a star, solved his lingering financial problems and expanded his opportunities, he was uneasy about its effects and continued working feverishly to develop what is now known as the Epic Theatre.

Sachlichkeit may not come to mind when thinking of *The Threepenny Opera*. Rather than direct and unaffected, 'factual', the play seemed complex, confusing, chaotic. The stories about its origins and methods invoke a plethora of sources from John Gay to Kipling to Villon, various styles of song and language, characters of multiple classes, eras and places, technical choices such as the half-curtain and projections, captions and sudden changes between singing and speaking. Countering the lore of its instant popular success, Elisabeth Hauptmann recalls that the premiere at the Theater am Schiffbauerdamm on 31 August 1928 had anything but a euphoric reception: 'No, the audience was peeved.'[80] Brecht's idea of having the viewer observe the re-arrangement of the set between acts was in particular met with scepticism and irritation. The critic for the *Neuen Preußische Kreuz-Zeitung* wrote, 'The whole thing is best described as literary necrophilia, the only remarkable thing the insignificance of the object it was committed on.'[81] Reporting for the other end of the

The Threepenny Opera, premiere, Berlin, 1928.

political spectrum, the *Rote Fahne* similarly observed a lack of coherence and significance:

> When one feels weak, one leans on the stronger; when facing the present more or less uncomprehendingly, one flees into the past. . . . No trace of modern social or political satire. But all in all a multifarious, entertaining mishmash.[82]

The Threepenny Opera was in many ways a thievish play. It began as an adaptation of John Gay's *The Beggar's Opera* (1728), which had been rediscovered and staged in the UK since 1920 with great success. In the winter of 1927–8, prompted by the press coverage of the play, Elisabeth Hauptmann translated Gay's text. Meanwhile, Brecht had been invited to mount something at Theater am Schiffbauerdamm. He had met the composer Kurt Weill in 1927 and collaborated with him on a couple of projects, and they set to work on a full-length opera using Gay's project as a blueprint. Brecht and Weill composed new songs and wrote new lyrics, constantly adding and scrapping material, Gay's as well as their own. Brecht and Weill even spent a summer in southern France working, as Weill's wife, the actress Lotte Lenya, recalled, 'like crazy, writing, changing, tossing, writing anew, taking a break only to walk down to the sea for a few minutes'.[83] The project's collaborative structure was made transparent to readers and audiences in both its first print publication with Verlag Felix Bloch Erben in June 1928 and the premiere's programme, which credited Gay, Villon, Kipling, Hauptmann, Weill, Erich Engel, Neher, Theo Makkeben and the Lewis Ruth Band. Gay's original was already a work of various sources and collective effort (Alexander Pope and Jonathan Swift had allegedly lent a friendly hand), to the extent that Gay (and later Brecht) was accused of plagiarism.

The Beggar's Opera was a 'poor play', its poverty, as in Brecht's *Lesebuch*, a means of justifying the appropriation of operatic forms, and as such a critique of the artificial 'nature' of high culture. It is a story about two men, a robber and a fence, who will do anything for money, turn anything – any person, feeling or desire – into a commodity in order to succeed. But Gay's opera is less a progressive critique of social circumstances, exploitation and alienation than a conservative lament about money as a vulgar tool of social mobility. Brecht's version, on the other hand, does not show the ascent of the rabble but, quite the opposite, shows that capitalism itself is a form of robbery. Werner Hecht describes the *Beggar's Opera* as a 'disguised critique of open grievances' and Brecht's project as 'an open critique of disguised grievances'.[84] In a letter to George

Grosz, Brecht writes of the *Threepenny Opera*'s plot, 'The main point: The robbers are *Bürger*.'[85] In allegorical fashion, Brecht displays how the struggle of the market and its Darwinian laws of survival are carefully hidden behind seemingly abstract bank trans-ferrals, boardroom meetings and stock-market numbers, as well as a cultural apparatus concerned with categorical questions of truth and meaning rather than a reflection of history and its making. Accordingly, the *Moritat* balladeer famously sings:

Oh, the shark has pretty teeth, dear
And he shows them pearly white
Just a jack knife has Macheath, dear
But he keeps it out of sight.[86]

In a London cobbled together from Brecht's reading of detective novels and a temporal setting far from authentically Victorian, Brecht produces an armature of juxtapositions, showing the relations among bourgeois traditions and their contemporary application, among social strata and the ideology that unites them, among old and new notions of progress, freedom and subjectivity. The prostitutes and cripples are shown as victims of interrelated circumstances – industrialization, warfare and modern forms of traffic as well as reparations and Weimar prosperity. Brecht's constructions of robbing and owning, of classes and experiences, drives and desires, truths and images reflect the Weimar Republic's rudderless, 'lawless' culture and ideological laissez-faire. The content and the formal devices of narration and representation emphasize the contradictions of the capitalist order; Weill's music, Neher's stage setting and Brecht's characters all lack harmony and coherence. The music is at times antithetical to the action on stage, veering between pop and jazz; the stage itself is a landscape of superficial construction, as are the protagonists, slipping in and out of roles, attitudes and convictions, accusing each other of being fakes, forgers, even 'artists'. Everything is constructed, lending insight into the mechanisms of how things are made. At the same time as being usable, everything is consumable. In his essay 'Zur Musik der *Dreigroschenoper*' (On the music of *The Threepenny Opera*, 1929), Theodor Adorno articulated this ambiguity:

> Society has many ways to deal with inconvenient works. It can ignore them, it can critically destroy them, it can swallow them, so that nothing is left of them. *The Threepenny Opera* has roused its last appetite. However, it remains to be seen how agreeable a meal it is.[87]

3

Work, Class and the Struggle with Marxism, 1929–33

Teaching and Learning

The late 1920s are usually considered to be the years of Brecht's politicization, a turn to Marxism and socialism prompted by his encounters with political theorists Karl Korsch and Fritz Sternberg, his collaborations with the musician Hanns Eisler and his sporadic studies at the Marxistische Arbeiterschule (Marxist workers' school). Yet this scholarly observation of the sudden appearance of the 'political' in Brecht's work is misleading on several levels. It assumes the earlier plays and writings to be void of concerns regarding the distribution and exercise of power, a view that has led many a post-war Brecht study to conveniently distinguish between the poet's aesthetic achievements and his political outlook. It also supports the notorious association of Brecht's Marx studies with Stalinism, a reading that got him into trouble with the House Un-American Activities Committee during his U.S. exile and made him a glamorous pawn in the totalitarian scheme of the East German Democratic Republic. In fact, Brecht's reading of political theory, of Marx, Engels and Korsch, as well as his concurrent interest in working-class culture and investigative journalism by 'muckraker' authors like Ida Tarbell and Gustavus Meyers, represent a step in the continuous transformation of his artistic method, which was always preoccupied with issues of ownership: who determines the terms of experience, for whom, and who changes them.

In 1929 Brecht took advantage of the financial success of *The Threepenny Opera* to focus on reading and writing, often under the guidance and auspices of Fritz Sternberg. The two men had become acquainted in 1927, and Brecht later gave Sternberg a copy of *Man Is Man* inscribed 'to my first teacher'. Brecht also sat in on classes at the Marxist Workers' School, where he developed a friendship with Marxist theorist Karl Korsch, who taught there. Brecht shared the classroom with workers of various professions, while through Korsch and the director of the school, Hermann Duncker, he came into contact with unionists and representatives of the German Communist Party (KPD). With the composers Weill, Paul Hindemith and later Hanns Eisler, Brecht began to write and stage the so-called *Lehrstücke* or learning plays, developing a body of performative and theoretical work that would prove crucial to the development of his mature methodology.

A pivotal experience of the time is recounted by Sternberg in his book *Der Dichter und die Ratio: Erinnerungen an Bertolt Brecht* (The poet and reason: memories of Bertolt Brecht, 1963). During the late 1920s Sternberg and Brecht met often, primarily discussing the diminishing role of the individual in capitalist society, and participating in a few published and radio-broadcast discussions about a 'new dramaturgy'. On the evening of 1 May 1929 – the annual Labour Day in Germany and many other countries, a celebration and commemoration of the working class and its struggles – Brecht observed from Sternberg's apartment the violent repression of an illegal Communist demonstration, which came to be known as the 'Berlin Blood-May'. Sternberg writes:

> As far as we could tell the people were not armed. The police fired a few times and at first we thought these were just warning shots. Then we saw how several demonstrators fell and were later carried away on stretchers. There were, as I remember, more than twenty dead demonstrators in Berlin. When Brecht

heard the shots and saw that people were being hit, he
turned paler than I had ever seen him. I think it was not least
this incident that drove him toward the Communists.[1]

For Brecht, democracy and the party that was in power defending
and enforcing it – the Social Democrats (SPD), a party supposedly for
and by the working people – enabled capital in the form of private
individuals and companies that, as Friedrich Engels put it, make production social without *socializing* it.[2] Capitalism is democratic in its
processes of exploitation and consumption and, as Brecht observed
from Sternberg's window, in its violent suppression of demands for
equality and fraternity. Yet this violence was not merely that of the
police. It was also embodied in the SPD's reformism, the party's
attempt to defend the Weimar constitution and its industrialist
sponsors rather than to fundamentally redistribute the rights to
physical, social and psychological property. And violence, to Brecht,
was further done to the oppressed by the ideological apparatuses,
justifying and naturalizing abuse and misconduct through religious,
moral and humanist tales of transcendence. To realize how these
tales are put to the test at a moment of crisis is to see a chance for
revolutionary change; this is the challenge of the political artist.

Brecht's play *St Joan of the Stockyards*, begun in 1929, reflects
the tensions between the working classes' claim to the ownership
of their labour, their right to organize and withhold it on the eve
of the Great Depression and the state's brutal defence of existing
economic relations. The story tells of Johanna Dark, a member of
the Salvation Army, who tries to aid a group of locked-out meat-
processing-plant workers but inadvertently helps their
industrialist employer, whose reformist gestures prolong rather
than ease the injustices meted out to those in servitude to him.
After herself experiencing a good measure of proletarian poverty
and the asocial hostility it begets, Johanna changes her opinion
about the 'nature' of humankind and kindness and realizes that

'only violence helps where violence rules', and that he who tells the needy that there is a God ought to have his 'head smashed unto the pavement until he expires'.[3] But her words are drowned out by the chorus's 'Hosanna' and the industrialist manages to have Johanna commemorated as a saint.

Brecht's critique of reformist politics and the pacifying effects of bourgeois humanism were the reasons that *St Joan* was never staged during the Weimar Republic – and not for a long time afterwards, for that matter (the play premiered at the Schauspielhaus Hamburg in 1959). An abbreviated version was broadcast on Berlin radio in 1932, prompting the critic Fritz Walter to write in the *Berliner Börsen-Courier*:

> It will count as one of the most remarkable, yet inglorious attributes of the cultural history of our time that the theatre had to leave the mediation of one of the greatest and most meaningful dramas of its epoch to the radio.[4]

St Joan is often misunderstood as an illustration of class struggle rather than a critical sociopolitical analysis. In fact, Brecht looked to Marxism not to visualize history's inevitable development but to articulate the workings and the limits of contemporary politics, economics and culture under capitalism: to stage property relations and labour, to dramatize economics, to communicate the workings of the market, the trading of and the conflict over the ownership of goods and productive capacities.

In two poems written in 1926 and 1935 respectively, and an originally unpublished text from the mid-1930s, Brecht describes consulting 'specialists and practitioners' while working on the play *Joe Fleischhacker* (1924–9), set at the Chicago wheat market: 'Nobody, neither a few well-known economists nor businessmen . . . could sufficiently explain to me the operations of the wheat exchange.' The work on *Joe Fleischhacker* came to a halt; the play remained a fragment. At that point, while neither his time in the workers and soldiers council and the accompanying USPD membership in 1918 nor Sergei Eisenstein's films and Piscator's theatre convinced him to pick up *Das Kapital*, Brecht declared, 'The planned drama was not written, instead I began to read Marx; there, and only then, did I read Marx.'[5]

Marx became central to the playwright's thinking about art and politics. In Marx, Brecht found less a doctrine than an attitude, an approach to reality or, as he called it, 'a great method'.[6] Brecht's own evolving method recalls, unsurprisingly, Eisenstein's plans to produce a filmic version of *Das Kapital*, as summarized in the filmmaker's notes from 1927–8:

> The most important task in a cultural revolution are not only *dialectical demonstrations but instruction in the dialectical method*. . . . The content of CAPITAL (its aim) is now formulated: *to teach the worker to think dialectically*.[7]

A similar sentiment can be gleaned from Brecht's writings, especially the oft-cited remark regarding Marx and audience:

> When I read *Das Kapital* by Marx, I understood my plays. . . . This Marx was the only audience I had ever seen for my plays. Because a man of such interests must be interested in precisely those plays. Not because of their intelligence but because of his.[8]

Brecht's reading of Marx and Engels, Lenin and Korsch affirmed his anti-individualism, his earlier observations that 'great art serves great interests' and the fallacy of Kantian aesthetic autonomy, as well as the subsequent question regarding art's usefulness: 'Who benefits from it?'[9]

Meanwhile, Brecht was working on the *Lehrstücke*, a number of plays devised between 1928 and 1932, including, strictly speaking,

The Flight of the Lindberghs (first staged in 1929), *The Baden-Baden Teaching Play on Agreement* (1929), *He Who Says Yes* and *He Who Says No* (1930), *The Measure Taken* (1930) and *The Mother* (1932). While Brecht studies commonly draw a bright line between the *Lehrstücke* and the playwright's other works, these plays represent a significant component of Brecht's methodology and contain the seeds of the Epic Theatre. The *Lehrstücke* developed out of Brecht's early collaborations with Weill, who wrote the so-called *Mahagonny-Songspiel* based on the *Mahagonny Songs* of the *Manual of Piety*. The *Songspiel* was performed to great acclaim at the Festival for German Chamber Music in Baden-Baden in 1927. This success in turn led Brecht and Weill to collaborate on the opera *The Rise and Fall of the City of Mahagonny*, set in a fictional American city where mankind's hedonistic pursuits and the resulting lack of solidarity leads to the society's violent demise: the orderly system of capitalism revealed as anarchy. The Leipzig premiere of 1930, in an actual opera house, was one of the greatest theatre scandals of the Weimar Republic. The critic Alfred Polgar recalls sights 'ugly and mean', observing a 'dignified man' and his wife, 'two thick fingers stuck in her mouth, the eyes closed, the cheeks bloated', whistling shrilly with all their might.[10]

Writings on Brecht and his Epic Theatre have often simplistically cast the task of transforming attitudes towards cultural production as the activation of a passive spectator. For the most part, Brecht's theorization of the Epic Theatre took place during the mid-1930s, from the distance of his Scandinavian exile. But his notes regarding the *Mahagonny* opera and its premiere, first published in the *Versuche* in the autumn of 1930, include a chart comparing the 'dramatic form of theatre' with the 'epic form of theatre', already demonstrating a nuanced, dialectical approach towards the role of the audience and its transformation. While the traditional theatre 'consumes the viewer's activity', the Epic Theatre 'makes the viewer an observer but rouses his activity'. The audience are supposed to

become aware of themselves as constantly transformed and trans-
formational, always in process, their thinking determined by social
being rather than their 'thinking determining their Being'. [11]

Weill's score – simple, balladesque, mimicking romantic chansons
yet dissonant, disruptive – refused to drive the action along, to
lend a formal totality that would turn *Mahagonny* into a
Gesamtkunstwerk. Instead, Weill saw the music as a means of reflection, putting emphasis back on what is being sung rather than its
melodic packaging. He described it as 'neither naturalistic nor
symbolic. It could rather be called "real" because it shows life as
it presents itself in the sphere of art.' [12] Music theorist and leading
member of the Frankfurt Institute for Social Research, Theodor
Adorno, wrote a long review in the literature and theatre journal
Der Scheinwerfer. 'The surrealist intentions of the *Mahagonny* are
carried by the *music*', he contends, 'directed from the first to the
last note at the shock caused by the realization of the derelict bourgeois world.' [13] This music, 'made from the rubble of past music, is
entirely present'. [14]

While working on *Mahagonny* and, subsequently, *The Threepenny
Opera*, Weill and Brecht pursued contributions to the Baden-Baden
festival of 1929, a forum for 'new music' offering more experimental possibilities than the German stage and its bourgeois audiences,
especially since the theme of that year's event was *Gebrauchsmusik*
(utilitarian music). The music had to be simple, in order to be
performed by laypeople. To Brecht and others, notably Ernst
Hardt, director of the Cologne radio station and in charge of audio
plays at Baden-Baden, the exploration of artistic participation was
inspired by the technological potential of the radio apparatus as a
new form of communication. Accordingly, Brecht and Weill's submis-
sion to the festival, *The Flight of the Lindberghs* – a play conceived
for the radio but first presented onstage at Baden-Baden – was to
celebrate collective progress through technology in both form and
content. The famous flight across the Atlantic was rendered as a

collaborative effort between the pilot, his machine and those who built it rather than an exposé of individual achievement, and the radio became the model for collective production translating the narrative presented onstage into communicative practice. Brecht explained his plans in a letter to Hardt: *Lindberghs* 'could at least demonstrate optically how the participation of the listener in the radio arts is possible'. The stage was divided into three parts: under a banner reading 'radio' assembled the narrator, the singers and the musicians; under a sign reading 'the listener', a man in shirtsleeves, sitting at a table holding the score and humming, speaking and singing 'the Lindbergh part'; and in the middle, a few maxims about the use of the radio were projected onto a large screen. These included, 'The thinking listener takes part in the music, following the basic principle: doing is better than feeling, as he reads the music, adds missing voices, follows quietly in the book, or sings loud with others.'[15] In a draft for a speech preceding the *Lindberghs* premiere, Brecht defines the role of the audience further: the listener is to 'take over the part that is suitable for his education'.[16] This emphasis on self-teaching instead of reproducing dependency and spectatorial passivity is informed by the Weimar discourse around *Reformpädagogik*. Brecht was familiar with the work of the educational reformer Johann Heinrich Pestalozzi and owned books on the subject by Jean-Jacques Rousseau and Franz Neumann, among others.[17]

The integration of experience into teaching means not only that knowledge is not solely derived from the outside – as if the students simply had to be made to see, their false consciousness stripped away as if removing a blindfold – but that it includes the experience of alienation: the relation between what is and what ought to be, between real and ideal, between ideology and the everyday. For Brecht, the goal was for a collective to examine its own conditions and to chart the parameters of its possibilities for change. This examination was an active, participatory process: 'The *Lehrstück* teaches by being played, not by being seen.' Here lies the essence of Brecht's remark that 'in principle, the *Lehrstück* needs no audience'.[18] The idea of doing away with the audience reflects the influence of Brecht's Marxist teacher Korsch, who had argued since the mid-1920s for a critical investigation of the relationship between theory and practice in Marxism.[19] The notion of *Eigentum*, or ownership, is specifically extended to the production of ideas based on experiences and needs rooted in the life of the proletariat. *Eigentum* is thus best translated as 'selfhood', and Brecht's goal of the *Lehrstück* the formation of *Eigensinn*, a 'sense of self' as a historically determined and changeable subject.[20]

At the same Baden-Baden festival, Brecht presented *The Baden-Baden Teaching Play on Agreement*, written with the musician Paul Hindemith. Here the dictum that the *Lehrstück* does not require an audience took a more radical incarnation. The play included intertitles and filmic projections, and its author and composer appeared onstage issuing instructions to the actors

Rehearsal for *The Flight of the Lindberghs*, Baden-Baden, 1929.

and musicians in an attempt to provoke the audience. These efforts drew harsh criticism. According to Hanns Eisler, one critic fainted in his seat and Gerhart Hauptmann walked out in disgust when, during an interlude, a clown had his limbs sawn off by two clown colleagues (even though it was obvious that all that was being cut were pieces of wood). And when the viewers grew restless during Neher's presentation of images of dead people, photographs that showed, as Brecht put it, 'how in our time humans are slaughtered by humans', the playwright had the announcer call out for a repetition of the pictures as soon as the projection had finished. *Die Menge* (the crowd), meaning the audience, listed in the score as one of the performers, was to answer the choir's question preceding the images of death as to whether human compassion exists with a united shout: 'Man does not help man!'[21] One writer pronounced that Brecht had created not a *Lehrstück* but a *Leerstück*, an 'empty' play.[22] But Brecht himself learned something: that the audience may intellectually know that art sublates all reality but nonetheless be outraged when confronted with any provisionally repressed experience.

The 'school opera' *He Who Says Yes* was written by Weill and Brecht for the 1930 festival 'Music Days' in Berlin, which was dedicated to 'music and education', showcasing projects that sought to integrate composition and performance with the reform-pedagogy movement's goal of community building. The opera was then revised in collaboration with students from the Karl-Marx Schule in Berlin, an institution run at the time by one of the leading figures in progressive German education, Fritz Karsen. Under Karsen, the institution offered workers the chance to earn a high-school degree through evening classes and in 1929 established a public comprehensive school that would develop a curriculum of 'productive collective work' in collaboration with its students.[23] The 'central project' of the new pedagogy, according to Karsen, was the 'transformation of society, its elevation through *gesellschaftliche*

Arbeit [social work]'. The content and method of education was to be gleaned from the students' *Lebensgebiete*, or areas of life, hence connected to the local and historically specific experiences and interests of those learning. This notion of the *Lebensgebiete* and, by extension, of *Lebenszusammenhang*, or 'relationality', a term used by Oskar Negt and Alexander Kluge in their 1972 exploration of proletarian public spheres, is key to the development of a progressive reconsideration of Marxism in Germany ranging from Korsch and Brecht to its renewed revision in the 1960s and '70s.

The premiere of *He Who Says Yes*, held at the Zentralinstitut für Erziehung und Unterricht (the state-run central institute for education and instruction) and broadcast live on Berlin radio, was a great musical success, with the youth choir, the instrumentalists and the composer euphorically celebrated. The critics praised what the sceptics had declared impossible: an aesthetically sophisticated utilitarian music. Brecht's text and the play's content, on the other hand, were greeted with universal hostility. Presenting another examination of individual surrender to the greater good, the 'school opera' took its cue from Japanese Noh plays, discovered in English translation and rendered into German by Elisabeth Hauptmann in the winter of 1928–9. Noh plays are highly stylized, anti-illusionist performances on open, bare stages showing tales and myths of the contradictory connection between the empirical and the metaphysical, and the ephemerality of earthly life, often finding expression in the Buddhist monk's acceptance of his caducity or the samurai's death in self-sacrifice. *He Who Says Yes* tells of an arduous mountain expedition led by a teacher in order to obtain much-needed medicine and medical advice for his community. A young boy whose mother is sick insists on joining the dangerous quest, despite being urged otherwise. When the climb indeed proves too strenuous for the boy and he can no longer be carried along, following an old custom, he agrees to be sacrificed and is abandoned to the abyss. Brecht's story was dismissed as 'reactionary' and teaching 'blind obedience'.[24] The play is geared towards the self-examination of those who perform actions; Brecht asks actors and audience alike to take ownership of their decisions, attitudes and behaviours. The *Einverständnis*, or 'agreement', is less a self-sacrifice than an acceptance of responsibility and agency. Brecht's description of the *Lehrstücke* as plays without an audience has led to an academic separation between this type of drama and the Epic Theatre, the former being viewed as works for a future, utopian-socialist society when the need for art as a mediation between the possible and the actual has been abandoned.[25] But this suspension of the distinction is best understood as an *Aufhebung*, a transcendence of the separation, in a unity of theory and practice. As Brecht explains in an unpublished text from 1930 titled 'The Great and the Small Learning', 'The Great Learning completely changes the role of acting. It sublates the reciprocal system of actor and spectator. It henceforth knows only players who are learners at one and the same time.'[26]

The second version of *He Who Says Yes* emerged in the spring of 1931 after the students at the Karl-Marx Schule had given their input. The students criticized the ritualistic sacrifice as neither realistic nor necessary. Some suggested, 'One could use the play to show the harmfulness of superstition.'[27] Others demanded more solidarity of the community with its weaker members. The revised play includes more deliberation among the members of the expedition, rational and emotional responses, and a broader discussion of principle and necessity, intention and circumstance, social and individual responsibility. Ultimately the boy, again, dies.

In the summer of 1931, Brecht offered a third version, *He Who Says No*, taking a crucially differentiated approach to *Einverständnis*. This time the boy specifically agrees before the trip that if anything were to happen to him, he would stoically accept his fate. But as he falls ill and is confronted with his promise, he corrects his agreement. When the others demand that 'he who says "a" must say "b"', the boy responds, 'The answer I gave you was wrong, but your question was even more wrong. He who says "a" must not say "b". He can recognize that "a" was wrong to begin with.' Against *Einverständnis* as obedience or acquiescence, he proposes 'the habit to think anew in every new situation'.[28] In this version the boy refuses to be sacrificed, and the group turns back.

Brecht's most notorious play, *The Measure Taken*, was conceived as yet another version of *He Who Says Yes*, a 'concretization' written in 1930 with Eisler and the director Slatan Dudow and, as both Brecht and Eisler claimed, 'in proximity' to the proletarian movement of the time. The producers submitted the play to the Neue Musik Berlin festival but withdrew it after the festival organizers expressed reservations about the text. In an open letter, they explain:

> We remove these important performances from any dependencies and let them be made by those who they are made for and who alone have use for them: workers' choirs, amateur troupes, students' choirs and school orchestras, hence those who neither pay nor get paid for art but who want to make art.[29]

The play premiered in December 1930 under the auspices of the so-called Internationale Tribüne, an organization for the 'promotion of international revolutionary art and literature', with a cast that included Brecht's wife Helene Weigel, the mechanic-turned-actor Ernst Busch and the former baker Alexander Granach, supported by three workers' choirs and a mixed orchestra, on a boxing-ring-like stage. In the programme, Brecht summarizes the play's content and goal: four young communist agitators are accused of killing a comrade and have to rehearse their actions, arguments and attitudes in front of a court represented by the choirs. Brecht writes, 'The purpose of the *Lehrstück* is therefore to show politically incorrect behaviour and teach appropriate behaviour. This performance is supposed to bring to discussion whether or not this type of event has pedagogical value.'[30] A questionnaire was appended, asking the viewer about the relations among play, actors and audience and inviting suggestions for the play. Sternberg recalls that Brecht would lead discussions with the audience after every performance, turning the acts of learning and teaching into reciprocal activities.

The Measure Taken was lauded for its innovative musical arrangements and the actors' performance. Given the general climate of the early 1930s in Germany, and the nationalist and fascist permutations of *Einverständnis* as totalitarian usurpation of individual participation in historical development in particular, it may come as no surprise that the critics either ignored Brecht's text and the content of the play, refused to discuss them or accused the writer of 'primitivism', 'instruction in communist militarism' or 'a dangerous contamination of our cultural values'.[31] After the Second World War, several critical voices judged Brecht even more harshly. In the late 1940s, Ruth Fischer, a former member of the Austrian Communist Party and publisher of the organization's journal *Der Weckruf – Die Rote Fahne* (The wake-up call – the red flag), denounced both her brother Hanns Eisler and Brecht, calling *The Measure Taken* 'an anticipation of the Moscow Show Trials of 1936'.[32] Hannah Arendt accused Brecht of defending the party's extermination of 'one's own comrades and innocent people': 'In *The Measure Taken* he shows how and for what reasons the innocent, the good, and those who are outraged and come running to help are being killed.'[33]

The early 1930s saw the working class weakened by unemployment and poverty, and leftist parties, fragmenting through infighting, failed to deliver the solidarity needed for revolutionary change. Meanwhile, the German bourgeoisie, ostensibly protectors of the ideals of freedom and equality, stood on the sidelines. Writers including Ernst Jünger and Carl Schmitt were busy laying the ideological foundations for a different sort of collectivism and

Einverständnis. Jünger was the author of celebrated books like *Stahlgewitter* (*Storm of Steel*, 1920) and *Der Kampf als inneres Erlebnis* (Battle as inner experience, 1922), based on his front-line experiences during the First World War. These works glorify battle as 'baptisms of fire' for an eternal Germany and death as a quasi-erotic form of spiritual unity.[34] In his book *Der Arbeiter* (*The Worker*, 1932), published the same year as Aldous Huxley's *Brave New World*, Jünger presents the working man as a force replacing bourgeois values such as individualism, democratic liberalism and social contracts with total mobilization, synchronization and obedience, offering homogeneity in a chaotic Weimar world.

The philosopher Schmitt, for his part, propagated a notion of the political as a struggle based on friend–enemy relations. To Schmitt, the state channels the natural struggle into obedience in exchange for protection. But Schmitt is less interested in making the exception the rule (as fascism will) than in taking antagonism to its extreme: for Schmitt, militarized struggle will abolish all false versions of conflict, be they in parliament, art or the economy. Writing about Schmitt in 1999, Slavoj Žižek memorably calls this 'politics proper'.[35] And here lies the difference between Brecht and Schmitt, between *Einverständnis* as agreement and as acquiescence: where Schmitt proposes an 'ultra-politics' pitting the state against an external enemy, Brecht insists on the internal struggle within the social body, the possibility for all members of society to carry out 'politics proper' through the ability and ownership of the material and immaterial means to participate in antagonism. For Brecht, there is no single, primordial struggle but only various, historically determined conflicts.[36]

The Measure Taken offered learning in self-awareness rather than Jünger's 'training in self-forgetting'.[37] Instead of a mastery of nature through sublimation, Brecht sought a mastery of relations. In his review in 1931 of several different performances of the play (which Brecht was constantly rewriting), the critic

Julius Bab remarks that what the playwright has accomplished is how to 'express a collective experience with dramatic means'.[38] More importantly, Brecht had provided an experience of collectivity wherein both experience *and* collectivity were subjected to critical enquiry, judgement itself judged, theory made material when shown applied to human beings and relations, to social reality, a reality right then and there produced and applied by the audience.

Wem gehört die Welt? – More Experiments in Ownership

Brecht began publishing the so-called *Versuche*, or experiments, in 1930, in the form of journals or booklets as part of his attempt to redistribute the means of cultural-political production. As cheaply printed and bound materials, they were to be disseminated beyond the realm of the traditional theatre and the avant-garde festival. The *Versuche* constituted a central part in Brecht's endeavour to respond to the struggle over power and meaning in a volatile and fragmented ideological and economic climate, to his experience of the Labour Day violence, and to the questions of how the workers, the parties and the arts could engage in revolutionary change. This meant prising the making and distribution of culture out of the hands of the bourgeoisie. It also meant redefining and redirecting the gain and profit from art. The first page of the first *Versuche* stated the project's intention:

> The publication of the *Versuche* comes at a moment when certain works are intended less as individual experiences (works as 'art works') than as a means of using (or transforming) specific institutes and institutions (works as 'experimental') and to that end explain individual, interconnected operations in their relationality.[39]

This notion of relationality is key for Brecht in his quest to politicize areas beyond 'politics', such as the social, the economic, the cultural and the private. The *Versuche* are an amalgam of intertextualities, including plays and poems, short stories and children's tales, instruction and documentations, charts and images, direct address and third-person narrative. The texts contain notes and comments, and words and phrases are crossed out and new ones inserted, as a way to lay bare and make available the forms and functions of authorship.

Brecht's experiments paralleled and were most certainly informed by the so-called Agitprop debate of the Weimar Arbeitertheater, or workers' theatre, a discussion within the KPD during the mid-1920s of 'how to politicize the everyday life and entertainment needs of the masses'.[40] Historian Hans-Jürgen Grune has argued that what was manifest in technological modernizations of much political drama (he mentions Wieland Herzfelde, John Heartfield and Piscator) – such as the removal of the fourth wall or bridging the orchestra pit – became political innovation in some proletarian performances like those of the *Rote Raketen* (Red rockets) or the Russian *Blauen Blusen* (Blue blouses): 'Here everything is present that makes those who experience into players. The contact is there because what is mere play onstage is at the same time very serious offstage.' Associations are made, situations applied, experiences included. Attitudes and ideas, types of speech and methods are played out and taken to the factory, the bar, brought back. The stage becomes an experiment in action informing and informed by what happens outside the theatre. The workers' theatre recruited actors from the audience, while the touring troupes, according to Grune, 'repeatedly and spontaneously' spawned new ensembles.[41]

Yet the influence of the Arbeitertheater and related organizations, such as choirs and the workers' press, was limited by the SPD's adherence to bourgeois ideals of aesthetic value and the KPD's unreflective dogmatism. To most workers, shopkeepers and clerks, the idea of redistributing ownership translated into accumulating private property, or participating in consumer culture – or rather, in culture through consumption. The goal, to Brecht, Steinberg and others, was not to pursue existing (bourgeois) ideals but to establish a proletarian consciousness through the experience of the failures of those ideals – the experience of alienation articulated as the dialectics between universal expectations and the possibility of individual achievement, rather than as a personal failure or moral shortcoming. As Walter Benjamin observed in his discussion of the *Versuche*, Brecht's characters derive their attitudes and behaviour from the experience of the abyss between what is and what ought to be: 'Brecht hopes to produce the revolutionary . . . from a mixture of poverty and nastiness.'[42]

Among more familiar Brechtian characters like Baal and Galy Gay was Herr Keuner, a figure who had made an appearance in several dramatic experiments and fragments, such as the incomplete *Fatzer* (1926–9) and an early version of *The Measure Taken*. The 'Stories of Herr Keuner', anecdotes or short parables, some no longer than a single sentence, were published in three issues of the *Versuche* and as part of the *Kalendargeschichten* collection of texts in 1948. Walter Benjamin, in his review 'Bert Brecht' (1930), offers the sole contemporaneous discussion of these texts, which cast their protagonist as an ambiguous practitioner and critical example of a dialectical attitude. From his earliest incarnation, Herr Keuner is presented as *der Denkende* (the thinker). Yet what he offers are not thoughts in the traditional sense of disembodied contemplation but attitudes or opinions prompted by an experience and immediately acted on. The first *Versuche* collection states that the stories are an attempt to 'make gestures quotable'.[43] In conversations with neighbours and shopkeepers, philosophy professors and enemy soldiers, Herr Keuner ponders the relation between belief and unemployment, the value of dwelling and the cost of furniture. Often he is referred to as a teacher, but he is also a learner, constantly and strategically adjusting his attitude in his commitment to reality rather than principle.

According to Benjamin, Herr Keuner derives his name from a mixture of local dialect and Greek mythology. Brecht recalled a teacher who pronounced 'eu' as 'ei', making 'Keuner' *Keiner* (nobody).[44] Benjamin thus relates Herr Keuner to Odysseus, who as a 'foreigner' with a distanced perspective explores 'the cave of the one-eyed monster "class state"'.[45] Furthermore, as Benjamin agrees with Lion Feuchtwanger, 'Keuner' has a Greek root, *choinos* – 'the universal, that which concerns all, belongs to all', which, according to Benjamin, makes sense for Keuner 'since thinking is the common'.[46] Indeed, thinking is the struggle between experience and knowledge, between opinions and universal truths; it means getting to the bottom of naturalized histories, institutionalized ideas and accepted points of view. The basis for the new collectivity, the common, is not a national identity, inherited customs, cultural conventions and traditional beliefs, but thinking as a way to move forward, to live in history. Herr Keuner has one vice: to question for the sake of alterity as attitude. The *Versuche* 13 (1932) contains the following anecdote:

THE REUNION

A man whom Herr Keuner hadn't seen in a long time greeted him with the words: 'You haven't changed a bit.'

'Oh', said Herr Keuner, and turned pale.[47]

Like Brecht, Herr Keuner is a scientist; here science serves, as Fredric Jameson explains, the pleasure of practical knowing and making, 'the manual amusement of combining ingredients and learning to use new and unusual tools'.[48] Brecht describes the 'audience of the scientific age' as those who seek to understand not the human being presented onstage but the 'operations' in their relationality: 'When I want to see Richard III, I don't want to feel like Richard III, but I want to observe the phenomenon in all its strangeness and incomprehensibility.'[49] And to Brecht the tools are not as new and unusual as they are to Jameson. The excitement of recovered labour comes not from novelty of form; the dialectically thinking worker is less curious than amateur, familiar with the objects and their production as they suit a proletarian interest and utility.

The relationality between making and purpose is at the core of proletarian emancipation. Regarding the connection between the 'bourgeoisie and technology', Brecht writes in 1930:

> Technology is foreign to the bourgeois. When building machines the proletariat has found an appropriation for the denied feelings of having-self-built. Observe a greasy worker climbing into a car for the first time: he understands it instinctively. A bourgeois almost never does.[50]

The stories of Herr Keuner are instruments in the construction of the new *Eigentum* and *Eigensinn*. Herr Keuner is part of what Brecht, in a letter to Korsch from January 1934, calls the *Handwerkszeug*, or 'set of tools', that 'needs to be fixed', made available, appropriated.[51]

The task of recovering labour as collective utility is central to Brecht's 1932 film *Kuhle Wampe*, whose subtitle 'To Whom Does the World Belong?' signals from the outset an enquiry into the ideological and pragmatic dimensions of ownership. *Kuhle Wampe* is Brecht's only realized film project, a work made for a new mass audience, heeding the collaborative character of the medium's production and reception. One crucial part of this endeavour led to the film's controversial reception prior and in response to its initial release in 1932 as well as its post-war influence on film-makers like Jean-Luc Godard and Rainer Werner Fassbinder, and critical film studies such as those initiated by the British journal *Screen* in the early 1970s. This crucial part was that *Kuhle Wampe* took advantage of the medium's formal means, such as montage, sequencing and sound, to articulate proletarian experience not only in relation to bourgeois, capitalist and outright fascist ideologies, behaviours and attitudes, but also to the petit-bourgeois longings of the working class and institutionalized proletarianisms as well.

Brecht had tried once before to make a film. In the spring of 1930, on the heels of the success of *The Threepenny Opera*, Brecht and Weill signed a contract with the Nero-Film-AG for the rights of a movie version of the play. The clash over the company's attempt to cash in on the opera's popularity and the artists' vision of how to adequately translate the work's 'social tendency', as Brecht called it, for a new medium and apparatus led to the infamous '*Threepenny* Process'. Brecht sued Nero-Film after he refused to cede control over the project and the company accused him of breaking the contract. During the trial, the playwright garnered much support from the press and solidarity from his peers but was accused by some, including Kracauer and Ludwig Marcuse, of egotism and opportunism when the procedures ended in a loss of rights but financial compensation for the artist.[52] In an essay published the following year, 'The *Threepenny* Process: A Sociological Experiment', Brecht declared that he had meant to lose the trial to begin with, to use the publicity and debate surrounding the proceedings in order to expose the absurdity of the traditional notion of the 'work of art'.[53] But whatever the playwright's ulterior motives may have been, the trial and the text – the latter itself a montage of Brecht's unabashedly biased recollection and interpretation of the events, quotes from the many articles published in response to them, excerpts from the hearings and theoretical ruminations on the cultural-industrial complex – forcefully lay bare the discrepancy between bourgeois ideology and its practice. Here, notions of ownership and authorship are cloaked in the rhetoric of individual freedom and artistic integrity, while the commodification of culture is protected by its judicial apparatus. At stake is the question of the proletarization of art – its availability and distribution to a constituency that brings its own habits of seeing. Rather than merely provide a celluloid version of a theatrical performance, a *Threepenny* movie had the potential to redefine cultural access and production beyond the dichotomy of authenticity and consumption precisely by playing the two against each another. Film would have to serve the deconstruction of artistic production as something made by individuals for individual contemplation or collective consumption instead of reinscribing old values and habits into a new technology. To Brecht, here and elsewhere, social progress was inextricably intertwined with technical progress.

The *Threepenny* Process garnered *Kuhle Wampe* much media attention throughout its production, and inspired by the Weimar arrival of revolutionary Russian cinema such as Vsevolod Pudovkin's *Mother* (1926), Eisenstein's *Battleship Potemkin* (1926) and *October* (1927) and Dziga Vertov's *Man with a Movie Camera* (1929), Brecht joined forces with the *Measure Taken* director Slatan Dudow, Hanns Eisler and the writer and KPD member Ernst Ottwalt. In 1931 Brecht and Dudow signed a contract with Prometheus Film, a production and distribution company with close ties to Moscow and the KPD, responsible for the German introduction to Soviet cinema and the making of eight feature and over 50 documentary films, including Dudow's short reportage project *Wie der Berliner Arbeiter Wohnt* (How the Berlin worker lives, 1930). Brecht regarded the collective work on *Kuhle Wampe* as an integral part of its process. In the context of the *Threepenny* lawsuit, he had declared collaborative filmic production a 'progressive' necessity: 'In fact, a collective can only make works that can make the "audience" into collectives.'[54] (Brecht's reference to plural collectives again emphasizes the historically contingent and circumstantial properties of new social formations rather than a single, static,

Brecht, seated, with Hanns Eisler and Slatan Dudow during the filming of *Kuhle Wampe*, 1932.

homogenizing principle.) Dudow recalled the working dynamic as one in which 'discussion rather than authority was the determining factor'.[55] The film-makers proclaimed in an announcement in 1932: 'Increasingly we found the organization of the film to be an essential part of the artistic labour. It was only possible because the work as a whole was a political one.'

The same text describes the film's content: *Kuhle Wampe* 'consists of four independent parts, separated by self-contained musical pieces that are accompanied by moving images of tenements, factories, or landscapes'.[56] The first part shows the competition for work and the suicide of an unemployed youth; the second his family's eviction and relocation to the tent colony 'Kuhle Wampe' on the outskirts of Berlin, where the daughter gets pregnant and subsequently engaged; the third portrays 'proletarian sport contests' which are 'certainly of political character', a 'mass leisure of fierce character' portrayed by 3,000 actual worker-athletes, among them the young couple of part two who, after an abortion, have given up their plans of marriage. The fourth sequence depicts a discussion in a crowded streetcar among young workers, office clerks and lower-middle-class types as well as more conservative, middle-class Germans regarding the destruction of overproduced goods and harvests.

What makes *Kuhle Wampe* a cinematic milestone, earning the undivided attention of the censors and infuriating critics on the Left and the Right while impressing future generations of artists, is its critical look at the production of social reality or, as film scholar Bernard Eisenschitz put it, the relationship between the 'typical' and the *Gestus* (elaborated below).[57] The typical comprises actions and behaviours that appear to result naturally from a set of given circumstances: in the instance of *Kuhle Wampe*, the suicide of young Bönike. Since the beginning of the Great Depression, the un employment numbers in Germany had risen precipitously. A statistic from January 1931 records the suicide of eight unemployed workers

Men playing cards at Kuhle Wampe, a tent camp at the Müggelsee in Berlin, 1929.

in a single day.[58] By February 1932, approximately 44 per cent of the
eligible population (more than 6 million people) was out of work.
Hunger and desperation were everywhere. In the film, a neighbour
of the Bönikes looks straight into the camera and says with a manner
of defeated matter-of-factness: 'One less unemployed.'

While Dudow's *Wie der Berliner Arbeiter Wohnt* showed the living
conditions of the metropolitan working class in direct comparison
with the opulence of those better off, cast as the cause of the proletarian plight, *Kuhle Wampe* presented a more nuanced picture of
class struggle, as a struggle *within* ideology. As opposed to the typical, the *Gestus* is the action that shows the 'natural' as determined,
as coming from somewhere and having its own repercussions. It
has a self-referential, enquiring effect: 'When you show: this is how
it is, show it in such a way that the viewer says: but is it like that?'[59]
When young Bönike jumps to his death, he pauses first to take off
his watch and carefully set it aside. According to director and critic

Bernhard Reich, when the film premiered in Moscow in 1932 the Russian audience did not understand why someone who owned a watch would commit suicide.[60] The anecdote is telling: *Kuhle Wampe* holds not only direct economic and political exploitation responsible for the injustices of the late Weimar Republic, but also the alienation caused by someone's perceived inability to live up to the social standards and ideological truths set forth in the bourgeois public sphere. The ideals of private ownership, property and success are as much at the root of Bönike's action as his inability to help feed his parents and sister. In the tent colony, each family has its own kitschy little property, tended to with the utmost care, and the moral horizon remains utterly *bürgerlich*. The idea of class consciousness as a struggle over attitudes runs throughout the work and, given the successes of the National Socialist party in the elections of 1930 and 1932, became an uncomfortable but crucial consideration in any concept of revolutionary social change.

Montage within specific sequences and as an overall formal device of the work's episodic structure suggests ambiguities and contradictions in proletarian attitude and outlook throughout the film. The scenes appear as moments or scenarios among many others, without any climactic resolution. Like Herr Keuner, Brecht assembles the typical, the available, while disassembling the origins of its typicality. Film historian Wolfgang Gersch remarked:

> For *Kuhle Wampe* the representation of the proletariat's miserable living conditions is not the goal but the precondition for a comprehensive, critical and mobilizing interpretation. The milieu acquires a new function. No longer does it, like previous social-critical films, uninterruptedly depict – it quotes.[61]

The practice of quotation further consists of the use of montage as repetition, panning shots against the action and still images emphasizing the act of picture-making. Eisler's music is partially in disharmony with the moving images. He explained, 'The contrast of the music . . . to the merely montaged pictures causes a type of shock, which, intentionally, calls forth more resistance than empathetic sentimentality.'[62] Resistance is the motto of the last part of the film, which ends with a 'right politician' in the streetcar sneeringly asking the young proletarians, 'And who will change the world?', to which one of the workers replies, 'Those who do not like it.'[63]

Kuhle Wampe articulates the contradiction and ambiguities of political struggle – a struggle between available worldviews and attitudes, between truths taken for granted and their relative dependence on construction, power and circumstance. The alienation created between expectations and experience is the site of disharmony, and the opportunity to repossess the means of making self and sense. In the chaotic early 1930s in Germany, such revelatory contestation caused considerable discomfort.

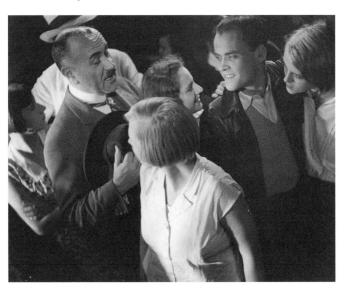

Still from the streetcar scene of *Kuhle Wampe* (1932).

Party lines demanded clarity, a respite from difficulties, economic, psychological, intellectual and otherwise. In March 1932 the Berliner Filmprüfstelle (Berlin Film Examination Bureau) refused to approve *Kuhle Wampe* for release, asserting that it needed to be edited in certain places as it 'threatened public safety and order and vital interests of the state'.[64] The relation drawn between young Bönike's suicide and state cuts in unemployment aid was considered especially problematic. After several hearings and public protests (against censorship in general and for *Kuhle Wampe* in particular), a few metres of celluloid were cut and the film was approved.

At the Moscow premiere in May, Brecht was disappointed by the cold reception, as both audience and critics expected and demanded a more celebratory and overt form of cinematic revolution. When it opened in Germany later that month, however, the film was a success. Its run at the Atrium theatre was extended and expanded to fifteen other Berlin cinemas as well as theatres in Paris, London and Amsterdam. The critics were divided along predictable lines. The bourgeois press called *Kuhle Wampe* 'openly Marxist party ballyhoo'.[65] The journalist Rudolf Olden, who spoke out on behalf of the film-makers during the censorship proceedings, lamented, 'No, the destitution, the real destitution is not being shown', while the author Heinz Lüdecke, writing for *Rote Fahne*, called the film 'an important attempt' but found fault with 'the partially skewed depiction of the proletariat, showing the petit-bourgeois lifestyle in focus while the working class is presented somewhat pale, sweeping and idealized'.[66] Some of the worker-athletes who had participated in the film wrote a letter to the film company protesting against the 'reform flick', asserting that the transition it portrayed from abject destitution to glorious nature was as little a part of their reality as the reduction of their class struggle to a discussion about coffee in the streetcar: 'As class-conscious workers we resolutely reject this film as it depicts our athletic life and life attitude in a completely butchered manner.'[67] On 26 March 1933, *Kuhle Wampe* and a number of other films were banned for the 'protection of *Volk* and state'.[68] A request for prohibition filed by the National Socialist Party's Bavarian film bureau included the work on a list of films with 'purely communist content'.[69]

Brecht had been on the Nazis' blacklist for several years, and at the beginning of the 1930s he found his work increasingly compromised by reactionary forces. Brown Shirts interrupted a performance of *Mahagonny* in 1930, and though the protests failed to lead to the cancellation of the play, other theatres retracted their commitments to stage the work. The premiere as well as subsequent productions of *Man Is Man* at the Berliner Schauspielhaus in 1931 had to be abandoned due to tumultuous disturbances staged by fascist members of the audience. And in January 1933, when the Kampfgemeinschaft der Arbeitersänger, a proletarian collective, performed *The Measure Taken* at the Reichshallentheater in Erfurt, the play was cancelled due to accusations of its being communist propaganda, and the organizers were sued for treason. At that point Brecht decided it was time to go. With access to theatres, journals and other apparatuses of creative work and communication further and further restricted, different producers chose different paths in response to their forcibly abandoned experiments: some left the country, others went into controversial 'inner exile' and a good number joined the fascists. Brecht and Weigel fled to Prague with their son Stefan on 28 February 1933, the day after the Reichstag fire. Brecht's books were burned on 10 May 1933, and the following day his entire oeuvre was banned.

4

Early Exile: 'Singing about Dark Times', 1933–41

Truth-Telling

In the *Unpolitical Letters*, presumably written in Denmark in the autumn of 1933 after only a few months on the run, Brecht took stock of his position as a writer in exile. Having left Germany behind, he feared that he had lost his language, his stage and his audience. He also contemplated whether words and images, poetry and theatre were adequate weapons in the fight against the Nazis, especially since these had done nothing to prevent their rise. In the *Unpolitical Letters*, his remarks about the developments in Germany have a bitterly satirical tone:

> I felt rather superfluous, and a careful survey of my surroundings as well as a few visits alerted me to the fact that, as happens occasionally in the life of *Völker* [the people], now a truly great time had begun, where people of my kind only disturb the great picture.[1]

Brecht cunningly and ambiguously positions himself between unwanted and useless, yet much scholarship has framed the sudden shift from celebrated Weimar playwright to poet without a people in terms of Brecht's own painful rejection of Marxism and his paralysing disillusionment in the face of a working class that failed to fulfil its revolutionary destiny, and an avant-garde art that foundered in its mission of social and spiritual progress.

Brecht's incredible productivity in a variety of genres, media and styles during the Scandinavian years – in Denmark, then later briefly in Sweden and Finland, with visits to Paris, London, New York and elsewhere – stems in part from his intellectual and pragmatic anxiety regarding the question of who was going to read, see and participate in what the arts still had to offer. He worked on more than ten plays during this first phase of his exile, devised radio programmes and flyers, produced books and photomontages and wrote hundreds of poems and more than 500 (most unpublished) essays, reports and other texts about any and every relevant topic, including human rights and the Moscow Trials, artistic resignation and resistance through reason, proletarian housing and utopia, war and realistic writing. His productivity is surely also an act of defiance, a *trotz alledem* (despite everything). But amid the uncertainties of his exile, his dedicated forays into the techniques and technologies of artistic production and communication only intensified during this period. He countered the literal and metaphorical speechlessness of many of his peers with a commitment to critical analysis and a penetrating dedication to a multiplicity of publics and audiences. Brecht answered the question of what ought to be done in the light of the overwhelming forces of fascism with the following lines published as part of the *Svendborg Poems* (1939):

In the dark times,
Will there still be singing?
Yes, there will be singing.
There will be singing about dark times.[2]

After leaving Berlin, Brecht and his family travelled from Prague to Vienna, where Weigel's family lived; there they met Eisler,

Sternberg, the publisher Peter Suhrkamp and Karl Kraus. But despite the relatively comfortable circumstances among family and friends, the playwright decided that Vienna was no place for him to work. After briefly contemplating an exile in Switzerland, he settled in Paris for a few months following the invitation of Kurt Weill, and worked with him on a ballet entitled *The Seven Deadly Sins*, which premiered at the Théâtre des Champs-Elysées on 7 June 1933. The playwright received some money for the play but regarded it as being otherwise of little importance. Brecht liked Paris, but the possibilities for work were slim, and the family moved to the small island of Thurø, Denmark, into a house owned by the writer Karin Michaelis, who was also hosting Brecht's *Kuhle Wampe* colleague Ernst Ottwalt and the author Hans Henny Jahnn.

Brecht had little money as his books were forbidden in Germany, while the publishers he had worked with were unwilling or unable to pay royalties. Many went bankrupt. The house that Brecht and Weigel bought in Denmark in August was in part paid for by their fathers. Elisabeth Hauptmann remained in Berlin dissolving the Brechts' household and taking care of any manuscripts left behind.

Brecht, centre, wearing a hat, at the house Karin Michaelis lent him, Thurø, Denmark, 1933.

She was briefly arrested by the Gestapo and fled to Paris in December, followed by a short falling-out with Brecht, who accused her of not having taken enough care of his things. Margarete Steffin, a young communist actress from a working-class background with whom Brecht had begun an intimate relationship, had also fled to Paris. Steffin was and would continue to be an important collaborator for Brecht's work, and he wrote a number of sonnets expressing his love for her, as well as his feeling of responsibility for her welfare, as she suffered from chronic tuberculosis. Their relationship almost cost Brecht his marriage to Weigel and remained a persistent strain on their bond.

Although Brecht had always considered himself an oddity or outsider even among those whose artistic and political convictions he shared, the alienation he felt from early twentieth-century German society and culture took on an existential dimension in exile. Brecht had become a nomad both literally and, most importantly, ideologically. The task of seeing things from the outside, finding a new perspective and descriptive language, had taken on an unprecedented urgency.

With *Kuhle Wampe*, Brecht had already articulated a differentiated notion of the public sphere, acknowledging a complex and fragmented proletariat reaching beyond conventional class lines to include young, organized labourers, white-collar workers, the unemployed and an older generation whose idea of a collective lifestyle and redistributed ownership were more *kleinbürgerlich*, or petit bourgeois, than revolutionary. This historically specific understanding of the public sphere as a relational and cumulative rather than substantive concept enabled Brecht to see and respond to the phenomenon of German fascism as a multi-pronged appropriation and exploitation of existing, if often latent, sociopsychological tendencies and traditions, hopes and fears, in a perverted yet comprehensible trajectory. The huge number of unemployed workers for one, many no longer unionized or otherwise organized, seem to have found the KPD's promises of the revolution's inevitability increasingly inadequate as a growing divide between everyday experience and ideology created an insurmountable alienation that in many cases ended in a turn to fascism, more specifically to its paramilitary arm, the Sturmabteiling or SA. The SA provided not only a new outlook on life, complete with comradeship, mythical past and glorified missions against internal and external enemies, but clothes, food and a place to sleep. For their part, the Weimar working-class parties, unions, clubs and organizations, as well as their numerous middle-class counterparts, were either unwilling or unable to discharge sufficiently the contradictions of history and provide a programme of immediate ideological gratification. Meanwhile, the Nazi Party succeeded in representing itself as radically anti-parliamentarian, as outside the system that had allegedly caused Germany's decline since 1918. While the ever more dreaded 'paper-ballot democracy' came to represent the people's feeling of alienation from abstract political processes, the Nazis offered a model of direct participation in everyday life and politics, blending public, semi-public and private spheres by assigning ranks and duties in all sorts of organizations.

Brecht's response to these developments was manifold, revealing both a sense of confusion as well as an acknowledgement of the situation's complexity. From the beginning of the Third Reich, he was well aware of the extent of fascist crimes, writing about concentration camps and orchestrated murder as early as 1933.[3] The same year he portrays Hitler as a 'Pied Piper' who misleads the unsuspecting masses with the sweet sound of false consciousness.[4] Another text written shortly thereafter discusses the temporary proletarian 'defeat' caused by and causing 'weakness' and the necessity of acknowledging and articulating those weaknesses, real and perceived, in order to continue the struggle.[5] Brecht also continuously and emphatically connected fascism with capitalism, arguing for a reconsideration of the causes of Nazism and the struggle

Soup kitchen, Berlin, 1934.

against it as a matter of ownership, profit and exploitation. In 1934 he wrote that 'fascism can only be fought as capitalism, as the most naked, brash, crushing and deceitful capitalism'.[6]

When it came to the Soviet Union, however, Brecht's position was marked by both fear and desire, hope and disappointment. He hoped to work in Moscow and wanted to retain the Soviet Union as a productive and inspiring example of an actual proletarian rule as well as a necessary power in world politics. After the success of *Kuhle Wampe* at its Moscow premiere in 1932, Brecht happily accepted Piscator's invitation to visit the USSR on the occasion of a 'Brecht evening'. The German playwright was euphoric about the technological progress he witnessed during the opening celebrations of the Moscow Metro on 17 April 1935, and as late as 1937, when the Moscow Trials and Stalinist purges were well under way, Brecht lauded the Russian 'liberation of productive resources' and abolition of profit, the source of all inequality, which despite its radical and dictatorial implementation he thought would ultimately provide collective as well as personal freedom.[7] Yet Brecht also rejected the very idea of a state as the 'source and product' of 'regulations' and 'hierarchies', despite the fact that 'those without possession had assumed power'.[8] His own dialectical approach to art and history clashed with the tenets of Socialist Realism and he remarked that the 'Russian comrades' were forced to engage in a two-sided battle: 'They have to fight the arid, abstract doctrinism and they have to turn against the mechanical, noncommittal naturalism.'[9] His criticism of Stalin increased, albeit in a very mediated, veiled form, as in the poem 'The Farmer Addressing His Ox' (the ox being Stalin) of 1938 and the *Book of Changes*, written during the mid- to late 1930s and published posthumously.[10] While he never embraced the Soviet regime, he never openly denounced it either. Consequently he was attacked by communist émigré artists and writers like Julius Hays and, beginning in 1937, had a falling-out with Georg Lukács and his fellow editors of the Moscow-based journal *Das Wort*, which had been founded on the heels of the 1935 International Writers Congress as a forum for anti-fascist writers and critics. Brecht's lingering scepticism concerning the truthfulness of Western media reports about the trials sustained a bitter blow when Russian authorities arrested and sentenced Ernst Ottwalt and the *Threepenny Opera* actress Carola Neher to five and ten years imprisonment respectively. Both would die while in prison camp. In a journal entry dated January 1939, Brecht describes the artistic-intellectual situation in Russia following the sentencing of his colleagues, the disappearance of the Constructivist writer and playwright Sergei Tretyakov and Vsevolod Meyerhold's loss of his theatre: 'Literature and art are shit, political theory gone to the dogs, and there is something like a bureaucratically propagated, thin, bloodless, proletarian humanism.'[11]

Despite his disillusionment, Brecht never doubted his own position as a critical instrument in the ongoing fight for emancipation. Others found such a commitment harder to maintain. The writer and publisher of the periodical *Die Fackel*, Karl Kraus, whom Brecht held in high regard for his incorruptibility and tireless battle against ignorance, remained silent when the Nazis seized power in the spring of 1933. Kraus could not bring himself to publish his already typeset text titled *Die dritte Walpurgisnacht* (The third Walpurgis night), a 300-plus-page reaction to the political events in Berlin. His colleagues and admirers were appalled. It was not until October of that year that an issue of *Die Fackel* carried a poem by Kraus addressing his speechlessness in light of incommensurable experiences: 'And there was silence, because the earth thundered. No word that fitted . . . The word passed away as that world awoke.'[12] Brecht was one of the few who sympathized with and defended Kraus's position. His poem 'Regarding the Significance of the Ten-Line Poem in Number 888 of *Die Fackel* (October 1933)' acknowledges the difficulty of finding adequate expression for the fascists' atrocities:

> Crimes boldly step out into the street
> And loudly defy description.
>
> He who is being choked
> The word sticks in his throat.[13]

The silence, Brecht continues, may appear to be a form of acceptance but in reality points to the crimes committed. The poem then takes a turn and asks: 'Is the fight therefore finished?', thus providing a critical enquiry into what ought to follow. But rather than providing a moral stance and idealized agenda for why the struggle must continue (Brecht states that, indeed, 'Injustice can triumph, even though it is injustice'), it is the material experience of the exploited and repressed, the hungry and the 'taxed', those who feel 'the boot on their neck', that will lead to a new resistance.[14] A first draft of the text is more insistent in its demand on Kraus to break his silence and pick up his pen: 'Therefore we ask you to continue the fight without delay as the darkness grows, to cease-lessly repeat what has been said.'[15] This early version also contains a reference to the question of speaking and language in general, of how to compete not only with the physical and psychological Nazi terror, but with its permeation of all discourse and its appropriation of the apparatuses of communication. Brecht refers to 'the louder ones', the party's orators like Rudolf Hess and Hermann Göring, and he knew very well that simply throwing one's voice into the mix would prove insufficient.

In 1938 Ernst Bloch assessed the ability of the Left to find 'the right word' in the fight against Nazism.[16] After contemplating Kraus's infamous silence with a patience and benevolence comparable to Brecht's, Bloch remarks that 'language is a historical-material refer-ence structure', allowing one to understand fascist language as both historically unique and continuous in its attempt to sever words, phrases and entire histories from their specific connotation, imbuing them with a mythical, naturalized and timeless validity and power. As a perverted extension of the bourgeois public sphere, the speeches travelling over the Third Reich's airwaves, delivered at its arcanely dramatic rallies and circulated in its inflammatory newspapers, aimed to provide a sense of belonging and participation across boundaries of milieu and age by utilizing a language general enough to span the various publics' experience and thus organizing them as 'masses'. According to Bloch, neither the strangeness of the grotesque nor the moralism of the novel's 'great language' is sufficient to take on the 'tremendous format of [the] petit bourgeois puniness' of fascist rhetoric. Instead, he presents the language of description, of science, as a possible 'instrument that hits the mark', an analysis that 'studies the Nazi and exposes him at the same time'. Brecht's work is invoked as a productive instance of reportage and montage:

> He pieces together . . . pointed situations and lets the tension,
> the meanness, and the tickling danger, the contradictions of the

regime itself emerge as educational; the reader has to make sense of it himself.[17]

Two examples of such strategic analysis are Brecht's comparative *re*-presentations of speeches by Göring and Hess, which had appeared during the 1934 holiday season in the *Baseler Nationalzeitung*. In each instance, particular parts of the original address are juxtaposed sentence-by-sentence, sometimes line-by-line, with the playwright's additions.[18]

A number of texts that Brecht wrote in 1934 address the obligation to reconstruct a politicized language. These essays are some of the most important writings produced by Brecht in response to the Nazis' near-complete occupation of all spheres of life. The *Pariser Tageblatt* asked German writers living in exile for contributions on the topic 'The Mission of the Poet 1934'. In the December issue, it printed answers by authors including Alfred Döblin, Lion Feuchtwanger, Heinrich Mann and Arnold Zweig. Brecht's essay 'The Poets Ought to Write the Truth' begins with the observation that few people would deny that poets shall tell the truth, but that the problem lies precisely with the fact that too often truth-telling, or at least the willingness to write with candour and honesty, is taken for granted, while its difficulties are rarely examined and taken into account. The leftist writer and artist readily declare solidarity with the weak and pledge not to bend to the demands of the powerful. But how to find the truth and to tell it so as to serve the transformation rather than the reproduction of reality? Johannes R. Becher's letter accompanying the copies sent to the members of the Schutzverband Deutscher Schriftsteller, or SDS (an association for the protection of German writers and writings), points out the 'excellent article by Bertolt Brecht'. To Brecht himself Becher wrote: 'This article is, in my opinion, one of the best "theor-etical works" I have read lately,' and he encouraged the playwright to expand on his thoughts.[19]

Brecht obliged Becher in his essay 'Five Difficulties When Writing the Truth', published in the German-language journal *Unsere Zeit* (Our time), run by Willi Münzenberg out of Paris, Basel and Prague. Brecht's ruminations were aimed both at exiled authors and the anti-fascist writers remaining in Germany. In addition to the original title, the SDS also issued printings disguised under the heading 'Practical Guide to First Aid', to be smuggled into Germany and distributed there. (Brecht was also involved in the printing and subversive distribution of pamphlets and leaflets in Nazi Germany.) Though its public impact at the time is difficult to gauge, the essay became widely known among the émigrés. Wieland Herzfelde wrote to Brecht that he had used the text as the foundation for a lecture given in Prague, while Münzenberg made it known that he had sent copies to André Gide, André Malraux, Heinrich and Thomas Mann and Lion Feuchtwanger. 'Five Difficulties' was translated into Polish as early as 1935, with Russian, Danish and English versions appearing over the following years.

To Brecht, who referred to the piece as a 'tract' or 'treatise', the difficulties of politicized speech were the very necessities that made truth-writing possible: the *courage* to write the truth; the *keenness* to recognize it; the *skill* to wield it as a weapon; the *judgement* to select those in whose hands the truth will be effective; and the *cunning* to spread the truth among the many.[20] Truth, to Brecht as to Bloch, is not something singular and general but something that is necessarily produced. Writing the truth is a matter of studying, discovering and articulating the relationship between thinking and action, of how events and experiences come about and how they are transformable. Truth is, according to Brecht, directly related to circumstances, following a maxim borrowed from Hegel and Lenin – 'The truth is concrete,' a sentence the poet had pinned to the roof beam of his Danish house. The 'untruth' of fascism is thus defined by 'the general, the grandeur, the ambiguity' that is manifest in the crimes committed.[21] The truth becomes concrete where the relationship between word and deed as forged in the fascist public sphere is uttered and thus exposed as a lie. But, Brecht writes, 'Truth is not merely a moral category . . . not only a question of ethos, but a matter of ability. Truth needs to be produced.'[22]

Brecht's concern with truth, knowledge, politicized speech and how to distribute it among specific publics grew more urgent as German society struggled with the aftermath of the First World War, the rise of fascism and rapid modernization, including advances in communications technology, which brought new social and political possibilities. He had written a number of essays and articles about radio and film prior to his exile. One of the most important such texts was delivered at a conference organized in 1930 by the Südwestdeutscher Rundfunk (Southwest German Broadcasting Service) and published in part in 1932. Rather than a last hurrah to Weimar modernity and techno-utopian emancipation, the essay is a pragmatic call for the appropriation and *Umfunktionierung* (refashioning) of the radio in light of the commercial and political massification of culture and life. 'The Radio as an Apparatus of Communication' demanded that technology and mechanization not merely distribute information but instead be utilized to enable dialogue and critical exchange. Remarking that 'The radio is one-sided where it ought to be two,' Brecht cautions that simply supplying a means of communication does not guarantee access to the production of culture.[23] Quite the opposite. The mass distribution of irrelevant subject-matter under the guise of public culture – in an earlier essay Brecht had lambasted 'the colossal triumph of technology to finally make Viennese waltzes and cooking recipes available to the entire world' – led to the isolation of the listener.[24] Instead, according to Brecht:

> the radio would conceivably be the greatest apparatus of commu-
> nication of public life, an enormous network of pipes, meaning, it

would be if it knew how to send out as well as to receive, hence, to make the listener not only listen but speak, to put him into relation rather than isolating him.[25]

Brecht understood that the bourgeois public sphere – and later its perverted extension, the fascist public sphere – were still operating under the Enlightenment ideals of direct cultural engagement but had exchanged infantilizing gestures of participation for genuine critical discourse and production as actions of agency. As technological advances were propagating new models of social formation and interaction, Brecht urged relationality, in a scientific-pragmatic as well as intellectual sense: he advocated the ability to literally talk back, to speak, to discuss via the apparatus of transmission. Yet he also implied that *what* is being communicated must have relevance to the listener and engage him as a speaker.

The radio was a rather young medium in Germany. Broadcasting began in October 1923 with the Berliner Funkstunde, while the first radio play was produced in the autumn of 1924. By 1932, radio programmes reached an audience of 12–15 million listeners in a population of 80 million. Historians generally distinguish three phases in the development of the radio play, exemplifying the changing use and demands put on the new technology.[26] The first radio plays were simply texts read over the air. Around 1926 came 'acoustic film', integrating sound and montage effects adapted from the moving-picture industry. Along with Brecht, it was Alfred Döblin who advocated a contemporary, critical radio and demanded a medium-specific radio art, appropriate to its technological potential.[27] The radio version of Döblin's famous novel *Berlin Alexanderplatz* was broadcast in 1930 and marks the transition to the third phase of Weimar radio, the attempt to create a form of communication that would adequately reflect and engage in its historical context. To Brecht, this meant using the radio in the collective production of a critical consciousness. His *Flight of the Lindberghs* demonstrated both onstage and to the listeners sitting in front of the radio apparatus the type of participation he had in mind: not only to speak and sing along, but to intellectually participate in current events and issues by rethinking and supplementing what was being presented.

In a parallel development, the Weimar workers' movement sought to expand the bourgeois public sphere by contributing different voices, outlooks and experiences to what was perceived to be the primarily entertaining function of the radio. In early 1924 union members, Social Democrats and Communists founded the Arbeiter-Radio-Klub (Workers' radio club) in Berlin, which was followed by several other organizations in the autumn. By 1932, the German workers' radio movement consisted of 267 local clubs.[28] The organizations had three goals: the DIY production of receivers, the exertion of influence over programming and the creation of proletarian broadcasting stations. While such stations were never established, the fabrication of receivers was so successful that even the industry profited (for little or no compensation or acknowledgement of the original labour). Further, influence over the content and format of broadcast time was exercised through a great number of publications by the 'workers' radio press', which printed reviews and editorials as well as a number of unbroadcast reportages as political and medium-theoretical contributions. As the media historian Friedrich Knilli put it, '[These publications] articulated what the capital's stations concealed.'[29] Other initiatives included collective listening evenings and letters to the studios and editors, as well as the formation of the agitprop group Rote Welle (Red wave), which aired readings and radio plays by working-class writers and broadcast Labour Day festivities. Like Brecht's own observations, these efforts aimed to make explicit that, yes, with the new technology one has the opportunity to say everything to everyone, but what is 'everything' and who is 'everyone'?

The National Socialists had a simple answer: the fascist public sphere and its institutions were able to unite the numerous publics and milieus under the notion of the *Volksgemeinschaft* (*Volk* community), which, not unlike its precursor, the bourgeois public sphere, merely glossed over class divisions rather than actually suspending them. The Nazis considered individualism under modernity a sort of second original sin and, accordingly, only what pertained to the *Volk* as a whole warranted utterance and dissemination. Under the Nazis, radio, like film, underwent a drastic monopolization, and Reichsminister Joseph Goebbels, in charge of propaganda and the 'people's enlightenment', declared, 'The press has to conform to the new state or it has to vanish.'[30] In the face of such obvious force, reorganization and censorship, radio in particular became what media historian Knut Hickethier has called an arena of 'parasocial interaction'.[31] The manufacture of the state's *Volksempfänger* (people's receivers), built to receive only local airwaves and guard its listeners against foreign voices, was stepped up, and the audience was presented with public events in the privacy of their own home. Live transmissions of speeches and festivals, and the experience of simultaneity they conveyed, created a spectacle of participation and community. The *Volksempfänger* were an integral component in half of Germany's households by 1937. Propaganda took the form of entertainment, and 'national values' were rehearsed in a playful manner. Musical interludes, sport reports and news saturated the living room with a carefully crafted programme of Germanic attitudes. The radio play, though in a form very different from the one practised and advocated by Brecht and Döblin, played a crucial role in the state's propaganda efforts.

Yet fascist control over the public sphere was far from undisputed. Accounts by the Sicherheitsdienst or secret service (SD), as well as letters and diary entries written by members of the listening public, attest to alternative and subversive 'readings' of programmes and articles and the persistence and use of foreign stations, as well as the interference of official transmissions by resistance organizations. Before 1933 Brecht had produced a number of radio plays and programmes and participated in on-air roundtables and discussions; a short version of *St Joan* was broadcast by the *Berliner Funkstunde* in 1932. After his emigration, Brecht kept writing pieces for German radio, like the *German Satires*, which were aired in 1937 by the Deutscher Freiheitssender, an anti-fascist radio station based in Madrid and targeting listeners in Germany. The radio, more easily accessed and utilized than film, remained an important and viable tool in the mission of truth-telling.

Walter Benjamin extolled Brecht's concern with more than simply displaying a correct attitude, or as Benjamin put it, the right 'political tendency'.[32] In the *Linke Melancholie* (Leftist melancholia, 1931), a review of Erich Kästner's latest collection of poems, Benjamin wrote that rehearsing revolutionary ideas was insufficient:

> The leftist-radical publicists of the type of Kästner, Mehring or Tucholsky are the proletarian mimicry of collapsed bourgeois ranks. Their function is to generate, politically speaking, not parties but cliques, literarily speaking, not schools but fads, economically speaking, not producers but agents.[33]

In his famous address in 1934 at the Institute for the Study of Fascism in Paris, entitled *Der Author als Produzent* (The author as producer), the philosopher demanded a consideration of form, or 'literary tendency', a call to take into account the quality of language and the ways in which it is transmitted. For Benjamin, only the direct engagement with and transformation of the apparatus that produces ideas and images at a specific place and moment in history would make for a political work of art. The mere expression of political ideals had to be replaced by an active change in how words were utilized, who had the power and the means to utter them, and to whom. Benjamin went on to single out Brecht's work as an example of such critical engagement.

Brecht and Benjamin spent time together in Paris in 1933, and when the playwright settled in Denmark, Benjamin visited for several weeks during the summers of 1934 and 1938, bringing his entire library, as he was himself unsure where to settle. The two men played chess and discussed politics and ongoing projects as well as children's theatre, the Moscow Trials and Soviet literature, among many other subjects. Their friendship and mutual admiration has been a thorn in many a scholar's side. Theodor Adorno determined Brecht's influence on Benjamin to be vulgar and restrictive, while Gershom Scholem called it 'baleful, and in some cases disastrous', Benjamin's Marxist turn an unfortunate misstep by an essentially religious thinker.[34]

The dialectics of progress were key to Brecht and Benjamin's attempts to appropriate technology in cultural production. Rather than glorify the machine per se, they realized that the liberating potential of the increasing mechanization of everyday life brought with it alienation and instrumental destruction, and that it furthermore had the potential to perpetuate bourgeois culture through the industrial production and distribution of commodities. Brecht's remark during the *Threepenny* Process regarding the 'proletarization of the producer' is illuminating: the disconnect between worker and means of production should not be remedied through a reproduction of an ultimately bourgeois notion of ownership, a redistribution of individual use and gain. Instead, the 'proletarian producer' was to be the active refutation and transformation of the traditional notion of authorship. Technology made it easier for members of the collective to use and utilize productive instruments because they no longer had to rely on conventions of access. The potential simplification of understanding the mechanisms of the apparatus (technical, social, political) ideally allowed for an eradication of bourgeois binaries of unequal exchange. Brecht, according to Benjamin, was the first to insist that intellectuals and artists ought not to 'merely supply the apparatus of production without, to the greatest extent possible, changing it in accordance with socialism'.[35] New communication technologies afforded the ability to reach the fragmented audiences of the mid-1930s while breaking up, adding to, repeating and juxtaposing the voices and views that determined the formal and topical homogenization of the public sphere.

The scholarly consensus is that both Brecht and Benjamin occupied rather naive, utopian positions in this regard. It has often been remarked that texts like Brecht's 'Five Difficulties' and Benjamin's 'The Author as Producer' and 'Das Kunstwerk im Zeitalter Seiner Technischen Reproduzierbarkeit' ('The Work of Art in the Age of Its Technological Reproducibility'), written in the early 1930s, retained some Weimar enthusiasm, which waned as the Third Reich gained strength. Yet such a retrospective interpretation risks overlooking some crucial nuances of their work. Rather than assume that all would be well if everyone would collectively shout back into the apparatus, for example, both writers relied on an idea of the public sphere as a site of struggle and as a constellation of interdependent multiple publics, with various and conflicting experiences, histories and desires, harbouring subversive and revolutionary potentials of alienation that escaped the smothering grip of systematic equalization, and that could be mobilized if given the opportunity, the proper tools and the incentive.

Technification

The heterogeneity of the public sphere and the necessity to employ keenness, skill and cunning to activate a plurality of voices and experiences in order to form a discourse, attitude and behaviour that would innovate rather than renovate social structures – all this was something that Benjamin had determined as an integral part of Brecht's oeuvre as early as 1920. He observed:

In the years 1920 until 1930, [Brecht] did not tire of putting the dramatic rules to the test of history over and over again. He took on various forms of the stage and the most disparate formations of audiences. He worked for the podium theatre as well as for the opera and presented his products to Berlin proletarians just as he did to the Western bourgeois avant-garde.[36]

This ability and commitment to specificity, according to Benjamin, as well as a notion of technification applied to all mediums and media, not only radio and film, made the playwright 'a specialist in beginning anew', an outstanding example of critical engagement in the fight against fascism.[37] In a way, the Weimar media experience provided an important basis for Brecht's participation in this specific struggle.

Another reason Brecht felt equipped to fight the new powers was that he considered fascism an extension, or extreme form, of capitalism. In the summer of 1935, he attended the International Writers Congress for the Defence of Culture in Paris. While speakers like André Gide and Heinrich Mann called on the approximately 250 delegates to 'save culture', Brecht demanded that they fight the 'root of evil'. In his speech 'A Necessary Observation Regarding the Fight against Barbarism', he argues that the rawness and fanaticism of fascism are not part of a repressed natural drive but instead fixed 'in the business transactions that could not be exercised without it'. It may be noble and necessary to save culture, but it was more important to save the people from the 'prevailing *Eigentumsverhältnisse* [property relations] whose sustainability make these atrocities necessary'.[38]

The audience was stunned. One attendee remarked that Brecht, like Georg Büchner's Woyzeck, had ripped through the congress like a straight razor. Others were furious, as the playwright's appeal for class struggle ran counter to the event's goal to unite socialists and communists in a common front. For his part, Brecht expressed his dismay with the congress in a letter to George Grosz: 'We just rescued culture. It took us 4 (four) days and we decided to sacrifice everything rather than let culture perish. . . . Fascism was generally condemned – because of its *unnecessary* cruelty.'[39] Brecht was fully aware that culture and ownership were deeply intertwined, especially since his own strategies and methods as a producer had to be adjusted in light of not only fascism and exile but also the economic crisis and the developments in Russia. At the second International Writers Congress two years later, he claimed (*in absentia*) that culture had to be defended, but was 'not solely a *geistige*, but also, and especially, a material thing, [and thus] has to be defended with material weapons'.[40] Based on his experiences at the first convention, Brecht observed that critical cultural production was not only possible but necessary, an additional public being the 'Tuis' he so despised. 'Tui' is an acronym derived from a play on the word 'intellectual': 'Tellekt-Ual-In'. About the Tui's function, Brecht writes, 'The Tui is the intellectual of this time of markets and commodities. He is the lessor of the intellect.'[41]

Written in 1935 and published in 1936 in the journal *Das Wort*, 'Questions of a Reading Worker' offered a set of provocative enquiries regarding the ownership of labour and history. The worker's perspective produces a tension between official narrative and counter-history, articulating the circumstances of alienation while actively combatting the myths of culture as the achievement of 'great men', a notion deeply engrained in both fascist and bourgeois narratives. Brecht asks, 'Who built the Seven Gates of Thebes? In the books one finds the names of kings. Was it the kings who hauled the rocks? . . . The great Rome is full of triumphal arches. Who erected them?' And the text broadens the canon of great men, adding Philip of Spain and Frederick the Great to the list. 'Every ten years a great man. Who pays the expenses?'[42] The audience for this text are the German intellectuals in exile who are reminded that history is both a material and a narrative pursuit, and that this pursuit is ongoing. To ask how someone contributes meant, at this moment, to acknowledge both the material plight of the masses as well as their contribution to extraordinary historical events, both progressive and destructive.

To address those masses directly, Brecht and Eisler (with Steffin and Hauptmann) published the collection *Songs, Poems, Choirs* in 1934 as an anti-fascist response to the appropriation of *Volk* culture in Germany. The added '32 Pages of Musical Scores' point to the intended use-value of the book, which was printed by Editions de Carrefour in Paris. It is tightly structured and starts with a chapter that examines the causes for the Weimar Republic's decline into fascism, including the First World War, with a reprint of 'The Legend of the Dead Soldier'. The chapter addresses the Nazis' exploitation of hunger, unemployment and class struggle and includes 'The Song of the SA Man' and 'The Song of the Class Enemy'. The next section opens with 'The Song of the House Painter Hitler', which, referring to the shape and economic appeal of the swastika, begins with the lines:

> They are carrying a cross in front
> On blood-red flags
> That for the poor man has
> A great hook.[43]

The poem is followed by texts addressing persecution, concentration camps and anti-fascist resistance in Nazi Germany. The next chapter includes songs of prior revolutionary struggle – a reminder at once nostalgic and pensive regarding a social transformation gone terribly awry, yet an encouragement to pick up where the struggle was left off. An addendum draws tentative connections to American capitalism and the role of the Tuis in the fascist ascent to power. A large number of the 3,000 copies was to be smuggled into Germany to be disseminated by the resistance. The success of this plan remains uncorroborated and was, under the circumstances, unlikely. Seven hundred pre-orders and a number of reviews, announcements and reprints of individual poems and songs in émigré publications tell of a smaller, narrower success. Klaus Mann praised the book's combination of poetry and politics, while Arnold Zweig declared that Brecht creates the 'social transparency of a mindset' and that the poems have 'the utility of tools, and they presuppose that the world is in flux, changeable by men and women, individually or acting in mass'.[44]

The *Svendborg Poems*, published as a collection by Wieland Herzfelde's Malik Verlag in 1939, presents a similar attempt to reach and construct multiple publics and attests to the languages, angles and strategies employed by Brecht despite his feeling of isolation in Denmark and the seemingly unassailable power of the Nazis to control all communication. The 'Children's Songs' were written in 1934 in response to the Nazi youth organizations and, like the children's story *The Three Soldiers*, illustrated by Grosz and published as an issue of the *Versuche* in 1932, were meant to elicit questions rather than further indoctrinate young minds. Most of the poems in the section 'German War Primer' were published during the years 1936 and 1937 in a variety of journals, including *Das Wort*. Written in a terse, anonymous tone, these texts sought to provide a form of publicity that would subvert Hitler's stories of peacekeeping, countering official images and proclamations made to the outside world on the occasion of, for example, the Olympic Games in Berlin, with voices and observations from the inside, of the deeds and an everyday experience of oppression. The 'German Satires' had originally been written for and were, in part, transmitted by the Madrid-based radio station Deutscher Freiheitssender in 1937. The texts in this chapter include biting comments on Göring's remark that 'cannons are more important than butter', to which Brecht adds that the state only needs more cannons when it runs out of butter and has to protect itself against its own people. In another piece he defends the regime's use of propaganda as a tool that, among other things, rather than fight hunger makes hunger seem appropriately chic, and notes that the construction of thousands of miles of highway instils in people 'a joy, as if they owned cars'.[45] The language is direct, irregular and generally unrhymed: 'The purpose [is] to throw single sentences into the distant, artificially dispersed audience.'[46] The *Svendborg Poems* had a print run of 1,000 copies and its actual reception is difficult to assess. Margarete Steffin recalled that, when in Copenhagen for a visit in 1938, her parents – politically engaged, union-organized and usually dismissive of poetry as too esoteric – were astounded by an early version of the collection. Her father remarked, 'What is written here is all true. This is so beautiful, it could have been a real book.'[47] Only with great effort could Steffin keep her parents from taking the poems back to Germany.

In exile, Brecht focused his project of truth-telling further on the complexity and ambiguity of historical circumstances, their presentation and perception, making directly apprehensible the concrete worldviews, policies and actions underlying them. The *Threepenny Novel*, for example, written over the course of a year and published in 1934, was an attempt to outline the contemporary reality of Nazi Germany through juxtaposition, collage and montage, obliging the viewer to look into the elements and arrangements that make up images and reality. The book extends the idea of business as crime, as robbers and thieves move up into the world of commerce, where they work according to its laws of deception and blackmail, corruption and murder. Justice remains a duplicitous ideal as the institutions – be they law, marriage or social status – favour the wicked and aid the repression of the already exploited. Brecht makes direct references to speeches by Hitler and the party programme: he exposes the commercial efforts of fascism by, for one, using the language employed to justify the nationalization of Jewish property and total monopolized control of the entire economy,

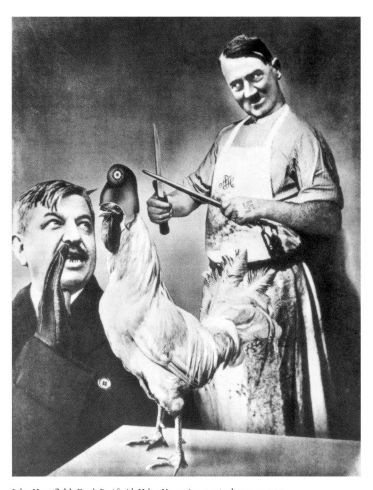

John Heartfield, *Don't Be Afraid, He's a Vegetarian*, 1936, photomontage.

declaring the creation of a 'healthy' middle class and the 'communalization' of prosperity. The structure of the novel (which has little to do with the original opera) was determined by what Brecht called 'film-seeing', the creation and perception of one's environment as shaped by the possibilities of technology. 'Irreversibly', according to Brecht, 'the technification of literary production' guides the author to use the available 'instruments' to adequately show reality but, more importantly, 'to lend his attitude when writing the character of employing the instruments'.[48] Unlike the traditional novel espoused and created by authors like Thomas Mann, with protagonists and action driven by accumulating, progressively binding characterizations, Brecht's figures' attitudes and convictions, their subjectivities, change according to the state of business. Filmic devices such as repetitions, close-ups, superimpositions and fast motion are adapted to the literary form to show these subjectivities to be causal, determined, rather than relativist. The mixture of genres, between kitschy romance and *Kaufmannromane* (a type of bourgeois novel), noir fiction and pornography, amplifies the strategy of *von-aussen-sehen* (seeing from the outside) to keep the reader at a distance and encourage the discernment of transactions and their motivations. The *Threepenny Novel* was a success: it was widely, and mostly positively, reviewed and was published in a number of different languages. The editor-in-chief for the *Europäische Hefte* in Prague, Willy Siegfried Schlamm, called the novel 'Brecht's Textbook for the Present', a work for teaching 'history and macroeconomics, sociology and psychology'.[49]

Meanwhile, Brecht's theatrical productions were as varied and specific as his other writings, and as exhortative. *The Round Heads and the Pointed Heads*, published in the *Versuche* in 1933 and staged in Moscow (1935) and Copenhagen (1936), addresses the notion of politics as theatre. As the world looked on in horror and incomprehension at the extreme transformation of an entire country, the play uses filmic devices, especially repetition and duplication of images, actions and characters, to explore the relationship between appearance and reality, rhetoric and action. The foregrounded artifice of the theatrical sheds light on what historians have referred to as the German *Doppelcharakter* (double character), the phenomenon of a people who know exactly what happens during the night and in the concentration camps, but lead an existence buffered by 'double morals' that allow for the persistence of two parallel worlds. It also exposes the duplicity of the Nazi machine – its ability to run in parallel the state's open violence and 'the bourgeois need for serenity, order and safety as well as its demand for masters and heroes' – and reminds those looking on from the outside that their own speech must be more than rhetoric, must be political speech, must transform rather than redouble the existing gap between words and action.[50]

With *Señora Carrar's Rifles*, staged in Paris in 1937, Brecht extends this looking-from-outside to the Spanish Civil War (1936–9). Brecht had been urged by Dudow to somehow contribute to what had become an international cause. A letter to Dudow written in 1937 outlines the plan: 'I am thinking of a very simple format for the performance. . . . Nothing fidgety, everything calm, prudential realism.'[51] The play portrays the story of the fisherwoman Carrar, who lost her husband in the bloody battles between the violent 'generals' (standing in for General Franco and his henchmen) and the rightfully elected government of the Second Spanish Republic. Carrar is a determined pacifist and despite her son's pleas refuses to aid the resistance. She joins the struggle only after her son is killed by the fascists while peacefully fishing. What is remarkable about the play, other than the parallels with the playwright's own reluctance to pick up a gun, is the directness of its form. Its focus on the central character and the emotional loss that begets her change of heart have led many scholars to consider this play more or less conventional, an effort based on empathy to rally support for a pressing cause, a divorce of poetry from politics where, according to Werner Mittenzweig, 'a direct appeal for action' justified 'concessions regarding [Brecht's] dramatic theory'.[52] Brecht himself called it 'Aristotelian' and 'technically speaking, a big step backwards . . . opportunistic'.[53] Yet from the beginning he aimed to keep the play straightforward for the sake of its call for action and involvement in an international war, addressing both the French public and his fellow writers. And while the appeal may be simple, the situation portrayed is anything but. Again Brecht interweaves personal fate and ongoing sociopolitical developments; the relationship between individual action and history, between stage and the immediate temporal, geographical and political proximity to 'outside' reality. The play is considered Brecht's greatest popular success after *The Threepenny Opera*.

At the same time, Brecht had been working with Steffin on a collection of press reports and eyewitness accounts about everyday occurrences and experiences in Nazi Germany since 1934. This collection provided the basis for *The Private Life of the Master Race*, published in 1938 and described by its author as a 'montage of 27 scenes': 'a tableau of gestures, precisely the gestures of falling silent, of looking over one's shoulder, of fright, etc.'[54] In a letter to Dudow, Brecht wrote, 'Here after all, I think, the entire brittleness of the Third Reich in all of its details will become visible and the fact that only violence keeps it together.'[55] The play weaves together a web of social, geographic and chronological pieces: from 1933 until 1938, Berlin to Vienna, the young and the old, peasants and workers to clerks, doctors and bureaucrats. 'The style I envision being like Goya's etchings about the Civil War . . . with something documentary in between.'[56] Other than the overall topic of violence and lies, scenes are connected through subjects like 'betrayal' and 'distrust'. In relation to one another, individual and ostensibly private actions exhibit their political dimension while collectivity (concerning the social body as much as the play's formal structure) is dismantled as brutal individuation. 'Character', states one of the protagonists, 'is a matter of time. It lasts for a while, just like a glove.'[57] Eight scenes premiered in Paris

Brecht and Helene
Weigel, in
Copenhagen,
Denmark, during
the autumn of 1936.

in 1938 under the title *99%*, with music by Paul Dessau and direction
by Dudow. Helene Weigel, who played three roles in this version,
remembered the premiere as 'a great success. . . . The people laughed
a lot, applauded a lot after the play.'[58] The German-language news
paper *Pariser Tageblatt* praised the performance as 'a work of
simultaneous contemporary relevance and great artistic maturity.
The visionary realism of a prophetically burning chronicler projects
the thousands of infamies, making up the complex of the perversities
of the Third Reich, into the night sky of eternal remembrance.'
Brecht built, the reviewer continues, 'a kaleidoscope of hell'.[59]

A print version of the play was to appear as part of Brecht's
Collected Works, volumes one and two of which had already been
published by Herzfelde's Malik Verlag, now located in Prague. The
text was advertised under the title *Deutschland: Ein Greuelmärchen*
(Germany: a horror tale), in direct reference to Heinrich Heine's
Deutschland: Ein Wintermärchen (Germany: a winter's tale, 1844).
Brecht shared Heine's anxiety over the country's fate as its people
abused abbreviated cultural traditions and fictional *völkisch* values
in a barbaric rejection of the social and psychological challenges of
modernization, an anxiety expressed by Heine on the eve of the

failed German revolution of 1848 with the famous lines: 'Thinking of Germany in the night, I lie awake and sleep takes flight.'[60]

But while it was published in excerpts in several journals around Europe and in Moscow, *The Private Life of the Master Race* never appeared as part of the Malik *Collected Works*. The publisher sent the proofs to Brecht for review, but even before Germany annexed Czechoslovakia in March 1939, fascist influence and actions in Prague forced Herzfelde to precipitous flight. The printing set for the text was presumably destroyed in late 1938 or early 1939. Brecht took Herzfelde's departure as a sign of his own situation's precariousness, observing in a journal entry in August 1938 that Hitler 'is preparing to conquer the world. Yesterday the great German manoeuvres began, the mobilization rehearsals.'[61] In October, he wrote that it was conceivable that the Czechs had to give Germany something, but that they gave 'pretty much everything to everybody. And the Jews and émigrés at that' – to Brecht, a situation easily fathomable in Denmark's case as well.[62] His one-act play *Dansen* (1939) chronicled these events and the playwright's fears and addresses the Scandinavian politics of neutrality in light of the Austrian and Czech invasions. Brecht called it a 'not-getting-involved play', about sticking one's head in the sand.[63] *Dansen* and another short play entitled *What Does the Iron Cost?* (1939) were cited in support of the playwright's official visa application, filed on the occasion of a request by a Swedish organization of amateur theatres for a series of presentations and discussions. In April 1939, Brecht accepted the invitation of Swedish sculptor Ninnan Santesson and moved with his family and Steffin into the artist's house on the island of Lindingö near Stockholm.

It was in this context that Brecht wrote *Mother Courage and Her Children: A Chronicle of the Thirty Years War.* Although the precise period of origin is disputed, Steffin's calendar marks the dates of working on *Mother Courage* as between September and November

1939, while Brecht recalled, 'I wrote my play for Scandinavia.'
There, he remembers,

> The theatre mattered, unlike in many other European countries.
> I envisioned, while writing, that from the stages of some big
> cities the warning of a playwright would be heard, the warning
> that he who wants to have breakfast with the devil must wield a
> long spoon . . . There never were any such performances. The
> writers couldn't write as fast as the governments were making
> wars . . . *Mother Courage and Her Children* came too late.[64]

As suggested in the play's subtitle, *Mother Courage* sets the story of
the widow Courage in the early seventeenth century, but references
to the volatile situation in twentieth-century Europe abound.
Courage, mother of three children by three different men, travels
the war-torn countryside in a journey of loss (first to die is the horse
that pulls the cart, then one child after another). Yet despite her
eyes being open to the horrors that so violently shape her as well as
her personal losses, Courage remains a cunning profiteer, valuing
her business interests above the compassion and truth she
nonetheless loudly proclaims, even when her deeds harm herself
and those around her. In contrast to her mute daughter Kattrin,
who selflessly aids others, Courage exemplifies the schism between
rhetoric and conduct as well as the capitalist egotism willing to
sacrifice not only any form of human solidarity but the very notions
of humanist moralism it espouses. Usually reserved for the history
of great men, Brecht turns the form of the chronicle into an account
from below, a plebeian perspective onto war and family, money and
perseverance. Like the 'Questions of a Reading Worker', this is a
story told in relation to, rather than in exchange for, existing tales
of greatness and honour. The play takes its cues from Johan Ludvig
Runeberg, a nineteenth-century Swedish-Finnish poet of wartime
ballads written as experienced by the common people, the soldiers

and peasants, and from Hans Jakob Christoffel von Grimmelshausen, the German author of a seventeenth-century picaresque novel about the Thirty Years War and the baroque tale of the duplicitous woman Courasche. Despite the obvious similarities, Grimmelshausen's influence on Brecht's play is primarily methodological, in the form of prepended synopses (asking the audience to focus on the 'how' rather than the 'what' of the performance), the insertion of songs (disrupting and defamiliarizing the action onstage) and the reversal of the ordinary (the appropriation of bourgeois values for the new 'normality' of war). Paul Dessau's final score of simple, popular songs and the open form of the play, reaching into the present through thematic allusions and parallels as well as the constant reminder of the play as an artificial, staged and narrated construction, aim to broaden *Mother Courage*'s impact beyond the confines of the theatre. The play premiered on 19 April 1941 in Zurich, with its author *in absentia*. The critical and public reception was favourable and Brecht was generally pleased with the outcome, even though most critics misunderstood the relation between war and Courage, in keeping with traditional expectations of a bourgeois theatre portraying the mother and her children as victims of the war rather than as being implicated in and by it. Three days after the premiere, Brecht wrote in his journal, 'It is brave that this theatre, made primarily by immigrants, is performing one of my works now. No Scandinavian stage was courageous enough.'[65] Only a few weeks later Brecht would board the Trans-Siberian Express to commence the long journey to his u.s. exile.

5

U.S. Exile: The Dialectics of Alienation and 'Culinary' Art, 1941–7

War Fare

As the war drew nearer and fascism tightened its grip on the Scandinavian peninsula, Brecht found himself crowded out of space to work: 'With every report of Hitler's victories, my significance as a writer diminishes.'[1] His Finnish journal records his anticipation of finding a place where he could continue what he started. An entry written on 18 April 1941 reads: 'I realize that it is impossible to avoid "*wishful thinking*", meaning to fearlessly analyse the facts. I find myself constantly thinking: this I will reassess in the USA.'[2]

Brecht, Weigel and the children, Barbara and Stefan, landed on American shores on 21 July 1941. They had moved to Finland only a year earlier, after German troops had invaded Denmark and Norway, and the Swedish police searched Brecht's house for political writings. The time spent in Finland is described in a journal entry as a period of suspension, marked by a feeling of increased isolation alongside the distracting pleasures of rural leisure at the manor four hours outside Helsinki where the family lived as guests of the Finnish writer Hella Wuolijoki:

When I listen to the news on the radio in the morning while reading Boswell's *Life of Johnson* and peering out at the birch-tree landscape with fog from the river, then the unnatural day

begins, not with discord, but without a chord at all. This is the
in-between time.[3]

The procurement of U.S. visas proved more difficult than
expected, but with the help of a number of friends, especially Lion
Feuchtwanger, the family, Ruth Berlau and Margarete Steffin
obtained the necessary papers. In May of 1941, the exiles began
their journey, taking an eastward route via Moscow, where Steffin's
tuberculosis took a turn for the worse. Brecht's notes tell of her 'collapse', attributed to the poor Finnish diet and Steffin's fatigue from
feverishly collecting and caring for his manuscripts.[4] She had to
be hospitalized but insisted that the rest of the travellers move on.
Brecht's journal records the news of her death immediately after,
as unembellished as the telegram he received while still on the train
to Vladivostok. But Brecht expressed his deep attachment to and
admiration for Steffin in a series of poems, including 'When It Was
Time', 'After the Death of My Colleague M. S.' and 'My General Has
Fallen' (all 1941). Brecht's journal, which contained only sporadic
entries throughout the 1920s and '30s, now becomes a detailed log
of displacement. Brecht came to the U.S. to flee the war and found
an environment that both affirmed and starkly clashed with the
fantastic Amerika of his Weimar plays. And although he tried to
adapt to the lifestyle and working conditions of his host country, he
found himself out of place. At the same time he discovered a pressing
continuity to questions of labour and ownership as the source of
psychosocial alienation and strategies of artistic defamiliarization,
and he began to expand on projects he had begun in Europe.

In many ways the U.S. of Brecht's exile turned out to be the
very land of his imagination: with gangsters and corruption, an
adventure in consumption and progress available to those who
could afford to live the fiction. For Brecht, America was a condition
in which the dialectics of modernity seemed suspended not in
synthesis but in the resolution of artifice as reality:

People have concluded that God,
Requiring both a Heaven and a Hell, didn't need to
Plan two establishments but
just the one: Heaven. It
Serves the unprosperous, the unsuccessful
as Hell.[5]

This realization of the U.S. as a land of fantasy is, as Fredric
Jameson has pointed out, specifically concurrent with the country's
period between the Depression and post-war McCarthyism, 'the
"moral equivalent" of revolution and socialist construction'.[6] But
rather than just the 'dreary reality of the 1930s–'50s continuum',
Brecht finds his host country to be not in a state of anomaly but
existing in relation to *alltäglich* (everyday) modern phenomena
like war and progress, collectivity and alienation. He sees it as
constructed, living its own precarious promise along with all the
contradictions that make it possible and that it enables.[7] Brecht's
period in America thus serves to confirm his assessment of the
relationship between capitalism and fascism, between the U.S. and
Germany, as well as his notion of historical scenarios as contingent
upon one another rather than exceptional. It was, after all, the
fabled Chicago wheat exchange of *Joe Fleischhacker* that led Brecht
to the study of Marxism in order to understand the mechanisms
at work in the capitalist economy and the economics of democracy,
to find in practice the conditions that would beget radical transformation. Not that the playwright did not express frustration and doubt
regarding his Hollywood experience, caused in part by the overall
failure of his attempts to find footing in the movie industry and his
very limited success on and off Broadway. But his sense of alienation and self-alienation can be seen as providing Brecht with
further, palpable impetus to adjust his theory and practice, his
method of getting history onto the stage.

Brecht may have been, as James Lyon put it, 'reluctant' to commence the American leg of his exile, as his youthful enthusiasm for the land of boxing and Chaplin, the Wild West and industrialization waned.[8] He was forced to confront his own stylization of that mythological place. Often his observations verged on self-pitying complaints, especially during the first months in Hollywood. Weeks after his arrival, Brecht remarked, 'In almost no other place was life for me more difficult than in this mortuary of "*easy going*". The house is too pretty, my job here gold-digging.'[9] One week later he wrote, 'I feel as if removed from my age; this is a Tahiti in metropolitan form.'[10]

Though averse to participating in what he considered the 'prostitution' of the film industry, Brecht tried hard to find work as a screenwriter, to forge collaborations and to sell scripts. But except for his tumultuous work with director Fritz Lang on the 1942 hit *Hangmen Also Die* – marred by their fundamentally different ideas regarding artistic merit and popular appeal – the German playwright had little employment and even less money. The family depended on the generosity of friends, including Feuchtwanger, Weill and Korsch, as well as subsidies from initiatives like the European Film Fund, established by European exiles to support other refugees. Weigel bought furniture and clothes from the Salvation Army and Goodwill. Since he could not afford a car, Brecht relied on others to drive him to meetings and appointments.

In the U.S. Brecht and his work were nearly unknown. In a letter to Heinrich Mann, Brecht describes the lack of opportunity to communicate in print, onstage and otherwise as a 'relapse to the Middle Ages'.[11] The *Hollywood Elegies*, a collection of poetic observations written in the late summer of 1942, lack the lyrical first-person narrator typically found in the lament's traditional form and instead cast a distanced, critical eye on the City of Angels. In this town, even the imaginary succumbs to the forces

of materialization – musicians hustle, writers get in line at the
'market of lies' and 'Dante sways his scrawny butt':

The angels of Los Angeles
Are tired from smiling. In the evening
Behind the fruit markets they buy,
Desperately, little bottles
Containing the odour of sex.[12]

The commercialization of art and the function of culture to
obfuscate the all-permeating powers of money were not new to
Brecht, yet he was surprised by the obvious and unapologetic
collapse of a dialectic that was supposed to provide a subtle yet
fundamental mechanism of modernity's potential for progress.
How to offer an estranging glance onto the world when estrangement loses the reality of its distance? But just as he had found that
the Nazis' undisguised violence was part of fascism's contradictions,
Brecht felt compelled to pursue the relationality between the
ever-transmuting given and the possible.

This relationality and its evolution is at the core of the *War
Primer*, which consisted of 'photo epigrams', as Brecht called the
combination of found published materials, mostly images from
news sources, and his own lyrical commentary. Brecht had begun
to cut out and collect newspaper clippings in the mid-1920s, and
in 1938 he had started pasting photos and found texts into his
journal. The first published photo epigram appeared in 1944 in
the literary section of the New York-based *Austro American Tribune*,
while the *War Primer* itself was not realized in its entirety until
1955. In 1945, a version of the primer sent to Karl Korsch in New
Orleans contained 66 collages, the original text and image re-
photographed separately and reduced in size, then mounted onto
a small piece of black cardboard and fastened into a folder marked
War Primer. Korsch's reply to Brecht praises the work as 'the best

thing there is about the war'.[13] The 1955 publication contains 69 photo epigrams plus an introduction and an epilogue as well as a dust jacket whose back picture shows students in a lecture hall at an East German university annotated with a poem that begins, 'Don't forget: someone like you struggled.'[14]

The choice of the photo epigram form, the overall composition and arrangements of the individual parts, and the subjects, subjectivities and perspectives included make the primer project much more than an expression of Brecht's distrust in the photographic image and a 'Marxist corrective to "Western" histories of the war'.[15] Whether in his oft-cited observation that photographs of the Krupp and AEG factories reify social relations or in his praise of Willi Münzenberg's proletarian journal *Arbeiter Illustrierte Zeitung*, famous for its publication of John Heartfield's photomontages, Brecht thought of images never simply as lies, as false consciousness or fabrication, but always as something that in their construction either enabled or denied access to reality as a totality of relations that included the image itself.[16] The *War Primer* is thus an enquiry into a type of speech, connecting images and ideas, myths and circumstances of war as production, progress and subjectivity. Chronologically arranged events include armament and preparation for battle; the Spanish Civil War; the occupation of and attacks on Poland, Norway, Denmark, France, England and Russia; war in Africa, Asia and the Pacific; the Jewish flight to Palestine; the American invasion in Northern France; and the German defeat, destruction of cities and the soldiers' homecoming. There is a separate focus on the powers and institutions being held responsible for the Second World War, including politicians, industry and the Catholic Church, as well as a look at the fighting in Russia, which is subsequently articulated as a fight between German and Russian 'brothers', whose respective victory and loss is over those who turned workers and farmers against one another.

Es war zur Zeit des UNTEN und des OBEN
Als auch die Luft erobert war, und drum
Verkroch viel Volk, als einige sich erhoben
Sich unterm Boden und kam dennoch um.

War Primer, 1938–55, plate 19.

To Brecht, this global event of horror and destruction is, at
its core, a class war, of those *oben* (on top) against those *unten*
(on the bottom).[17] At times, this constellation between top and
bottom is direct: photo epigram 19 begins with the line, 'It was
the time of BELOW and ABOVE,' followed by a textual juxtaposition
of conquered airspace and uprising with taking cover, staying
low, hiding out.[18] Other panels speak of *Herren* (masters), whose
constitution as such is not bound to national boundaries but

determined by ownership, and tell of those kept 'under the boot'. The word *erobern* (to conquer) and its association in German with *oben* runs throughout the *War Primer*, as an incentive to gain advantage and occupy as an attitude transcending barriers of language, culture, history and nationality. This transgression of the particular is juxtaposed with the visual uniformity of the black-and-white press photographs taken from German propaganda materials, Scandinavian newspapers, *Life* magazine and various other sources.

It is here, precisely, that Brecht's project enquires about the differentiation between generality and specificity: whereas the media images project a generalization through formal similarities, turning the war into a humanist disaster of exceptional circumstance, the *War Primer* finds specificity in the treatment of people in relations of power. Panel 43 shows a *Life* picture of a blinded Australian soldier being led by a loincloth-clad helper, whom the magazine describes as a 'kindly Papuan native'. The caption ends with, 'Both men are barefoot.'[19] Within the context of the *War Primer* the blindness of the infantryman and the touching humanism of the common shoelessness is compared to the class-based commonality shared by the Russian and the German soldiers. This commonality is, in Brecht's project, unavailable to the American soldiers depicted therein, whose war is regarded as an essential battle between good and evil, as if on a Wild West stage: 'One pulled a gun. I pulled mine. I killed him. It was just like in the movies.'[20] It is also unavailable to the readers of *Life* magazine, whose insight into the totality, the complexity of the war and its portrayal, is incomplete. For Brecht, the war was a competition over ownership of images and perspectives as much as land and power. Accordingly, the *War Primer* functions as a series of 'tableaux', a term used by Roland Barthes, offering both the war and its representation as driven by essentially national, cultural and quasi-ethnic or *Volkish* traits rather than by a historically

Als nun für mich die lange Schlacht vorbei
Half mir ein Mann zurück, der freundlich war.
Aus seinem Schweigen lernte ich, er sei
Wohl des Verstehns, doch nicht des Mitleids bar.

War Primer, 1938–55, plate 43.

determined constellation of economic agendas and pursuits. Barthes writes that Brecht's tableaux are 'clearly projected, privileging a meaning but manifesting the production of that meaning, achieving the coincidence of the visual projection and the ideal projection'.[21]

Brecht refused to see the war as a state of exception. He was interested in its underlying mechanisms, the acquisition and maintenance of power, determined by questions of profit, expansion and monopolization to which the rhetoric of honour, race and

Lebensraum served as barbaric legitimization. In order to fight fascism and establish a post-war Germany that would be truly liberated from the oppressive machines of violent mass exploitation, Hitler had to be understood as a *Bürger* and the system of free-market democracy, even or especially that of the U.S., as thoroughly 'bourgeois'. To Brecht, American capitalism and German fascism differed dramatically in the quality of violence applied to maintain hegemony, but shared certain basic political motivations and tactics. One similarity was the ideological projection of the enemy as entirely other. In a text from 1939 Brecht asks why the petit bourgeois and even the proletariat threaten to join the fascists.[22] One answer given is that communism is denounced as both utopian and dangerous to those constituencies and their individual (and individuating) belongings, and that fascism promises the protection of property through expansion and constitutive difference (ours–theirs) rather than the abolition of the very concept of property through a complete redefinition of social relations. When Brecht portrays Hitler as a gangster in a milieu of corruption and murder, intrigue and seduction, as in the play *Arturo Ui* (1941), he not only draws parallels between capitalism and fascism but also de-mythifies and repoliticizes the German dictator.

At many a gathering in the Hollywood Hills, according to Brecht's journal, the discussion of the fate of fascism included the impression of Hitler as an 'insignificant thespian' or *Hampelmann* (jumping jack) in the service of the German *Reichswehr*, as 'Feuchtwanger and others' referred to him.[23] In contrast, Brecht was 'unreservedly willing to treat Hitler as a great bourgeois politician', certain that the despot was 'a revision of the bourgeois idea of a *great man*'.[24] Hitler was to be understood not as a villain but 'as the perpetrator of immense political crimes, which is something completely different'.[25] For Brecht, neither the Nazis nor their methods were to be relegated solely to the ahistorical bin of the insane and unspeakable, but they were to be confronted as social, economic and psychological constructions that could be studied and thus fought and avoided in the future: 'Anti-Semitism is likewise not something *sinnlos* [pointless, absurd], even though it is something abominable.'[26] When 'German reports', as the newspapers put it, announced that the Reichswehr's march on Moscow was paralysed 'by zero weather', Brecht remarked dryly, 'At the time that the world's greatest industrial power joins the war, Hitler realizes that the Russian winters are cold.'[27] When a few months later snow and ice make for images of frozen soldiers and amputated limbs, Brecht spends many days and pages arguing for a differentiation between 'class' as a notion, a consciousness, and 'class' as an existing social formation. As German and American intellectuals were at odds about how an entire population could succumb to murder and mass delusions of grandeur, Brecht argued that 'the war economy with its closure of the job market has damaged the economic idea of class. What remains is class itself. Luckily it is not a concept.' He continues, 'It is wrong to deduce that because a war cannot be fought without the proletariat [as labour power], a war unsympathetic to the proletariat cannot be fought.'[28]

And this war was being conducted on two fronts – inside Germany and outwards, with other countries ('the German people', Brecht wrote, were the 'first conquered'). His essay 'The *Other* Germany: 1943' was an attempt to convince the American public that there was, in fact, a resistance movement in Germany and that its population should not be simply equated with the Nazi apparatus: 'Hitler ravaged his own country before he ravaged other countries . . . He made prisoners of war in his own country. In 1939 these armies numbered 200,000 – more Germans than the Russians took at Stalingrad.'[29] (The essay was translated by Eric Bentley, who, at Brecht's behest, tried in vain to get it published in a popular magazine 'like the *Saturday Evening Post*'; it did not appear in print until 1966.) Brecht went on to point out that even though the Nazis took advantage of the economic situation of the Weimar Republic to turn the proletariat against itself in competition over jobs and food, the German people did indeed have as much of an interest in the war as its regime, as they fight for work and land: 'Somewhere near Smolensk a Silesian soldier points his gun at a Russian tank that will crush him if it is not stopped. There is hardly any time to realize that what he is pointing his gun at is unemployment. . . . War demands everything, but it provides everything too. It provides food, shelter, work.' Yet, according to Brecht, there is what he calls 'an enormous miscalculation somewhere'. He continues:

> The regime had to choose war because the whole people needed war; *but the people needed war only under this regime and therefore have to look for another way of life.* The road to this conclusion is a long one. For it is the road to social revolution.[30]

This refusal to equate the Nazi regime with the German people had consequences for the role of the country's population in the fight against fascism and the international community's involvement in the destruction of Hitler. Together with other exiles, Brecht composed a number of public declarations regarding the actions to be taken by Germans within and outside the Reich's boundaries. When on 1 January 1942 the Anti-Hitler Coalition, consisting of the U.S., Great Britain, the Soviet Union and 23 other states, declared the isolation of Nazi Germany through the coalition's political-military unity, Brecht participated in the formulation of a list of suggestions of how best to aid the intra-German opposition: Goebbels's propagated myth of 'Hitler and Germany being one' was to be countered by an 'honest propaganda'.[31] This propaganda would come from the opposition outside, at a moment when the regime was weakened by military setbacks, taking the opportunity to remind the population of its sovereignty. On 19 March 1942, the

Intercontinent News in New York published a telegram signed by Brecht, Feuchtwanger and Heinrich Mann, which opens with, 'Germans! This appeal is a call for salvation, for everyone and for you too, Germans! You have plunged the world and yourselves into calamity. . . . Only you can abort the most ruinous and senseless of all wars.'[32]

Other émigrés had trouble believing in the people's ability and willingness to throw off their fascist yoke. In 1943 Brecht organized a meeting of writers and intellectuals to write a position paper in reaction to a manifesto from the NKFD, an organization of German prisoners of war and émigrés in the Soviet Union, calling on the German people and soldiers to end the war. The response, composed and signed by Heinrich and Thomas Mann, Feuchtwanger, Bruno Frank, Ludwig Marcuse, Brecht and others, supported the NKFD's appeal to 'the German *Volk* to force its oppressors to surrender unconditionally' and the 'necessity to sharply distinguish between the Hitler regime and the social strata connected to it on the one hand and the German *Volk* on the other'.[33] But the next day, Thomas Mann and Bruno Frank retracted their signatures. According to Brecht, Mann felt that the declaration was a 'patriotic statement' that was 'stabbing the allies in the back' and did not necessarily object to the idea that the allies would 'castigate Germany for ten or twenty years'.[34] This rekindled Brecht's old disdain for Mann. Brecht wrote a bitter poem titled 'Upon the Nobel Prize Winner Thomas Mann's Authorizing the Americans and the English to Punish the German People Ten Years for the Crimes of the Hitler Regime' (1943) and reminded himself in his personal notes of the debilitating 'resolute woefulness of these "bearers of culture"'.[35]

Realism(s)

Since the mid-1930s, Brecht had made several attempts to stage his plays on and off Broadway, but repeatedly ran into sharply binary expectations with regard to the roles of art and politics. To some U.S. producers, his work was overtly propagandistic, while to others it was not sufficiently populist. The production of *The Mother* by the New York Theater Union, at the time the most prominent U.S. 'workers' theatre', ended with Brecht's being thrown out of rehearsals and the organization financially ruined.[36] The Theater Union had shipped Brecht in from his exile in Denmark but during rehearsals, realizing that *The Mother* had been stripped of his concerns for the defamiliarization of theatrical experience, Brecht threw tantrums and yelled, 'This is shit!' until he was removed from the theatre. The simplified, palatable version of *The Mother* was dismissed by the press as 'didactic' and 'pretentious', 'amateurish' and 'affected', 'an entertainment for children, for it is a simple kindergarten for Communist tots'.[37] In the climate of Popular Front alliances and the economic successes of the New Deal, the American Brecht reception was a divorce of tendency and technique. Rather than acknowledging the dialectical interplay of the commitment to social change and the cognitive-aesthetic politics of form, the reception of Brecht's work was marked by either the rejection of its revolutionary content as 'Communist infantilism' or the dismissal of its anti-illusionist dramaturgy and prose as elitist and over-intellectualized.[38]

Aware of this split reception, Brecht tailored his next two plays to be, as he later admitted to the set designer Mordecai Gorelik, explicitly directed at an American middle-class audience. Essentially the playwright aided his critics in separating his revolutionary intentions from his poetic and dramatic work. This tailored approach would determine the critical response to Brecht's theatre and aesthetic politics in general. Despite his concessions, including the dramatic resolution of a 'happy ending', and despite his contract and his presence in New York writing and working on the play in 1944, *The Caucasian Chalk Circle* was never performed during his American years. Meanwhile, *The Private Life of the Master Race*, staged in the U.S. in the 1940s, received favourable reviews that recast Brecht as a pacifist playwright rather than one devoted to class struggle.[39]

Only a small faction of the American Left maintained a concern for socialist content *and* form in Brechtian aesthetics. Among these, critic and novelist Eva Goldbeck elaborated on the revolutionary importance of the *Lehrstück* in an article published in *The New Masses* in 1935. Goldbeck argued that to instruct the worker on how to think dialectically, not to present him with some sort of illusionist and affected spectacle, was at the heart of Brecht's original effort:

> The emotional excitement that is always present in the theatre is of course not ignored; but it is minimized and used not to obscure but to clarify the intelligence. Significantly . . . this new dramaturgy is called the Study play (*Lehrstück*).[40]

Meanwhile, Goldbeck's husband, the composer Marc Blitzstein, had found in Brecht the 'solvent of his career'.[41] In 1936 Blitzstein produced the famous play *The Cradle Will Rock*, fusing his interest in popular music and speech with radical social consciousness. Dedicated to Brecht, *The Cradle Will Rock* resulted from a conversation with the playwright concerning prostitution as a modern condition permeating all areas of ideological production, including the press, the clergy and intellectual life. The next year, Brecht's friend Gorelik published his own translation of some early Brechtian theoretical tracts under the title 'Epic Realism: Brecht's Notes on *The Threepenny Opera*', with some of his own elaborations on those theories.[42] Gorelik would go on to discuss Brecht's theatre at length in his influential book *New Theatres for the Old* (1940).[43] One of the first historical discussions of Brechtian theatre, Gorelik's study drew parallels with related phenomena such as Soviet theatre, Erwin Piscator's political theatre and the Living Newspaper, an American Federal Theater Project 'producing organization' established in 1935 and sponsored by the national union of newspaper workers.[44]

Brecht made far fewer concessions to his methods in discussions with other Marxist exiles, especially the members of the Institute for Social Research, or 'Frankfurt School', who had settled on the West Coast in 1941, having been in New York since 1934. Brecht's journals during the American years recount several social encounters with Theodor Adorno, Max Horkheimer, Friedrich Pollock and other 'Tuis'. Despite their shared concern with the production of culture under capitalism and fascism, Brecht and the members of the Frankfurt School regarded one another with respectful suspicion and at times outright hostility. Adorno and Horkheimer considered Brecht's materialism vulgar and simplistic, his notion of class struggle and faith in the working class as a historical revolutionary force dated and undialectical. Though Adorno accused the playwright of anti-intellectualism, he himself was not averse to the odd crude, personal remark. He notoriously noted that Brecht spent hours every day pushing dirt under his fingernails in order to appear more proletarian.[45] But it was Brecht who, judging by his journal entries, constantly baited and ridiculed the Tuis. He despised their elitism and accused them of leading a pseudo-revolutionary struggle that had nothing but disdain for regular people and their experiences. Within weeks of his arrival in Santa Monica, he met what he called the '*Doppelclown* Horkheimer and Pollock' at a garden party:

> With their money they keep afloat about a dozen intellectuals, all of whom have to turn in their work without the guarantee

that the *Zeitschrift* [the Institute's journal] ever publishes them. They can therefore claim that 'to save the Institute's money was their main revolutionary duty during all these years'.[46]

Brecht saw the Institute as part of the problem, their lack of concern for how to productively battle the monsters of mass culture beyond negative critique as a sign of complicity.

Brecht had been planning to write a 'Tui novel' for some time, gathering more and more inspiration and material during the California exile. The project remained a fragment, but its ruminations found affirmation in every encounter with the 'Frankfurtists'.[47] In June 1942, Brecht attended a seminar initiated by the Institute and reported that Horkheimer registered 'with alarm' an announcement by u.s. vice-president Henry Wallace that after the war, every child in the world ought to receive a pint of milk daily. 'The Institute is wondering if this is not the dawn of a gigantic threat to culture, should capitalism dispense that much milk (which, according to the economist Pollock's expertise, it certainly could).'[48] Echoing his Paris address in 1935 at the International Writers Congress for the Defence of Culture, Brecht questioned the effectiveness of saving culture in light of what was considered culture and how it related to the needs of those suffering from a lack of control over their own fates. To him, the preservation of the concept of culture as the disinterested, trans-historical realm of moral preservation was counter-revolutionary. Eisler proposed to Brecht that the plot of the Tui novel should be based on the history of the Frankfurt School:

A rich old man dies, troubled by all the misery in the world. He bequeaths a large sum of money for the establishment of an institute that is supposed to discover the misery's source, which is, of course, the old man himself.[49]

Brecht's confrontations with the members of the Frankfurt School regarding the quality of the relation between cultural production and popular experience had a precedent in the so-called *Expressionismusdebatte*, or Expressionism debate, of 1938, which began when *Das Wort* published a heated exchange between Ernst Bloch and Georg Lukács about the relation between Expressionist art and social reality. The debate soon extended to include other voices, most prominently Brecht, Benjamin and Adorno, the latter two peripherally involved in the actual discussion, yet developing it along the pivotal issue of aesthetics and politics, the role of an avant-garde and that of the populace.[50] Though Brecht had been originally named as one of the journal's three main editors, his contributions were never published in *Das Wort*; the publication was effectively run by Fritz Erpenbeck, a journalist with close personal and ideological ties to Lukács. Brecht was both politically and geographically removed from what he disdainfully referred to as the 'Moscow Clique', and he was looking to provide an alternative in form and attitude to the 'Moscow realism' of Lukács and the renowned Russian director Constantin Stanislavski. He found his letters unanswered and his recommendation in 1937 that the journal ought to publish Benjamin's essay 'The Work of Art in the Age of Its Technological Reproducibility' rejected, and he complained that the formalist character of the Expressionism debate, once under way, was 'highly harmful and confusing'.[51]

What united the contributions to this Popular Front publication was their intent to devise the parameters for an anti-fascist literature. But as Brecht had observed in Paris, fascism was condemned in a general manner, undifferentiated with regard to a historically specific notion of class, while the cultural climate in the USSR since 1936 had shifted to an aggressive and sometimes violent campaign 'Against Formalism and Naturalism'.[52] This fundamental reorientation of artistic guidelines coincided with

the years of Stalinist terror, and a number of writers associated
with *Das Wort* and contributors to the Expressionism debate
fell victim to the so-called cleansings, among them Ernst Ottwalt,
Brecht's *Kuhle Wampe* collaborator, and Herwarth Walden, one
of Expressionism's leading theoreticians. To Brecht, the fight
against fascism was always also a fight for the proletariat and for
the popular, and it was with an attempt to redefine the notions
of *Volkstümlichkeit* and *Realismus* (popularity and realism) that
he sought to join Bloch and Lukács's argument.

With the condemnation of Expressionist art and literature
having been brewing among exiled German intellectuals for
some years, *Das Wort* published Bloch's 'Diskussionen über den
Expressionismus' (Discussions of Expressionism) as a response to
Lukács's assault on Expressionism. Bloch saw in literary as well as
pictorial Expressionism a reflection of a common experience of
fragmentation and alienation amid the shattered holistic humanist
and artistic ideals of a bankrupt bourgeois universe. Modernist and
contemporaneous, as opposed to traditional and trans-historical,
Expressionism, according to Bloch, allowed for aesthetic tools to
become available to the struggle of the masses. It would only
seem like an 'irrationalist . . . pseudo activism', as it did to Lukács,
if the fissures in the ideological surface of bourgeois capitalism
were not filled with possibility but rather feared as the decay of an
abstract, ahistorical totality.[53] Lukács, in fact, argued for a realism
that would 'mirror objective reality'.[54] He felt that capitalist reality
was unitary, total and continuous and that aesthetic forms such
as collage and montage only mimicked the psychological and
social effects of capitalism (alienation) instead of presenting the
working class with a coherent and comprehensible understanding
of reality as a whole. While to Bloch, 'realism' was the expression of
a historically authentic experience, to Lukács it meant the removed
articulation of the rather stable and coherent circumstances that
begot this experience.

Brecht saw this removal, the unidirectional disconnect between ideal and real, between theory and practice, replicated in the discussion itself. He accused Lukács of formalizing class struggle:

> For Lukács, there is in the early bourgeois novel (Goethe) a 'broad richness of existence', and the novel arouses 'the illusion of shaping the entire existence in its completely unfurled breadth'. Imitate! It's just that nothing is unfurling and no existence acquires breadth!

The dialectic of aesthetics and politics, of image, imagination and action, had to evolve. Those like Lukács who stunted this development effectively obstructed public agency: 'The Realism debate is blocking production.'[55] When Benjamin, to whom Brecht complained about his encounters with the Moscow circle, remarked that 'with these people [one] could not make state' (a German idiom for turning ideas into political consequences), Brecht replied, 'Or *just* a state, but no collective. They are simply enemies of production. They are suspicious of production. One can't trust it. It has something unpredictable. You never know what comes out of it.'[56] And Brecht ascribed this fear of popular production to the Soviet enterprise: 'In Russia, what you have is a dictatorship *over* the proletariat.'[57]

One of Brecht's unpublished contributions to the debate was his essay 'Popularity and Realism', of June 1938, in which he argued that a repressed people had to shake off the yoke of barbarism themselves rather than reproduce a structure of compliant dependency. The making of this resistance had to be collective rather than assigned. It had to be popular rather than populist, not in the name of the people but by them, a task of not insignificant difficulty given the Nazis' mythology of *Volkstum* and *Brauchtum* (rituals and customs). The artist's role was thus to facilitate collective production as a historically specific transformation of material and immaterial ownership. The concepts of popularity and realism are defined very carefully and warrant citation in their entirety:

> *Popular* means: intelligible to the broad masses, adopting and enriching their forms of expression / assuming their standpoint, confirming and correcting it / representing the most progressive section of the people so that it can assume leadership, and therefore intelligible to other sections of the people as well / relating to traditions and developing them / communicating to that portion of the people that strives for leadership the achievements of the section that at present rules the nation.

> *Realistic* means: discovering the causal complexes of society / unmasking the prevailing view of things as the view of those who are in power / writing from the standpoint of the class that offers the broadest solutions for the pressing difficulties in which human society is caught up / emphasizing the element of development / making possible the concrete, and making possible abstraction from it.[58]

Thus an anti-fascist, proletarian art is concerned with, to use Jacques Rancière's term, 'the distribution of the sensible . . . of doing and making'.[59] It seeks to understand and reconfigure the ways in which politics are made visible, tangible, and in which doing and making are governed by the contested powers of tradition and history, fantasies and experiences, ethics and ethos. The role of the artist, the poet, the playwright is not to provide alternate truths but to reveal the contest over competing voices and perspectives, thus enabling proletarian production, the redistribution of productive capacities. This is also the point where Brecht and Benjamin meet, aesthetically and politically. And it is maybe no surprise that both *Das Wort* and the Frankfurt-ists rejected the ideas articulated in 'The Work of Art in the Age of

Its Technological Reproducibility'. The now-infamous distinction between the aestheticization of politics and the politicization of aesthetics drawn by Benjamin has been read repeatedly as a strategy of anti-aesthetics or, as Adorno put it, the 'liquidation of art'.[60] Though the essay was published with alterations in the Institute's *Zeitung für Sozialforschung* in 1936, Adorno took issue with what he felt was a simplistic and infantile notion of participatory culture.[61] The proletarian culture that Benjamin saw as being the result of reproductive mediums like photography and film's destruction of the artwork's 'aura', which he equated with 'disinterestedness' and 'autonomy', was not, according to Adorno, a utopian socialization of art but an already available mass culture that generated passivity and conformism: 'The laughter of the audience at the cinema . . . is anything but good and revolutionary; instead, it is full of the worst bourgeois sadism.'[62] Even Brecht was, at points, sceptical about this technological optimism: '[It is] mystical, while maintaining an attitude against mysticism.'[63] Brecht never engaged with Adorno in writing about Benjamin and their respective views on art and politics, though it was no secret that Adorno blamed the poet for Benjamin's perceived naivety. Brecht, for his part, followed a note pondering Benjamin's suicide with a journal entry about the Frankfurt School as 'survivors' and 'academic palm trees'. In the note Brecht wrote about the last work Benjamin sent to the Institute, about the author's rejection of history as 'a sequence, of progress as the forceful enterprise of rested heads'.[64]

Instead of attempting here what after Fredric Jameson could be considered an 'ill-advised' comparison between Adorno and Brecht, a few words regarding art, politics and technology will have to suffice. Both men saw the ills of mass culture, though they read their causes and resistance to them differently. As Jameson himself observed, 'What they share is evidently a sarcasm, a dialectical cynicism, about the present; what separates them is the principle of hope.'[65] To Brecht, mass culture was less the production of false

H MIT BERT BRECHT

eutung und Schaffen des meistgelesenen aller in Deutschland illegalen Dichter

Brecht featured in the exile paper *Der Arbeiter*, New York, 23 November 1938.

consciousness than the avoidance of 'real thought' with no thinking at all or a mere 'culinary' version of it on the part of the bourgeoisie at a time when critical analysis and its alleged project of growing, liberatory popularity ran counter to economic interests.[66] Rather than merely blind faith in technological reproduction as a harbinger of socialist (cultural) production, Brecht and Benjamin shared an interest in the technification of art that did indeed encompass the new apparatuses of image-making as a direct means of access to the tools of production and wide dissemination. But this also meant looking at the 'making and doing' of culture through the lens of technology, of technological parameters and possibilities – hence asking, analysing and expanding on questions of labour and distribution, usefulness and functionality.

Constellations

Despite limited resources and opportunities, Brecht proceeded to apply and develop his notion of popular realism as a fight against fascism and for the proletariat. Visiting Ruth Berlau in New York, he had the opportunity to meet and work with John Houseman, head of the Office of War Information's Radio Program Division of Overseas Broadcasting. The men raised enough money to hire a few musicians and the singer Lotte Lenya to record a number of songs. Brecht's brief and only note regarding the recordings states that Dessau composed the music and that 'the German desk sabotages it'.[67] The works, including the only surviving recording of Lenya singing 'Song of a German Mother', were never broadcast, since the State Department's German division and British Intelligence feared that programmes like these would incite hostility in their German audiences. In April that same year, Brecht participated in an expansive anti-war event held at New York's Hunter College, featuring a reading of his 'Children's Crusade 1939' and the *War Primer*, with slide presentations prepared by Piscator as well as Lenya and Kurt Weill singing songs from *The Threepenny Opera* and *Happy End*. Brecht also joined the Council for a Democratic Germany, which aimed to assist the resistance movement, improve the treatment of anti-fascist prisoners in German POW camps in the U.S. and influence Allied policy on rebuilding post-war Germany and Europe. The council was attacked in the American press for its silence about the atrocities committed by the Germans on other countries and the systematic destruction of Jewish lives. It has been argued that the members of the council, including its Jewish ones, shared Brecht's view of fascism as a monopolization of power and property that used racial and other forms of persecution as the justification rather than the cause of its actions, and thus needed to be comprehended as integral to fascism as a political phenomenon.[68] Yet Brecht's relative public silence on the matter remains problematic, as his work argues for historical specificity at the core of political thought and action and is more differentiated regarding individual responsibility as well as the relationship between thinking, attitude and action than his official declarations regarding the universal suffering bestowed by the Nazis on the German people as a whole.

In further efforts to assist the fight for liberation, Brecht was one of the founding editors of the German exile press *Aurora*, together with Wieland Herzfelde and F. C. Weiskopf, a writer and former editor of the *A-I-Z*. He insisted on publishing a type of literature that would aid the development of an anti-fascist, revolutionary consciousness among German prisoners of war and the German-speaking population in Europe. Although Brecht's plans to use the press to contribute the literature to the council-led re-education program in German POW camps in the U.S. failed, *Aurora* published twelve books between 1945 and 1947 in editions ranging from about 1,000 to 4,000, including Brecht's play *The Private Life of the Master Race*.

Brecht also continued to work on experiments in strategic communicative form, notably three projects begun prior to his arrival in the U.S.: the *Refugee Dialogues*, the theoretical treatise *Buying Brass* and the play *Galileo*. The *Refugee Dialogues*, a project whose beginnings were recorded in 1940 as 'a small satiric novel of contemporary subject', developed during the American exile into a conversation between two fugitives from fascism, the worker Kalle and the 'academic', the physicist Ziffel.[69] The work is part autobiography in exile, part polemic against the bourgeois notion of democracy. Its leitmotif is the dialectic, both as subject and as method, as the two men argue about the Popular Front and revolution, ideas and material truth, humanism and labour and, as part of Brecht's ongoing Tui critique, the necessity of reallocating the role of the intellectual in class struggle. The dialogue begins with Ziffel raising his glass of beer and 'seeing through it', remarking that 'the beer is not a beer' but that a passport must be a passport in order for it to work, to get across the border, out of harm's way.[70] The negotiation of concept and thing, of thought and experience, of possibility and necessity was, to Brecht, the embodiment of a plebeian or popular perspective, and the awareness or understanding of this negotiation was the very essence of class consciousness.

The dialogue form as open, experimental, relational method and plebeian practice was also at the core of *Buying Brass*. Begun in 1939, the project was an attempt to articulate a comprehensive dramatic theory, itself inspired, as its author notes, by *Galileo*'s dialogues.[71] *Buying Brass* must furthermore be regarded in the context of Brecht's *Expressionismusdebatte* attempt to offer an alternative to Stanislavski's 'Moscow realism'. Brecht's anti-Aristotelian Epic Theatre, with its emphasis on producing agency instead of empathy, found in the influential Russian director its methodological nemesis. On the occasion of Stanislavski's death in 1938, Brecht wrote with disdain about 'the mendacity of the Stanislavski school with its art temple, word service, poet cult, its inwardness, purity, exaltedness, its naturalism'.[72] *Buying Brass* is not only a critique of empathetic dramaturgy but, in the context of Socialist Realism's officiating embrace of Stanislavski's methods and the purging of more experimental aesthetic enterprises (from the likes of Tretyakov and Meyerhold), provides an exegesis of Socialist Realism's Marxist canonization. Whereas the Epic Theatre, especially in light of the cold war's active depoliticization of revolutionary, avant-garde forms, is often equated with a simplistic, agitational illustration of class struggle, *Buying Brass* applies as much as articulates its dialectical method of contingent analysis and transformation. The play comprises a conversation at a theatre between a philosopher of unorthodox Marxist conviction and the 'theatre people', each of whom brings a specific interest in the theatre: the philosopher wants to present the public with true images of social mechanisms and thereby produce agency; the actor seeks self-expression and embodies the illusionistic, empathetic theatre; the actress demands an educational and socially progressive art. The dramaturg, one of the most vocal participants in the discussion, aims to define a new place for the drama in history and is eager to work with the philosopher. And the stagehand, a 'worker and discontent with the world', is a different form of labour in the theatre and presents, significantly, 'the new audience'.[73]

The philosopher describes himself as a 'brass merchant who comes to an orchestra not to buy a trumpet but to buy only brass'.[74] He is interested in the material function of the aesthetic tools. To the reader it is made explicit that the emulation of the theatre is supposed to enable a critique of the emulated. The distance of the *Verfremdungseffekt*, Brecht's strategy of estrangement, is the articulation of the relations among dependent elements like the stage and the audience, fiction and reality, material and immaterial labour. Yet the key is not to look at such relations from the outside but precisely to find a place within them. *Buying Brass* is structured as four 'nights'. On the first, the philosopher criticizes dramatic naturalism not because it tells convincing lies but because of the way it implicates the individual in the workings of the world: it portrays history as unalterable and defies social consciousness. 'We all have very unclear ideas regarding the impact of our actions,' contends the philosopher. 'Indeed, we rarely know why we take them. Science does little to challenge the prejudices in this matter. Repeatedly it procures questionable motives such as greed, ambition, wrath, jealousy, cowardice, etc.' Then, looking back upon deeds done, it appears as though circumstances and actions were guided by factors 'that lay outside of our sphere of influence'. In a time when few take action so drastic as to alter the course of history, it is art's responsibility to qualify the connections between attitudes and agency, to contribute a particular type of science:

> [People] know why the stone falls this way and not the other when thrown, but they don't know why the person who threw it acted the way he did and not differently. They can deal with earthquakes but not with one another.[75]

The theatre of the scientific age needs to denaturalize and expand the human sphere of influence.

During the second night, the philosopher introduces two different types of drama that are crucial to Brecht's aesthetic method: the *planetarium*-type or P-type, and the *karousel*-type or K-type, designating the new and the old theatre respectively. The K-type carries the viewer placed on 'wooden horses or cars or airplanes past all kinds of landscapes painted on the walls. . . . Fictitiously we ride, fly, steer ourselves.' The audience is swept along unquestioning, and the direction of movement never changes. In contrast, the P-type offers an arena that charts a material world according to its own laws and perspectives. It presents constellations as constellations; it includes the relationships and possible configurations of the elements as well as the space perceived as a symbolic and thus determined form. While the K-type turns its audience 'artfully into kings, lovers, and class fighters', the P-type affirms 'the audience as what they are: an audience. And they see their enemies and allies.'[76] A notation accompanying the 'Second Night' reads: 'The P-type / Contradiction: the not only observing but also the acting person as viewer / the critical, regrouping, sovereign viewer.'[77] Despite being repeatedly painted as an agitprop artist, Brecht differentiates between certain kinds of activity and passivity: in the theatre, before it can abolish its mediating function and thus be integrated into everyday life under socialism, everyone is a spectator.[78] Political agency is a mode of critical seeing, which then turns into action outside the theatre. To simply apply a different narrative to the audience does not suffice. The emancipation of the spectator consists of understanding existing narratives and seeing their relations to other stories, experiences and fantasies. When the actor accuses the philosopher of moralism and indoctrination, of wanting to send the audience back to school, the philosopher replies, 'Your schools must be terrible if people hate it so much. But why should I be concerned with your terrible schools? Abolish them!'[79] Marxism as a form of pedagogy had to come under scrutiny itself. According to Brecht, a doctrine dedicated primarily to social behaviour needed its main propositions to be applied and applicable to individual action as it relates to collective being and consciousness, all in a constant process of transformation.

A great number of stalwart principles are therefore to be taken off course, such as the sentences 'Money makes the world go round' and 'Great men make history' and 'One = one'. They will by no means be replaced by opposite, similarly stalwart sentences.

The philosopher describes Marxism as a way of seeing and acting: 'It teaches *eingreifendes Denken* [thinking as a form of action] vis-à-vis reality, inasmuch as it depends on social action. It criticizes human practice and lets itself be criticized by it.' Unlike other worldviews, it is built not on the principle of harmony but on that of struggle and engagement: 'You have to analyse everything and prove everything.'[80]

Questions regarding the roles of the philosopher and the actor are renewed in the remaining *Buying Brass* nights. The third night brings demonstrations and exercises, the negation of the old method and applications of the P-type. A 'street scene' tests the limits of the relational method of bringing the masses onto the stage and the latter back to the masses. The presentness of the performance is emphasized, as citations, gestures and repetitions mark the parameters of imaginary and actual construction. Both the story and its telling are historicized. Shakespeare, Schiller and 'the Augsburger's theatre' (hence, Brecht's theatre) make appearances on the fourth night, adding yet another historical dimension. Within this trajectory, the strategy of estrangement is nothing new: 'The V-effect is an old artistic tool, familiar from comedy, certain branches of popular art and the practice of the Asian theatre.' Further links are drawn to Charlie Chaplin, Georg Büchner, Frank Wedekind and Karl Valentin, to the history of carnival and Pieter Bruegel the Elder. To the philosopher nothing less than the changing of the world is at stake: 'The experiments of [Shakespeare's] Globe Theatre, just like Galileo's, who treated the globe in a very particular manner, corresponded to the transformation of the globe itself.'[81]

Changing the world through seeing it differently, changing its position vis-à-vis other planets, perspectives and ideas that determine its place, was also at the heart of Galileo's work. Brecht's play chronicling the Renaissance physicist's life and work focused on the tension between perspective and position, science and politics, heavenly constellations and earthly matters as it pondered the theatre of the scientific age. Brecht had finished a first version of *Galileo* (then entitled *The Earth Moves*) in 1938 at a time when

Germany was descending further into darkness and civilization's progress and rationality were to be employed in unprecedented mass destruction. The play recounts the trials of Galileo's discoveries, his rise and fall, the allegiances formed and broken over money and commitment, and his beliefs as he chooses to recant his *Dialogo* concerning the replacement of the old, Ptolemaic model of the heavens with the heliocentric Copernican one under the Inquisition's threat of torture. Growing blind and held under house arrest, the scientist manages to compose his most significant tract, the *Discorsi* which, like the *Dialogo*, consists of conversations about and experiments in physics. The end of *Galileo*, entirely of Brecht's imagination, tells of the successful smuggling of the work across the border by Galileo's former pupil Andrea. Like the exiled Brecht, Galileo and his work are nomads, constantly displaced and dependent on their location within spheres of multiple forces. The Inquisition bears obvious resemblance to the Nazis, while the play and Galileo's struggle between the autonomy of science and the barbarism of worldly rationality in the name of enlightenment and progress shine a critical light onto the Stalinist regime as much as the growing forces of a capitalist culture industry.

There are many reasons why Brecht chose to rework the play in the mid-1940s while residing in California. As the war continued and the *War Primer* grew more substantial, the question of technology wielded for geographical and ideological gain and human destruction grew increasingly pertinent. At this point in his fourth residence in exile, the playwright found himself in a place where progress meant the production of desires rather than emancipation from them. In his role on the Council for a Democratic Germany, he was also deep in ruminations regarding the character of a post-war nation. On a more pragmatic level, *Galileo* was a way to engage the actor Charles Laughton, whom James Lyon has called 'the single most important person [for Brecht] in his American exile', and a chance finally to conquer Broadway.[82] The two men had met in

1944 and taken an immediate liking to each another. Laughton admired Brecht as a writer, while the latter found in the actor a Baal-like directness and honesty, and even wrote a verse about his protruding belly, 'carried forth like a poem', meticulously cultivated.[83] Each had a temper, and while the German was irritated by the American's lack of political engagement, Brecht's Marxism made Laughton uncomfortable. Brecht also wrote a poem about Laughton's painstakingly tended yard, admiring the cohabitation of various species and their ways of growth, a metaphor extended to civilizations and the relation between plan and reality, social as well as botanical: 'But as the garden grows with the plan, the plan grows with the garden.' Yet the collective paradise, or the miniature version of it, is in danger: Native American artefacts refer to civilizations destroyed while the plot's location on a cliff high above the ocean, 'built on brittle stone', suggests its precarious state.[84] As Brecht records in his journal, one day part of the garden indeed collapses and Laughton, already insecure and prone to depression, takes this event as a sign of his creative and professional demise. He shows up at the playwright's house, dispirited and apologetic for 'imposing on people who have not had a proper roof over their heads for a decade'.[85] Brecht encourages Laughton to read lines, to work, and soon after the incident introduces him to *Galileo*. The journal records a true co-production between the two men, in which Laughton's acting and gestures often determine the new text. *Galileo* premiered in the U.S. on 30 July 1947 at the Coronet Theater in Beverly Hills (the first version of the play had been performed in Zurich in 1943) and travelled to New York with Laughton again in the lead role.

The end of the Second World War appeared to have little direct impact on the work on *Galileo*, the notes scattered throughout Brecht's journal themselves providing a form of spherical dramaturgy. The entry for 8 May 1945 reads: '*Nazi Germany surrenders unconditionally*. Early, at six o'clock, the president gives a radio address. While listening, I look out at the blooming Californian backyard.' One week later: 'With *Laughton* back at *Galileo*.'[86] Shortly after that a poem:

And thus came the month of May
A thousand-year-old empire finished.

And walking down Hindenburg lane,
Boys from Missouri with bazookas and cameras

And asked for direction and some loot
And for a German who regretted the Second World War.

In roadside ditches field marshals rotted.
Butcher asked butcher to deliver the verdict.

The vetches bloomed. The roosters stood in affected silence.
The doors closed. The roofs open.[87]

What *did* drastically alter *Galileo* were the detonations of the atomic bombs over Hiroshima and Nagasaki on 6 and 9 August 1945. The events themselves were not recorded by Brecht, but he recalls Laughton's fear that under the circumstances science could be discredited and its Galilean birth lose all sympathy: 'The wrong kind of publicity, old man.'[88] The following week Brecht remarked, 'The atomic bomb has in fact turned the relationship between society and science into a life-and-death problem.'[89] It appears that within this context, the rewrite of *Galileo* before its u.s. premiere was motivated by a concern for truth-telling as the tension between a distanced, scientific objectivity and pragmatic historical events and actions. Already in the 1938 version Galileo declares, 'Truth is the child of its time, not of authority', thus appealing to every scientist's responsibility.[90] Yet the repercussions and limits of this burden to tell

the truth at the appropriate moment become apparent when
Galileo's reluctance for martyrdom is rewarded, at least in Brecht's
version of the story, with the smuggling and distribution of the
Discorsi across national boundaries, which enabled its timely impact.
After all, telling the truth included the judgement to select those in
whose hands the truth will be effective and the cunning to spread
the truth among the many. So when Brecht bestows unto the 1947
Galileo greater doubt and pain about bending to the Inquisition,
he directly addresses the changed expectations of the viewer, implying the need for resolve and heroic wilfulness, a timeless and thus
'scientific' behaviour that posits rational, empirical control over the
instinctual, the 'natural' fear of death. When Andrea, Galileo's pupil
who had lost faith in the great scientist after he recanted, is presented
with a copy of the *Discorsi*, a work that in his eyes will 'found a new
physics', he apologizes to Galileo for his lack of faith and enthusiastically lauds his teacher's selfless guile and 'contribution'. But
Galileo replies:

> Contribution to whom? Welcome to my gutter, brother
> scientist and fellow traitor. I sold out, you are the buyer.
> The first sight of the book! His mouth watered and the
> scoldings were drowned. Blessed be our bargaining,
> whitewashing, death-fearing community.[91]

Truth evolves, and discovery is a human product. To the *Buying
Brass* philosopher, to Brecht and to Galileo, truth is relative but
not relativist. The fight for truth is ongoing, a matter of seeing the
constellation while finding oneself in it, in a history that includes
the moment of viewing the stage. When Galileo famously declares,
'Unhappy is the land that needs a hero', he directly addresses the
audience's perspective on the play, the cathartic security that, to
Brecht, art and science with their assertion of the binary between
the subjective and the objective traditionally provided. Walter

Benjamin was right, in a sense, when he remarked that in this play, the hero is the people. But its heroism is unconventional. It resides, as Jean-Paul Sartre has remarked, in the ambiguity of taking action.[92] Galileo's actions are political, rather than based on principle.

Brecht himself never saw the New York production of *Galileo*. He and his family left for Europe the day after he testified in front of the House Un-American Activities Committee (HUAC) on 30 October 1947. In March Brecht had secured exit and re-entry permits for Switzerland, signalling his resolve to return to Europe and find a temporary platform of operation and observation outside his home country. He felt compelled to play a role in filling the political and aesthetic vacuum in Germany, fearing a resurgence of Nazism or, as he had observed among émigrés in the UK, the creation of a reactionary, pseudo-progressive state, a continuity of the lethal Weimar combination of democracy and capitalism. The Russian-occupied eastern part of Germany literally appealed to him – a letter written to Caspar Neher in December 1946 states, 'I also have offers from Berlin to use the Schiffbauerdamm Theater for certain things.'[93] But before he could avail himself of such invitations, Brecht had been summoned to appear in front of the HUAC following Hanns Eisler's hearings in Los Angeles as part of a broader inquiry into an alleged communist infiltration of the movie industry.

Eisler had refrained from mentioning Brecht's name, but the playwright had been the subject of an FBI investigation, including possible wiretapping of his phone, for years, and thus the known connection between the two men sufficed as an excuse to deliver a summons. The playwright became part of what came to be known as the 'Hollywood nineteen', a group of artists and writers, all, except for Brecht, part of the film industry and all of purported communist sympathies, but with a definite resolve to openly and loudly oppose the very existence of the HUAC. Though Brecht sympathized with his fellow defendants and their disdain for the

Red witch-hunt, he felt less compelled to step in front of the tribunal in an act of patriotic refusal, as the others had agreed to do. In arguably Galilean fashion, he performed a clever way of telling the truth, driven as much by self-preservation and a desire to be able to leave the country and pick up his work in Europe as by the conviction that steadfast principles in politics are foolish, if not outright reactionary.

The testimony, which one observer compared to a zoologist being interrogated by a bunch of apes, was carefully prepared by Brecht, who refused to get caught in a lie while never saying what the committee wanted to hear.[94] When asked by one of the chairmen whether or not he had written revolutionary texts, he answered, 'I have written a number of poems and songs and plays in the fight against Hitler and, of course, they can be considered, therefore, as revolutionary because I, of course, was for the overthrow of that government.'[95] And when the same chairman read aloud the English translation of Brecht's overtly proletarian 'Forward, We've Not Forgotten' of 1929 and wanted to know if Brecht was the author, the poet, eliciting laughter from the audience, replied, 'No, I wrote a poem in German, but that is very different from this.'[96] After about an hour, the exchange was concluded and Brecht was free to go while other members of the 'Hollywood nineteen' were subsequently imprisoned following the failure of their efforts to expose the unconstitutionality of the HUAC and its activities. On 31 October 1947, Brecht boarded a plane to Paris; Helene Weigel, Ruth Berlau and daughter Barbara followed by ship.

6

Realpolitik: Theatre of Socialism, 1947–56

Upon his return to Europe, Brecht made Zurich his temporary base of operations. Like many homecoming exiles, he was apprehensive of what he would find in Germany, what would be left and what would arise out of the material as well as ideological rubble. Brecht had anticipated this moment and the destruction that came before it in the 1943 poem 'The Return':

> The father city, how will it receive me?
> Before me come the bombers. Deadly swarms
> Announce my return. Blazes of fire
> Precede the son.[1]

The Swiss city was an obvious choice for Brecht, not only because of the country's declared neutrality during the war, but because the Zurich Schauspielhaus had premiered no fewer than three of his plays in 1941 and 1943 during the playwright's Scandinavian and u.s. exile. The theatre had also hired his old friend Caspar Neher as set designer for the 1946–7 season. But when the family arrived, the first iterations of Cold War politics made it difficult for the artist to pick up where he had left off. Brecht was denounced again by the former communist Ruth Fischer, sister of his old colleague Hanns Eisler, leading to constant surveillance from the Swiss authorities. Brecht was furthermore denied an entry permit to the u.s. Sector, including West Berlin. These circumstances and the fact that most of the important German theatres, including the Theater am Schiffbauerdamm, the Deutsches Theater and the Volksbühne, all lay in what would soon become East Berlin were pragmatic reasons for Brecht to set up shop in the officially socialist part of Germany, as he did in late 1948. But there were other reasons as well. For one, the playwright had long believed that his audience and the future of Germany consisted in a unified people. In a letter to the Austrian composer Gottfried von Einem, he wrote, 'I can't just sit in some part of Germany and therefore be dead to the other.'[2] He also believed that this future would have to be socialist and that he needed to participate in its realization. Brecht travelled to Berlin frequently to survey the scene. He met with students and workers to inform himself first-hand about the tasks that lay ahead, and he visited the theatre, expressing his disgust with what he saw. Attending the rehearsals for *Woyzeck* in 1948, he remarked, 'Even before I see the ruined theatres, I get to see the ruined acting. . . . [It] is desperate and ham-handed; one finds neither observation nor a dramatic thought.'[3] He found the artistic atmosphere 'provincial' and in many cases marred by the language and habits of the Nazi era.[4] The ways in which the past lingered on the one hand and was simply cast aside on the other would prove to be one of the greatest difficulties in constructing a new sociopolitical formation.

Brecht had applied for and in 1950 received an Austrian passport, leading to a major scandal that rocked the cultural scene of the Alpine nation and resulting in a concerted anti-Brecht campaign in Vienna. Brecht's successful pursuit of Austrian citizenship subsequently raised questions about the playwright's allegiances. This and his contract with the West German publisher Peter Suhrkamp was seen by many of his contemporaries as well as Brecht scholars as evidence of opportunism, even hypocrisy. To some, Brecht's foundation of the Berlin Ensemble on East German soil, his apparent defence of the East German state's violent repression of the infamous workers' uprising of 1953, and his acceptance of the

Brecht, standing front centre, and members of the *Berliner Ensemble*, Chemnitz, 1951.

Stalin Peace Prize in 1954 made him the lackey of a totalitarian regime. Others attribute to his actions and words a continuity of Galilean cunning, justified under the circumstances by the difficulties of telling the truth in complex times. Still others see his return to Europe as an ongoing condition of exile, of artistic and political homelessness, an existence alienated by the hopes for progressive social transformation and the limits of its historical reality, resulting in disillusionment and resignation. But the last years of Brecht's life and work were palpably marked by an ongoing, committed struggle with the possibilities and limits of establishing a socialist culture. He no longer saw the times as 'dark' but he certainly saw the times ahead as difficult, given the overwhelming project of *Vergangenheitsbewältigung* (a national project of coming to terms with the past), the fight against a capitalist and, possibly, fascist renewal under the guise of a renovated bourgeois idealism and the creation of a socialist state with a people who had no hand in a revolution that is supposed to be its founding condition. In the poem 'Perception', written in February 1949, Brecht describes the terrain ahead:

When I returned
My hair was not yet gray.
So I was happy.

The trials of the mountains lie behind us
Ahead of us lie the trials of the plain.[5]

Brecht famously claimed that he chose to reside in what on
7 October 1949 was officially christened the German Democratic
Republic (GDR) because while the West offered him a 'seat at the
table', the East 'invited him into the kitchen', where 'I was needed'.[6]
But in reality, the Social Unity Party (SED) and its cultural functionaries, as well as the constituencies of the newly erected 'Workers
and Farmers State', were unwelcoming, and Brecht had to fight
hard for support. His journal records a meeting with Berlin's mayor
in January 1949 regarding the plans for the Berliner Ensemble, 'my
theatre project concerning the recruitment of great émigré actors',
where his ideas met a less than enthusiastic response: 'The mayor
neither greeted me nor said goodbye, never even addressed me,
but uttered a single sceptical sentence about uncertain projects
destroying the already-existing. . . . For the first time I feel the
stinking breath of the provinces.'[7] Still, Brecht staked out his own
role in the new socialist reality, one that was not supposed to be
exclusively located on the Eastern side of the Cold War divide.
After the Berliner Ensemble, or BE, was officially sanctioned by
the SED in April, the playwright continued his efforts at an all-
Germany, even international, theatre, staging *Mother Courage*
in Munich and giving permission for productions in Hamburg,
Rome and Milan. There were even plans of establishing another
Ensemble in Augsburg so as to ensure the steady exchange of
productions and actors, perspectives and ideas. The BE debuted
in November 1949 at the Deutsches Theater with a production
of *Herr Puntila and His Servant Matti*. Between 1949 and 1951 the

company staged several plays, including *Mother Courage*, J.M.R. Lenz's *The Tutor*, *The Mother* and Maxim Gorki's *Vasya Shelesnova* to acclaim and official approval. Yet relations between the socialist reality and Brecht's vision of it remained contentious. Though the Epic Theatre received public support, a number of East German critics voiced their doubts about its attention to formal concerns, reprising charges of elitism and esotericism that had first surfaced during the *Expressionismusdebatte*. In 1950, the GDR's Cultural Advisory Board for the Publishing Industry refused the publication of the *War Primer* on the grounds that the book was 'only generally pacifist', while the head of the SED decried it as 'absolutely unqualified'.[8] That same year Brecht's *Future Song* (1948), a play celebrating the socialist future while warning of the misleading powers of masters old and new, was removed from the programme for the German Youth Meeting for Peace and Friendship because, according to the officials in charge, it did not conform to the state's pedagogical agenda, and Paul Dessau's music was deemed 'atonal and utterly incomprehensible'.[9] In 1951, Brecht's opera *The Trial of Lukullus*, another collaboration with Dessau, came under scrutiny and was cancelled after its BE premiere in March at the Deutsche Staatsoper in Berlin. The playwright's unpublished reactions to the renewed charges of formalism range from resigned incomprehension to bitter but pointed critique of the cultural apparatchiks: 'The fighters against formalism . . . know exactly what their *Volk* wants and recognize their *Volk* because it wants what they want.'[10] In fact, the new state's *Volk*, the workers and farmers, seemed to care rather little about the BE's projects, and the plays were mostly attended by party functionaries and West German audiences.

Brecht's artistic and political agenda increasingly clashed with the perspectives onto the past and the plans for the future advocated on either side of the Cold War divide. He strongly condemned the Marshall Plan and the founding of the Federal Republic of Germany, fearing the replacement of a critical reflection of the country's fascist

John Heartfield, poster for *The Mother*, 1951.

history with blind consumerism and a repetition of capitalist exploitation under a democratic guise of equality. The establishment of the West German state also destroyed all remaining hopes for a united country under a new, progressive and revolutionary form of government. Though Brecht was similarly critical of the GDR's attempt to go it alone, he maintained a position of sceptical commitment. He still believed in the possibility of a better, truly socialist state, and in poems, songs and public appeals he emphasized the necessity for the people to carry the burden of both past and future deeds. Brecht's vehement differentiation between the Nazis as perpetrators and the German people as their first victims, a position that the artist held for most of his time in exile, became increasingly nuanced in light of the Allies' de-Nazification programmes, which consisted mostly of the symbolic removal of former prominent fascists from economic and bureaucratic posts. Brecht demanded a language and a discourse that would critically engage with the circumstances that had made German fascism possible. To him, to de-Nazify Germany meant to rid it of bourgeois ideals and capitalist actions: 'Only when [one] is no longer a *Bürger* is [one] no longer a Nazi.'[11] To Brecht, understanding the people as victims of fascism did not mean denying that they supported the regime and in many cases committed unspeakable crimes in its name. But to come to terms with individual actions under fascism, rather than fascism as an extension of capitalism, with each and every German citizen's direct or indirect responsibility for the atrocities committed in Auschwitz and other camps, on the Russian Front and in every city and town all over the German Reich, and to acknowledge it publicly, remained what Andreas Klement has called a *Leerstelle*, a void in Brecht's oeuvre.[12] What is present throughout his work, in his plays and notes, poems and journal entries, is a profound ambiguity with regard to the role of the people in politics and the extent to which they are both product and producers of history – an ambiguity that the post-war experiment in socialist reality would only perpetuate. On the one hand, Brecht claimed, 'What happened in Auschwitz, in the Warsaw Ghetto, in Buchenwald cannot without a doubt abide a description in literary form. Literature was not prepared and has not developed any means for such events.'[13] Like Kraus before and Adorno after him, he found conventional means of addressing the barbaric outcome of fascist ideology in practice inadequate. On the other hand, he stated that a 'real critique of National Socialism is missing because it is treated as "beneath criticism". . . . National Socialism has to be regarded as the socialism of the petit bourgeois, a crippled, neurasthenic, perverted people's movement.'[14] The 'people' are reminded on several occasions that the decision regarding how to act and situate themselves vis-à-vis the narratives of history, power and progress lies with them. Addressing students in East Germany, he writes:

> That you can sit here: many a battle
> Was dared for it. You would happily forget them.
> But know: others have sat here
> They sat on humans then. Beware![15]

Just as Herr Keuner pales upon hearing from an old acquaintance that he has not changed much in all these years, Brecht's attitude towards the present is one of necessary and continuous transformation. But progress and emancipation, as in Galileo's case, are not inevitable, historical perpetuations – they are the product of self-guided actions. Thus the question of German unity and its future needed to be stripped of a mythical nostalgia for a national identity that never was, as rhetoric of 'German will' and 'destiny' resurfaced in both Eastern and Western parts of the country. Brecht proposed that one ought to speak of *Bevölkerung* (populace) rather than *Volk* and that:

Germany has to emancipate itself not as a nation but as a people, more precisely as a proletariat. It never was 'not a nation', but it was a nation, meaning, it played the nations' game for world dominance and developed the stench of nationalism.[16]

The poet's proposal for the official youth song for the construction of the socialist state demanded agency instead of empathy:

Better than being moved is: to move
Because no leader will lead us out of this mess!
Ourselves we'll lead finally:
Away with the old, in with the new state![17]

In 1951, the GDR's economic and political situation took a turn for the worse, and with it East–West relations and visions of a viable socialist future. The less successful the actualized dream of a more perfect society appeared to a population suffering from shortages of food and other everyday amenities, the more its policies were enforced and its victories declared. Brecht was torn about this 'socialism from above' – on the one hand he abhorred the idea of a prescribed collectivity, one not owned by the proletariat and thus reproducing traditional class structures; on the other he was afraid of the Western commodities' lure, a forceful material and ideological tool that could easily thwart the arduous revolutionary project. Unlike in other Soviet Bloc countries, the political purges in the GDR were at the time not accompanied by death penalties, yet many writers and activists lost their jobs, were expelled from the party or publicly ostracized, and many, if they could, moved to the West. The SED's *Kulturpolitik* began more and more to resemble propaganda, encouraging hateful glares towards all that was different and unquestioning gazes on truths declared to be self-evident. Brecht increasingly clashed with the authorities. He spent time devising state-school curricula and textbooks, all the while emphasizing that learning ought to be pleasurable, the result of a critical engagement with images of reality, and that the class's struggle was no longer *against* an enemy but *for* the construction of a new society. He organized discussions with students and workers and with the members of the BE, always seeking two-sided communication, and while his poems and songs still encouraged collective agency in order to arrive at a new social formation, his journal entries and letters record an impatience with his comrades' lack of political and aesthetic reflection and motivation. In an open letter to the BE, Brecht lamented the troupe's 'weakness' with regard to political and artistic interest and asked for 'unreserved advice' and 'suggestions' for improvement.[18]

The events of 17 June 1953 drove home the schism between the state and its subjects and made clear that the proletarian revolution would have been the decisive step in reallocating the ownership of the means of material, intellectual and spiritual production. In May, the SED had announced the increase in industrial workers' hours by at least 10 per cent, a desperate bureaucratic measure in response to an ongoing decline in national production and the growing exodus of the East German population. Almost half a million people left for the Western part of the country in the first six months of 1953 alone in response to the deteriorating economic climate and the state's increasingly draconian policies. On 17 June, after weeks of smaller strikes and demonstrations, thousands of East German workers, clerks, shopkeepers, teachers and students took to the streets in Berlin and other cities protesting the SED's decree and demanding free elections. The government responded by unleashing the *Volkspolizei*, the 'people's police', and Soviet tanks, killing more than 70 demonstrators.[19] Throughout the day Brecht tried to rally the BE to set up conversations in relation to the unfolding events, and later he sought radio airtime, which was denied. During the morning he wrote letters to the prime minister, the Russian ambassador, a member of the Office for Art and

The East Berlin Uprising: Russian tanks advancing toward Potsdamer Platz, 17 June 1953.

Culture and the head of the SED, Walter Ulbricht. Only the last sentence of the note to Ulbricht was published on 21 June in the party organ *Neues Deutschland*, leading to an enduring storm of outrage, especially among the West German literary and political establishment. Brecht's plays disappeared from repertoires and the reception of Brecht's work was affected for decades to come. The dispatch read:

> The National Prize Laureate Bertolt Brecht has sent the General Secretary of the Central Committee of the SED, Walter Ulbricht, a letter in which he declares:
> 'It is my desire to express to you at this moment my allegiance
>   to the Socialist Unity Party of Germany.
> Yours, Bertolt Brecht.'[20]

The rest of the letter clarifies Brecht's position. While the messages written to the prime minister and the Office for Art and Culture offered the services of the BE for political dialogue, for example in the form of radio programmes, the note to Ulbricht emphasized that holding the country's course meant seeking productive exchange with its people and historical self-reflection on behalf of the party:

> Dear Comrade Ulbricht,
> History will respect the revolutionary impatience of the SED. The great dialogue with the masses regarding the tempo of socialist construction will lead to an assessment and assertion of socialist achievements.[21]

With a typically Brechtian choice of words, the original text sought to remind the party of its responsibility to its constituency and the dynamics of this particular revolutionary project. Seeing only part of his text in print, Brecht was horrified at his public misrepresentation and sought to rectify his position. On 23 June *Neues Deutschland* published texts by Brecht, Slatan Dudow and others under the header 'There can be no mercy for fascists!' Brecht's contribution stated that he had declared his solidarity with the SED because he felt that on 17 June the justified discontent of the workers had been misused and misdirected by fascist provocateurs, a threat that needed to be confronted. Urging differentiation between those provocateurs and the proletariat, he called for 'the so pressing great dialogue about the mistakes made on all sides'.[22]

Brecht remained very critical towards the government, though often only in writings that remained unpublished or in private conversations. Former members of the BE have recalled how the playwright praised and encouraged those who expressed scepticism towards the party's rhetoric and actions.[23] Brecht's endorsement of the proletariat's self-government as a critique of a socialism from above now took the form of poetic warnings, advising the state not to govern without or against 'the wisdom of the people':[24]

> Always check: what and when?
> Step out into the street and see
> Which way the wind blows.[25]

And as Andreas Klement has pointed out, in a text recalling his 'Questions of a Reading Worker', the poet asks: 'What are cities built / Without the wisdom of the people?'[26] In a draft for the foreword to his play *Turandot*, written in direct response to the events of 17 June 1953, Brecht went so far as to speak about the continuity of fascism in the GDR, tolerated by the political and intellectual elite: 'Under the new command the Nazi apparatus was again set in motion. . . . Unpersuaded, but cowardly, hostile, but cowering, ossified officials began governing against the people anew.'[27]

These and other texts had far less public resonance than Brecht's obituary note for Stalin published in *Neues Deutschland* in March 1953 and his acceptance of the Stalin Peace Prize in Moscow in 1955. Brecht had long viewed the Russian despot with a somewhat mystifying ambivalence, stemming from the playwright's fierce commitment to the working class. Walter Benjamin's diary recalls a conversation from 1938 in which Brecht denounced the USSR's rendition of communist governance as a dictatorship *against* the proletariat, but one that ought to be tolerated as long as it benefited the working class.[28] To what degree Brecht knew of the scale of the Gulag is uncertain, but he certainly was aware of the Show Trials and early purges, having registered with great concern the disappearances and imprisonment of some of his colleagues. A journal entry in 1943 records the poet's disappointment with the Russian regime after reading a critical biography of Stalin:

The rise of fascism does indeed shed a new light on the
transformation of a professional revolutionary into a
bureaucrat, of an entire revolutionary party into a body
of civil servants. . . . In fascism, socialism sees its distorted
mirror image. With none of its virtues, but all of its vices.[29]

And while Brecht feared the fascist side of socialism, he feared the
fascist potential of the masses just as much. Following the events
of 17 June 1953, Brecht had told his West German publisher Peter
Suhrkamp that neo-fascist inklings were making their way back
into the heads of his fellow comrades, who were eager to follow
once again any Pied Piper promising collective, national better-
ment in the form of ideological and material gratification, a rise of
the type of petit-bourgeois urges so pointedly portrayed in *Kuhle
Wampe*. Elsewhere he calls the demonstrations an affirmation of
class, though the proletariat is 'without direction' and of a 'pitiful
helplessness . . . its slogans confused and feeble, instilled by the
class enemy'.[30]

In light of remarks like these, the *Buckow Elegies* (1953), verses
written in response to the repressed uprising, provide a more
nuanced perspective on their author's attitude than the traditional
interpretation of disillusioned withdrawal. Only six of the 22 poems
were published during Brecht's lifetime, and with titles like 'The
Flower Garden' and 'Rowing, Conversations' they were taken as
signals of a melancholic turn to nature. Even the unpublished,
more overtly critical and political pieces like 'The Solution' seemed
to confirm the poet's disenchantment with socialist reality and
thus many a Brecht scholar's notion of an artist who could not bear
the government's betrayal of its own subjects and of the revolution.
'The Solution' famously asks, since the regime's declared loss of
faith in its subjects, if it would not be easier for the government to
dissolve its *Volk* and elect a new people.[31] But what is usually seen
as a mocking condemnation of the authorities' role in the ongoing

socialist project could be read, as Slavoj Žižek indicates, as a critique of the people's inability or unwillingness to follow the path of emancipation. Žižek writes:

> One should bravely admit that it *is* a duty – *the* duty even – of a revolutionary party to 'dissolve the people and elect another', i.e. to bring about the transubstantiation of the 'old' opportunistic people (the inert 'crowd') into a revolutionary body aware of its historical task. Far from being an easy task, to 'dissolve the people and elect another' is the most difficult of all.[32]

Freedom, Žižek argues, is '*only* for those who *really think*, even if differently, not for those who blindly (unthinkingly) act out their opinions'.[33] Brecht's decision not to publish 'The Solution' may have been due in part to the text's potential interpretation as a justification of state violence. But Brecht's oft-noted melancholia may have been rooted less in the absurd reality of the existing, prescribed socialism than in his own failure to productively aid the people in their revolutionary transformation.

The play *Turandot or The Congress of the Whitewashers* (1953) reflects as much on Brecht's role as an artist in a revolutionary society as it does on the place of intellectuals in politics in general. Brecht had planned a work with this title since the 1930s. The play would be his last, and although its realization was triggered by the workers' uprising, it was informed by the Tuis' function under capitalism, fascism and socialism in the Weimar Republic, the Third Reich and the GDR: to offer an ahistorical assessment of the subordination of art, thinking and the political to doctrinaire politics and principles. In an unpublished foreword, the playwright observes that since the war 'socialist measures' had led to a 'drastic transformation of the *Lebensweise* [way of life]' – but 'a similarly significant change of the *Denkweise* [way of thinking] had indeed not occurred'.[34] Based on a Chinese fable and subsequent adaptations by Carlo Gozzi and Schiller, Brecht's *Turandot* tells of an emperor who in times of economic crisis and unrest seeks to appease his subjects. The regime's intellectuals, the scribes and scholars, artists and bards, have run out of ways to justify and exalt the government's policies of inequality and oppression, whereupon the emperor promises his daughter to the Tui who can embellish the predicament that the others could not. Death awaits those who fail to conceal the truth. In a letter dated June 1953, Brecht writes, 'The whitewashing is fully under way. And what a chance to become a good Communist!'[35] Brecht felt that history had been moved ahead too fast, that for the sake of old and new forms of monopolized power a thorough and imperative understanding of past relationalities between political ideals and political reality had been carelessly pushed aside. On either side of the Iron Curtain, artists and writers were busy, but with the wrong tasks: 'All too soon', he wrote in *Neues Deutschland*, 'we turned our backs on the immediate past, eager to devote ourselves to the future. But the future will depend on our working through the past.'[36] The sad verdict read, 'A revolution never happened.'[37]

Turandot ends with the irrevocable severance of the link between emperor and people. The Tuis have failed and the history of progress allows for no other constellation than the people leading themselves. The play thus ends on a cautiously utopian note, true to its author's assessment of art's dialectical usefulness vis-à-vis reality: 'Things will continue for a while longer until the intellectuals do not stand opposite the people but the entire populace is intellectualized.'[38] Brecht is fully aware of the contradictions in his scientific universe. His statement, 'Buckow. *Turandot*. Next to it the *Buckow Elegies*. June 17th has alienated the entire existence,' is less an expression of existentialist, personal dissociation than an acknowledgement of history unhinged.[39] A revolutionary state without a revolution, a new social constellation built on renovated mindsets and refurbished relations of ownerships, experiences of reality beset by ideals fabricated in words and images – this is the existence alienated.

When Brecht died on 14 August 1956 from a heart attack, he was buried quietly, in a simple zinc coffin, in Berlin's Dorotheen-städtischer Friedhof cemetery, across from Hegel. His grave marker bore only his name, despite the fact that he had, throughout his life, composed multiple epitaphs for himself. The most famous, written in 1933, reads, in part: 'He made suggestions / We accepted them.'[40] His idea of where he stood with regard to history and its trajectory is perhaps best captured by a late poem, 'Changing the Wheel' (1953):

> I sit on the side of the road
> The driver changes the wheel
> I don't like where I came from
> I don't like where I am going.
> Why do I watch the changing of the wheel
> With impatience?[41]

Brecht saw himself as a co-driver on the wagon of history – maybe holding a map, but dependent on the drivers and the material forces that moved it forward. Though in the end he was increasingly unsure of where they would go together, he kept a critical eye on the darkness of the past and on the difficulties of the future, and was always eager to continue.

References

Introduction

1 Hans Mayer, *Brecht in der Geschichte* (Frankfurt, 1976), pp. 154–5.

2 'The Epic Theater and Its Difficulties' (1927), in Bertolt Brecht, *Große kommentierte Berliner und Frankfurter Ausgabe*, vols I–XXX, ed. Werner Hecht, Jan Knopf, Werner Mittenzwei and Klaus-Detlef Müller (Berlin, 1989; hereafter GBA), XXI, p. 210. Trans. John Willett and Ralph Manheim with Erich Fried, eds, *Bertolt Brecht: Poems, 1913–1956* (New York, 1976), p. 23. Unless noted as here, all translations are my own.

3 Roland Barthes, 'Brecht and Discourse: A Contribution to the Study of Discursivity' (1975), reprinted in *The Rustle of Language* (New York, 1986), pp. 212–22.

4 'Theater for Pleasure or Theater for Instruction?' (1935), GBA, XXII, p. 110.

5 Herbert Marcuse, 'Art as a Form of Reality' (1969 lecture at the Guggenheim Museum), reprinted in Arnold J. Toynbee et al., *On the Future of Art* (New York, 1970), p. 123.

6 Sylvia Harvey, 'Whose Brecht? Memories for the Eighties: A Critical Recovery', *Screen*, 23 (1982), pp. 45–59.

7 Fredric Jameson, *Brecht and Method* (London and New York, 1998).

8 Jacques Rancière, 'The Emancipated Spectator', *Artforum* (March 2007), p. 275. See also Rancière, *The Ignorant Schoolmaster: Five Lessons in Intellectual Emancipation* (Stanford, CA, 1991).

9 Jameson, *Brecht and Method*, p. 89ff.

10 *Versuche*, 4–7, vol. II (1930), reprinted in *Brecht: Versuche*, 1–12 (Berlin, 1959), p. 141.

11 Cited in Mayer, *Brecht in der Geschichte*, p. 85.

1 Poet of Crisis, 1898–1923

1 Hannah Arendt, *Men in Dark Times* (New York, 1955), p. 218.
2 *GBA*, XI, p. 119; trans. John Willett and Ralph Manheim with Erich Fried, eds, *Bertolt Brecht: Poems, 1913–1956* (New York, 1976), p. 107.
3 Hans Mayer, *Brecht in der Geschichte* (Frankfurt, 1976), p. 29.
4 Ibid.
5 Cited in Christian Graf von Krockow, *Die Deutschen in ihrem Jahrhundert, 1890–1990* (Reinbek, 1990), p. 17.
6 James J. Sheehan, *German History, 1770–1866* (Oxford, 1989), p. 1.
7 Thomas Mann, *Betrachtungen eines Unpolitischen* (Frankfurt, 1956), p. 239.
8 Krockow, *Die Deutschen in ihrem Jahrhundert*, p. 43.
9 Jürgen Habermas, *Sturkturwandel der Öffentlichkeit: Untersuchungen zu einer Kategorie der bürgerlichen Gesellschaft* (Frankfurt, 1990).
10 *GBA*, XXVI, p. 14.
11 Werner Frisch and K. W. Obermeyer, eds, *Brecht in Augsburg* (Frankfurt, 1976), p. 56.
12 Hans Otto Münsterer, *Bert Brecht: Erinnerungen und Gespräche aus den Jahren 1917–22* (Zurich, 1963), p. 82.
13 Jan Knopf, ed., *Brecht Handbuch in fünf Bänden* (Stuttgart, 2001), vol. II, p. 3.
14 *GBA*, XXVI, p. 16.
15 Frisch and Obermeyer, *Brecht in Augsburg*, p. 174.
16 Walter Brecht, *Unser Leben in Augsburg, damals* (Frankfurt, 1984), p. 124.
17 Journal, 26 August 1920, *GBA*, XXVI, p. 141.
18 *GBA*, XXI, p. 35.
19 'The Ballad of François Villon' (1918), *GBA*, XIII, pp. 114–15.
20 Lion Feuchtwanger, *Erfolg* (Berlin, 1930), vol. I, p. 291.
21 *GBA*, XII, p. 84; trans. Willett and Manheim, *Poems*, pp. 316–17.
22 *GBA*, XI, p. 292.
23 Ibid., p. 39.
24 Ibid., pp.49–53; trans. Willett and Manheim, *Poems*, pp. 100–4.
25 'Regarding Rhetoric' and 'On Expressionism' (1920), *GBA*, XXI, p. 49.
26 'Karl Valentin' (1922), ibid., pp. 101–2.
27 Ibid.

28 See Werner Hecht, 'Der Augsburger Theaterkritiker', in *Sieben Studien über Brecht* (Frankfurt, 1972), pp. 7–24; and Manfred Voigts, *Brechts Theaterkonzeptionen: Entstehung und Entfaltung bis 1931* (Munich, 1977).

29 'Reply to the Open Letter by the Personnel of the Stadttheater' (1920), *GBA*, XXI, p. 86.

30 Roland Barthes, 'The Task of Brechtian Criticism', in *Critical Essays*, ed. Roland Barthes (Evanston, IL, 1972), p. 71.

31 Thomas Anz and Joseph Vogel, eds, *Die Dichter und der Krieg: Deutsche Lyrik 1914–1918* (Munich, 1982), p. 12.

32 Ronald Speirs, 'Gedichte 1913–1917', in Knopf, *Brecht Handbuch*, II, p. 24.

33 Reinhold Grimm, *Brecht und Nietzsche, oder Geständnisse eines Dichters* (Frankfurt, 1979), pp. 73–4.

34 *GBA*, XXI, p. 10.

35 Ibid., p. 11.

36 'Augsburg War Letter' (20 August 1914), *GBA*, XXI, p. 14.

37 The poem remained unpublished until 1922. See *GBA*, XI, p. 322.

38 Ibid., p. 323.

39 Kurt Tucholsky, 'Bert Brechts Hauspostille', *Weltbühne* (28 February 1928), reprinted in *Gesamtausgabe* (Reinbek, 1999), vol. X, p. 87.

40 Journal, n.d., *GBA*, XI, p. 322.

41 Ibid., p. 113.

42 *GBA*, XIII, p. 101; trans. Willett and Manheim, *Poems*, p. 10.

43 *GBA*, XIII, pp. 102–4; trans. Willett and Manheim, *Poems*, pp. 5–7.

44 *GBA*, XXVI, p. 146.

45 Journal, 24 September 1920, *GBA*, XXVI, pp. 169–70.

46 'Choral of the Man Baal' (1918), *GBA*, XI, p. 108.

47 Journal, 24 August 1920, *GBA*, XXVI, p. 139.

48 See especially *GBA*, XXVIII, pp. 63–278; and *GBA*, XXVI, pp. 121–286.

49 Kurt Tucholsky, 'Das Lied vom Kompromiß', *Weltbühne* (13 March 1919), reprinted in *Gesamtausgabe*, vol. III, p. 81.

50 'Literatur' (1921), *GBA*, XXI, pp. 99–100; Journal, 29 August 1920, *GBA*, XXVI, p. 145.

51 Letter to Hans Otto Münsterer, Munich, 5 May 1918, *GBA*, XXVIII, p. 51.

52 Cited in Simon Williams, 'The Director in the German Theater: Harmony, Spectacle and Ensemble', *New German Critique*, 29 (Spring–Summer 1983), p. 108.

53 Ibid., p. 110.

54 Cited in Gordon A. Craig, *Politics and Culture in Modern Germany: Essays from the New York Review of Books* (Palo Alto, CA, 1999), pp. 15–16.

55 Cited in Hans-Jürgen Grune, 'Dein Auftritt, Genosse! Das Agitproptheater – eine proletarische Massenbewegung', in *Wem Gehört die Welt – Kunst und Gesellschaft in der Weimarer Republik*, ed. Neue Gesellschaft für Bildende Kunst (Berlin, 1977), p. 434.

56 *GBA*, XXVI, p. 121.

57 Letter to Paula Bannholzer, Augsburg, 4 April 1919, *GBA*, XXVIII, p. 77.

58 Cited in Knopf, *Brecht Handbuch*, I, pp. 86–7.

59 *GBA*, I, p. 228.

60 Ibid., p. 229.

61 Arendt, *Men in Dark Times*, p. 228.

62 Reprinted in Hans Ostwald, *Sittengeschichte der Inflation* (Berlin, 1931), p. 219.

63 Herbert Ihering, review, *Berliner Börsen-Courier* (5 October 1922), reprinted in *Brecht in der Kritik*, ed. Monika Wyss (Munich, 1977), pp. 5–6.

64 Alfred Kerr, review, *Berliner Tageblatt* (21 December 1922), reprinted in Wyss, *Brecht in der Kritik*, pp. 10–11.

65 Wyss, *Brecht in der Kritik*, p. 10.

66 Alexander Abusch, review, *Bayrische Arbeiterzeitung* (23 December 1922), reprinted in Wyss, *Brecht in der Kritik*, p. 8.

67 Rosa Luxemburg, 'Der Anfang', *Die Rote Fahne* (18 November 1918), reprinted in Rosa Luxemburg, *Gesammelte Werke* (Berlin, 1974), vol. IV, p. 397.

68 Eugene Lunn, *Marxism and Modernism: A Historical Study of Lukács, Brecht, Benjamin, and Adorno* (Berkeley and Los Angeles, CA, 1984), p. 5.

2 'Mehr guten Sport': Brecht in Berlin, 1924–8

1 Journal, 1925, *GBA*, XXVI, p. 286.

2 Oswald Spengler, *Der Untergang des Abendlandes* (Munich, 1923), p. 44.

3 Quoted in Christian Graf von Krockow, *Die Deutschen in ihrem*

Jahrhundert, 1890–1990 (Reinbek, 1990), p. 151.

4 Journal, July 1921, *GBA*, XXVI, pp. 282–3.

5 Peter Sloterdijk, *Critique of Cynical Reason* (Minneapolis, MN, 1987).

6 Journal, July 1921, *GBA*, XXVI, p. 282.

7 Journal, 6 December 1952, *GBA*, XXVII, p. 339.

8 *GBA*, I, p. 438.

9 Joseph Stolzing, review, *Völkischer Beobachter* (Munich edition) (5 May 1923), reprinted in *Brecht in der Kritik*, ed. Monika Wyss (Munich, 1977), p. 19.

10 Wyss, *Brecht in der Kritik*, pp. 19–20.

11 Journal, September 1921, *GBA*, XXVI, p. 236.

12 'Don Carlos', *Der Volkswille* (15 April 1920), reprinted in *GBA*, XXI, p. 59.

13 *GBA*, XXI, pp. 59–60.

14 Cited in Patty Lee Parmalee, *Brecht's America* (Miami, FL, 1981), p. 13.

15 Journal, July 1921, *GBA*, XXVI, p. 283.

16 *GBA*, I, p. 587.

17 On Rimbaud and the critique of the bourgeois novel, see Kristin Ross, 'Rimbaud and the Resistance to Work', *Representations* (Summer 1987), pp. 62–86.

18 'Looking through My First Plays' (1953), *GBA*, XXIII, p. 244.

19 Journal, 1925, *GBA*, XXVI, p. 285.

20 *Geistig* is notoriously untranslatable but can generally be read as 'intellectual' or 'spiritual'. *GBA*, XI, p. 39.

21 Ibid.

22 Herbert Ihering, 'Drei Brecht-Bücher', *Berliner Börsen-Courier* (30 April 1927), reprinted in *Von Reinhardt bis Brecht*, ed. Rolf Badenhausen (Reinbek, 1967), p. 248.

23 Walter Benjamin, *Gesammelte Schriften*, II/2, ed. Rolf Tiedemann (Frankfurt, 1991), pp. 667; 557–60.

24 *GBA*, XI, p. 157.

25 Walther Rathenau, *Gesamtausgabe*, II, ed. Ernst Schulin (Munich, 1977), p. 69.

26 Friedrich von Gottl-Ottlilienfeld, 'Fordism' (1926), reprinted in *The Weimar Republic Sourcebook*, ed. Anton Kaes, Martin Jay and Edward Dimendberg (Berkeley, CA, 1994), p. 401.

27 Hans Ostwald, *Sittengeschichte der Inflation*, reprinted in *The Weimar Republic Sourcebook*, ed. Kaes, Jay and Dimendberg, p. 77.

28 *GBA*, XXI, p. 436.

29 See, for example, Brecht's autobiographical notes and Journal, 1919–20, *GBA*, XXVI, pp. 113–72.

30 *GBA*, XIII, p. 157.

31 *GBA*, II, p. 123.

32 Bernhard Diebold, review, *Frankfurter Zeitung* (27 September 1926), reprinted in Wyss, *Brecht in der Kritik*, p. 56.

33 *GBA*, XXIV, p. 41.

34 'Looking through My First Plays' (1953), *GBA*, XXIII, p. 245.

35 Fritz Sternberg, *Der Imperialismus* (Berlin, 1926), p. 513.

36 *GBA*, XI, p. 165.

37 *GBA*, II, p. 117.

38 Oskar Negt and Alexander Kluge, *Geschichte und Eigensinn* (Frankfurt, 1993).

39 Leslie A. Adelson, 'Contemporary Critical Consciousness: Peter Sloterdijk, Oskar Negt/Alexander Kluge, and the "New Subjectivity"', *German Studies Review*, X/1 (February 1987), p. 64.

40 Ostwald, *Sittengeschichte der Inflation*, p. 77.

41 See John Fuegi's *Brecht & Co.: Sex, Politics, and the Making of the Modern Drama* (New York, 1994); cf. Sabine Kebir, *Ich fragte nicht nach meinem Anteil: Elisabeth Hauptmanns Arbeit mit Bertolt Brecht* (Berlin, 1997) and Sabine Kebir, *Abstieg in den Ruhm: Helene Weigel – Eine Biographie* (Berlin, 2000).

42 Sara Lennox, 'Women in Brecht's Works', *New German Critique*, 14 (Spring 1978), pp. 95–6.

43 Angelika Führich, *Aufbrüche des Weiblichen im Drama der Weimarer Republik* (Heidelberg, 1992), p. 26.

44 *GBA*, XXI, p. 287.

45 'The Addiction for the New' (1926), *GBA*, XXI, p. 183.

46 Theodore F. Rippey, 'Athletics, Aesthetics, and Politics in the Weimar Press', *German Studies Review*, XXVIII/1 (February 2005), p. 85.

47 Siegfried Kracauer, 'Sie sporten', *Frankfurter Zeitung* (13 January 1927), pp. 1–2, reprinted in *Aufsätze 1927–1931: Schriften*, V/2, ed. Inka Mülder-Bach (Frankfurt, 1990), p. 14.

48 Siegfried Kracauer, *Die Angestellten* (Frankfurt, 1971). The essays were first published as a series in the *Frankfurter Zeitung* in 1930.

49 Siegfried Kracauer, 'Asyl for Obdachlose', in *Die Angestellten*, pp. 91–101.

50 'There Is No Big City Theater' (1926), *GBA*, XXI, p. 134.

51 'More Good Sport', *Berliner Börsen-Courier* (6 February 1926), *GBA*, XXI, p. 119; John Willett, trans. and ed., *Brecht on Theatre* (New York, 1964), p. 6.

52 David Bathrick, 'Max Schmeling on the Canvas: Boxing as an Icon of Weimar Culture', *New German Critique*, 51 (Autumn 1990), p. 132.

53 *GBA*, XXI, p. 119.

54 Alain Badiou, *The Century* (Cambridge, MA, 2007), p. 39.

55 Ibid., pp. 39–40.

56 Ibid., p. 45.

57 *GBA*, XXI, pp. 224–5.

58 'On the Occasion of the A-I-Z's Tenth Anniversary', *Arbeiter Illustrierten Zeitung*, 41 (October 1931); *GBA*, XXI, p. 515.

59 Roland Barthes, *Mythologies* (New York, 1997), p. 142.

60 Ibid., pp. 146–7.

61 *GBA*, XXI, pp. 192–3.

62 'Bert Brecht's Reply', *Die Neue Zeit*, 5/6 (May–June 1927); *GBA*, XXI, p. 200.

63 Klaus Mann, 'Die neuen Eltern' and Thomas Mann, 'Die neuen Kinder: Ein Gespräch', *Uhu*, XXI (August 1926).

64 *GBA*, XXI, pp. 159–60.

65 'Squibs about Crime Novels' (1926), *GBA*, XXI, p. 131.

66 'Word to Old Age' (1926), ibid., p. 168.

67 'A Bit of Advice for Producing Documents' (1926), ibid., p. 165.

68 Alfred Döblin, 'Unbekannte junge Erzähler', *Literarische Welt*, XI (1926), reprinted in *100 Texte zu Brecht*, ed. Manfred Voigts (Munich, 1980), p. 51.

69 *GBA*, XI, p. 164.

70 Ibid., pp. 175–6.

71 Benjamin, *Gesammelte Schriften*, V/1, p. 243.

72 *GBA*, XXIX, p. 351.

73 'Ruhrepos' (1927), *GBA*, XXI, pp. 205–6.

74 *GBA*, XIII, p. 376.

75 'Tendency of the Volksbühne: Pure Art', *Berliner Börsen-Courier* (31 March 1927); *GBA*, XXI, p. 195.

76 'The Primacy of the Apparatus' (1928), *GBA*, XXI, p. 226.

77 'The Relationship of the Augsburger to Piscator' (1939), *GBA*, XXII, p. 763.

78 'Piscatortheater' (1927), *GBA*, XXI, p. 197.

79 'Sociological Perspective' (1928), *GBA*, XXI, p. 234.

80 Cited in Kebir, *Ich fragte nicht nach meinem Anteil*, p. 107.

81 GI (author's initials), *Neue Preußische Kreuz-Zeitung* (1 September 1928), reprinted in Wyss, *Brecht in der Kritik*, p. 80.

82 er (author's initials), *Die Rote Fahne* (4 September 1928), reprinted in Wyss, *Brecht in der Kritik*, pp. 82–3.

83 Cited in Siegfried Unseld, ed., *Bertolt Brechts Dreigroschenbuch* (Frankfurt, 1960), p. 223.

84 Werner Hecht, *Sieben Studien über Brecht* (Frankfurt, 1972), pp. 84, 87.

85 *GBA*, XXVIII, p. 484.

86 *GBA*, II, p. 231. My translation is adapted from Marc Blitzstein's 1954 translation.

87 Theodor Adorno, *Musikalische Schriften v/Gesammelte Werke*, vol. XVIII (Frankfurt, 1984), p. 539.

3 Work, Class and the Struggle with Marxism, 1929–33

1 Fritz Sternberg, *Der Dichter und die Ratio: Erinnerungen an Bertolt Brecht* (Göttingen, 1963), p. 25.

2 Friedrich Engels, 'Socialism: Utopian and Scientific' (1880), reprinted in *The Marx-Engels Reader*, ed. Robert C. Tucker (New York, 1978), pp. 705, 716.

3 *GBA*, III, p. 224.

4 Fritz Walter, review, *Berliner Börsen-Courier* (12 April 1932), reprinted in *Brecht in der Kritik*, ed. Monika Wyss (Munich, 1977), p. 154.

5 'Draft to an Introduction to a Reading' (1935), *GBA*, XXII, Part 1, pp. 138–9.

6 'The Only Viewer for My Plays' (1928), *GBA*, XXI, p. 256.

7 Sergei Eisenstein, 'Notes for a Film of *Capital*' (1927–8), reprinted in *October – The First Decade*, ed. Annette Michelson et al. (Cambridge, MA, 1987), pp. 138, 122. Emphasis in original.

8 'The Only Viewer for My Plays' (1928), *GBA*, XXI, p. 256.

9 'Regarding the Suitability of a Viewer' (1926), *GBA*, XXI, p. 127; and 'Demands of a New Criticism' (1929), *GBA*, XXI, p. 332, respectively.

10 Alfred Polgar, review, *Das Tagebuch* (22 March 1930), reprinted in

Wyss, *Brecht in der Kritik*, p. 110.

11 *GBA*, XXIV, pp. 78–9.

12 Kurt Weill, 'Vorwort zum Regiebuch der Oper *Mahagonny*' (1930), reprinted in *Kurt Weill – Ausgewählte Schriften*, ed. David Drew (Frankfurt, 1975), p. 59.

13 Theodor Adorno, in *Der Scheinwerfer*, III (13 April 1930), reprinted in Wyss, *Brecht in der Kritik*, p. 114.

14 Wyss, *Brecht in der Kritik*, p. 115. Emphasis in original.

15 'To Ernst Hardt' (1929); *GBA*, XXVIII, pp. 322–3.

16 Reprinted in Reiner Steinweg, ed., *Brechts Modell der Lehrstücke: Zeugnisse, Diskussion, Erfahrungen* (Frankfurt, 1976), p. 40.

17 See *Die Bibliothek Bertolt Brechts*, published by the Bertolt-Brecht-Archiv (Frankfurt, 2007).

18 'Regarding the Theory of the Learning Play' (1937), *GBA*, XXII, p. 351.

19 See specifically *Marxismus und Philosophie* (1923) and 'Die Krise des Marxismus' (1931), translated as 'The Crisis of Marxism', *New German Critique*, 3 (Autumn 1974), pp. 7–11.

20 'Regarding the Theory of the Learning Play' (1937), *GBA*, XXII, p. 351. For a discussion of *Eigensinn* and its relation to history, see Oskar Negt and Alexander Kluge, *Geschichte und Eigensinn* (Frankfurt, 1993).

21 *The Baden-Baden Teaching Play on Agreement* (1929), *GBA*, III, p. 30.

22 Elsa Bauer, review, *Badische Zeitung* (30 July 1929), reprinted in Wyss, *Brecht in der Kritik*, p. 97.

23 Fritz Karsen, 'Die soziale Arbeitsschule als Lebensgemeinschaft' (1930), reprinted in *Das Problem der Unterrichtsmethode in der pädagogischen Bewegung*, ed. Georg Geissler (Weinheim, 1970), p. 112.

24 Frank Warschauer, review, in *Die Weltbühne* (8 July 1930), reprinted in Wyss, *Brecht in der Kritik*, p. 128.

25 See Reiner Steinweg, *Das Lehrstück: Brechts Theorie einer politisch-ästhetischen Erziehung* (Stuttgart, 1972); and Heinrich Berenberg-Gossler, Hans-Harald Müller and Joachim Stosch, 'Das Lehrstück: Rekonstruktion einer Theorie oder Fortzetzung eines Lernprozesses?', in *Brechtdiskussion*, ed. J. Dyck et al. (Kronberg/Taunus, 1974), pp. 121–71.

26 *GBA*, XXI, p. 396.

27 *GBA*, XXIV, p. 94.

28 *GBA*, III, p. 71.

29 'Open Letter to the Artistic Directors of the *New Music Berlin 1930*,
    Heinrich Burkard, Paul Hindemith, Georg Schünemann', *Berliner
    Börsen-Courier* (12 May 1930); *GBA*, XXIV, p. 98.

30 *GBA*, XXIV, p. 96.

31 From reviews in *Deutsche Allgemeine Zeitung, Münchener Neueste
    Nachrichten* and *Berliner Tageblatt*, respectively, cited in *GBA*, III, p. 441.

32 Ruth Fischer, *Stalin und der deutsche Kommunismus* (Frankfurt, 1948),
    p. 760.

33 Hannah Arendt, *Men in Dark Times* (New York, 1955), pp. 240–41.

34 Ernst Jünger, *Der Kampf als inneres Erlebnis* (Berlin, 1922), p. 12.

35 Slavoj Žižek, 'Carl Schmitt in the Age of Post-Politics', in *The Challenge
    of Carl Schmitt*, ed. Chantal Mouffe (London, 1999), p. 27.

36 Ibid.

37 Peter Sloterdijk, *Critique of Cynical Reason* (Minneapolis, MN, 1987),
    p. 465.

38 Julius Bab, review, *Die Hilfe*, 5 (January 1931), reprinted in Wyss, *Brecht
    in der Kritik*, p. 134.

39 *Versuche*, 1–3, vol. I (1930), reprinted in *Brecht: Versuche*, 1–12 (Berlin,
    1959), p. 6.

40 Hans Jürgen Grune, 'Dein Auftritt, Genosse! Das Agitproptheater –
    eine proletarische Massenbewegung', in *Wem Gehört die Welt – Kunst
    und Gesellschaft in der Weimarer Republik*, ed. Neue Gesellschaft für
    Bildende Kunst (Berlin, 1977), p. 435.

41 Ibid., pp. 436, 437, 439.

42 Walter Benjamin, 'Bert Brecht' (1930), reprinted in Walter Benjamin,
    Gesammelte Schriften, II/2, ed. Rolf Tiedemann (Frankfurt, 1991), p. 665.

43 *Versuche*, 1–3, reprinted in *Brecht: Versuche*, 1–12, p. 6.

44 Walter Benjamin, commentary to 'What Is the Epic Theater?' (1931/9),
    reprinted in *Gesammelte Schriften*, VII/2, p. 655.

45 Walter Benjamin, 'What Is the Epic Theater?' (I) (1931), reprinted in
    Gesammelte Schriften, II/2, p. 523.

46 Benjamin, 'Bert Brecht' (1930), p. 662; commentary to 'What Is the
    Epic Theater?', p. 655.

47 *Versuche*, 13, vol. V (1932), reprinted in *Brecht: Versuche*, 13–19 (Berlin,
    1959), p. 101.

48 Fredric Jameson, *Brecht and Method* (London and New York, 1998), p. 2.

49 'Dialogue Regarding the Art of Acting', *Berliner Börsen-Courier* (17 February 1929); *GBA*, XXI, p. 279.

50 'Bourgeoisie and Technology' (1930), *GBA*, XXI, p. 373.

51 *GBA*, XXVIII, p. 407.

52 See Siegfried Kracauer, 'Ein soziologisches Experiment? Zu Bert Brechts Versuch: "Der Dreigroschenprozeß"' (1932), reprinted in *100 Texte zu Brecht*, ed. Manfred Voigts (Munich, 1980), pp. 138–45; and Ludwig Marcuse, 'Brecht ist Brecht', *Das Tagebuch*, XXII/7 (1931), reprinted in *Wie Alt Kann Aktuelles Sein?* (Zurich, 1989), pp. 35–9.

53 'The *Threepenny* Process: A Sociological Experiment', *Versuche*, 10, vol. III (1931), reprinted in *GBA*, XXI, pp. 448–514.

54 *GBA*, XXI, p. 479.

55 Cited in Bernard Eisenschitz, '*Who Does the World Belong to?* The Place of a Film', *Screen* (Summer 1974), p. 69.

56 'Sound Film *Kuhle Wampe* or *Who Does the World Belong to?*' (1932), *GBA*, XXI, p. 545.

57 Eisenschitz, '*Who Does the World Belong to?*', p. 65.

58 Cited ibid.

59 'The Second Helping' (1930), *GBA*, XXI, p. 390.

60 Reich's observations are cited in Wolfgang Gersch and Werner Hecht, eds, *Kuhle Wampe oder wem gehört die Welt? Filmprotokoll und Materialien* (Leipzig, 1971), p. 215.

61 Wolfgang Gersch, *Film bei Brecht* (Berlin, 1975), pp. 120–21.

62 Theodor Adorno and Hanns Eisler, *Komposition für den Film* (Hamburg, 1996), p. 48.

63 *Kuhle Wampe*, GBA, XVIII, pp. 570–71.

64 Cited in Jan Knopf, ed., *Brecht Handbuch in fünf Bänden* (Stuttgart, 2001), III, p. 440.

65 Review, *Deutsche Allgemeine Zeitung* (31 May 1932), cited in *GBA*, XIX, p. 727.

66 Rudolf Olden, '*Kuhle Wampe*', *Berliner Tageblatt* (2 April 1932); Heinz Lüdecke, 'Der Fall *Weekend Kuhle Wampe:* Tonfilm weiterhin für Kitsch und Lüge reserviert', *Die Rote Fahne* (3 April 1932), both cited in *GBA*, XIX, p. 727.

67 Cited in *GBA*, XIX, p. 727.

68 Cited in Knopf, *Brecht Handbuch*, III, p. 443.

69 Ibid.

4 Early Exile: 'Singing about Dark Times', 1933–41

1 *GBA*, XXII, p. 13.

2 *GBA*, XII, p. 16.

3 See, for example, 'About the Defeat' (1933), *GBA*, XXII, p. 19; and 'Argument against Hitler' (1933), *GBA*, XXII, p. 29.

4 'The Communists' Habit' (1933), *GBA*, XXII, p. 18.

5 'Questions after a Defeat' (1933), *GBA*, XXII, p. 20.

6 'Five Difficulties When Writing the Truth' (1934), *GBA*, XXII, p. 78.

7 'Liberation of Productive Resources' (1937), *GBA*, XXII, p. 302.

8 'Regarding the State' (1937), *GBA*, XXII, p. 304.

9 'Regarding the Programme of the Soviet Writers' (1935), *GBA*, XXII, p. 136.

10 'The Farmer Addressing His Ox' (1938), *GBA*, XII, p. 52; and *Book of Changes* (1934–40; first published 1965), *GBA*, XVIII, pp. 45–194.

11 *GBA*, XXVI, p. 327.

12 Karl Kraus, poem, *Die Fackel* (October 1933), p. 4.

13 *GBA*, XIV, p. 196.

14 Ibid., pp. 196–7.

15 'Appeal to Karl Kraus' (1934), *GBA*, XIV, pp. 560–61.

16 Ernst Bloch, 'Der Nazi und das Unsägliche' (1938), reprinted in Ernst Bloch, *Politische Messungen, Pestzeit, Vormärz, Gesamtausgabe*, vol. XI (Frankfurt, 1970), p. 185.

17 Ibid., pp. 186–91.

18 'General Göring Regarding the Defeat of Communism in Germany' (1934), *GBA*, XXII, p. 92; and 'Christmas Address by the Deputy Führer (Hess) in the Year 1934' (1934), *GBA*, 22, p. 93.

19 Letter from Johannes R. Becher to Brecht, December 1934, cited in *GBA*, XXII, p. 904.

20 'Five Difficulties When Writing the Truth', *Unsere Zeit*, 2–3 (April 1935), p. 23; *GBA*, XXII, p. 74.

21 *GBA*, XXII, pp. 76–7.

22 'Regarding the Truth' (1934), *GBA*, XXII, p. 96.

23 *GBA*, XXI, p. 553.

24 'Radio – An Antediluvian Invention?' (1927), *GBA*, XXI, p. 217.

25 'The Radio as an Apparatus of Communication' (1930/32), *GBA*, XXI, p. 553.

26 See Norbert Schachtsiek-Freitag, 'Bertolt Brechts Radiolehrstück *Der Ozeanflug*': *Bertolt Brecht – Text und Kritik*, Sonderband 2 (1973), pp. 132–3; and Hermann Pongs, 'Das Hörspiel', *Zeichen der Zeit*, 1 (1930), pp. 1–48.

27 Schachtsiek-Freitag, 'Bertolt Brechts Radiolehrstück *Der Ozeanflug*', p. 132.

28 See Friedrich Knilli, 'Die Arbeiterbewegung und die Medien: Ein Rückblick', *Gewerkschaftliche Monatshefte* (June 1974), p. 359.

29 Ibid.

30 Cited in Ricarda Strobel, 'Film- und Kinokultur der 30er und 40er Jahre', in *Die Kultur der 30er und 40er Jahre*, ed. Werner Faulstich (Munich, 2009), p. 150.

31 Knut Hickethier, 'Hitler und das Radio: Der Rundfunk in der NS-Zeit', in Faulstich, *Die Kultur der 30er und 40er Jahre*, p. 196.

32 Walter Benjamin, 'Der Autor als Produzent', an address delivered at the Institute for the Study of Fascism in Paris, 27 April 1934, reprinted in *Gesammelte Werke*, II/2, p. 684.

33 Walter Benjamin, 'Linke Melancholie', *Die Gesellschaft*, 8, vol. I (1931), reprinted in *Gesammelte Werke*, III, p. 280.

34 Cited in Peter Mayer, 'Die Wahrheit ist konkret: Notizen zu Benjamin und Brecht', *Bertolt Brecht – Text und Kritik*, Sonderband I (1972), p. 5.

35 Benjamin, 'Der Autor als Produzent', p. 691.

36 Walter Benjamin, 'Das Land, in dem das Proletariat nicht genannt werden darf: Zur Uraufführung von acht Einaktern Brechts', *Die neue Weltbühne*, 38 (1938), reprinted in *Gesammelte Werke*, II/2, p. 515.

37 Ibid.

38 *GBA*, XXII, pp. 144, 146.

39 Letter to George Grosz, June–July 1935, *GBA*, XXVIII, p. 510.

40 Speech at the Second International Writers Congress for the Defence of Culture (1937), *GBA*, XXII, p. 325.

41 Notes for *The Tui-Novel* (1935–7), *GBA*, XVII, p. 153.

42 *GBA*, XII, p. 29.

43 *GBA*, XI, p. 215.

44 Klaus Mann, review, *Die Sammlung* (May 1934), and Arnold Zweig, review, *Neue Deutsche Blätter* (1934–5), both cited in *GBA*, XI, p. 372.

45 'The Necessity of Propaganda' (1937), *GBA*, XII, p. 66.

46 'Regarding Unrhymed Poetry with Irregular Rhythms', *Das Wort*, 3 (1939), reprinted in *GBA*, XXII, p. 364.

47 Cited in *GBA*, XII, p. 358.

48 'The *Threepenny* Process' (1931), *GBA*, XXI, p. 464.

49 Willy Siegfried Schlamm, review, *Europäische Hefte*, 30 (8 November 1934), cited in *GBA*, XVI, p. 423.

50 Christian Graf von Krockow, *Die Deutschen in ihrem Jahrhundert, 1890–1990* (Reinbek, 1990), pp. 209, 213.

51 Letter to Slatan Dudow, late July 1937, *GBA*, XXIX, pp. 35–6.

52 Werner Hecht, et al., *Bertolt Brecht: Sein Leben und Werk* (Berlin, 1969), pp. 118–19.

53 Journal, 25 February 1939, *GBA*, XXVI, p. 330.

54 *GBA*, XXVI, pp. 319.

55 Letter to Slatan Dudow, April 1938, *GBA*, XXIX, p. 84.

56 Letter to Erwin Piscator, March/April 1933, *GBA*, XXIX, p. 83.

57 *The Private Life of the Master Race* (1938), *GBA*, IV, p. 388.

58 Cited in *GBA*, IV, p. 531.

59 P. Br. (author's initials), *Pariser Tageszeitung* (21 May 1938), reprinted in *Brecht in der Kritik*, ed. Monika Wyss (Munich, 1977), p. 189.

60 Heinrich Heine, *Nachtgedanken* (1843), in *Sämtliche Gedichte* (Frankfurt, 1993), p. 446; trans. Hal Draper, *The Complete Poems of Heinrich Heine* (Frankfurt, 1982), p. 407.

61 *GBA*, XXVI, p. 319.

62 Ibid., p. 326.

63 *Dansen* (1939), *GBA*, V, p. 295.

64 'Courage Learns Nothing' (1953), *GBA*, XXIV, p. 272.

65 *GBA*, XXVI, p. 476.

5 U.S. Exile: The Dialectics of Alienation and 'Culinary' Art, 1941–7

1 Journal, 20 April 1941, *GBA*, XXVI, p. 475.

2 *GBA*, XXVI, p. 474. English in original.

3 Journal, 19 August 1940, *GBA*, XXVI, p. 414. The book referred to is James Boswell's *The Life of Samuel Johnson* (1791).

4 Journal, 13 July 1941, *GBA*, XXVI, p. 485.

5 *Hollywood Elegies* (1942), GBA, XII, p. 115; trans. John Willett and Ralph
   Manheim with Erich Fried, eds, *Bertolt Brecht: Poems, 1913–1956*
   (New York, 1976), p. 380.

6 Fredric Jameson, *Brecht and Method* (London and New York, 1998),
   p. 16.

7 Ibid.

8 James K. Lyon, *Bertolt Brecht in America* (Princeton, NJ, 1980), p. 5.

9 Journal, 1 August 1941, GBA, XXVII, p. 10. English in original.

10 Journal, 8 August 1941, GBA, XXVII, p. 10.

11 Letter to Heinrich Mann, 20 December 1944, GBA, XXIX, p. 342.

12 GBA, XII, p. 115.

13 Cited in Anya Feddersen, 'Kriegsfibel', in Jan Knopf, ed., *Brecht
   Handbuch in fünf Bänden* (Stuttgart, 2001), II, p. 384.

14 GBA, XV, p. 291.

15 Cf. J. J. Long, 'Paratextual Profusion: Photography and Text in
   Bertolt Brecht's *War Primer*', *Poetics Today*, XXIX/1 (Spring 2008),
   p. 197.

16 'The *Threepenny* Process' (1931), GBA, XXI, p. 496; 'On the Occasion
   of the A-I-Z's Tenth Anniversary' (1931), GBA, XXI, p. 515.

17 Anya Feddersen discusses this relationship in 'Kriegsfibel' in Knopf,
   Brecht Handbuch, II, pp. 388–9.

18 GBA, XII, p. 167.

19 Ibid., p. 215.

20 Caption of a *Life* magazine photograph, used for photo epigram no. 40,
   GBA, XII, p. 209.

21 Roland Barthes, 'Brecht, Diderot, Eisenstein' (1973), reprinted in
   Roland Barthes, *The Responsibility of Forms: Critical Essays on Music,
   Art, and Representation* (Berkeley, CA, 1991), pp. 90–91.

22 'Why the Threat of Petty Bourgeois and Even Proletarian Strata
   Changing Over to Fascism?' (1939), GBA, XXII, pp. 587–8.

23 Journal, 27 and 28 February 1942, GBA, XXVII, pp. 58 and 63,
   respectively.

24 Journal, 28 February 1942, GBA, XXVII, p. 63.

25 'Remarks regarding *Arturo Ui*' (1953), GBA, XXIV, p. 316.

26 Journal, 28 February 1942, GBA, XXVII, p. 64.

27 Journal, 12 December 1941, ibid., p. 34.

28 Journal, 8 January 1942, ibid., p. 46.

29 'The *Other* Germany: 1943' (1943), *GBA*, XXIII, p. 24. A shorter essay with the same title in German was published in *The German American*, 9 (January 1944), *GBA*, XXIII, pp. 30–31.

30 *GBA*, XXIII, pp. 27–8.

31 'Regarding the Declaration of the 26 United Nations' (1942), *GBA*, XXIII, p. 7. The remark regarding Goebbels's mythical unity of *Volk* and *Führer* is taken from Journal, 2 August 1943, *GBA*, XXVII, p. 163.

32 *GBA*, XXIII, p. 423.

33 Journal, 1 August 1943, *GBA*, XXVII, p. 161.

34 Quoted in Journal, 2 August 1943, *GBA*, XXVII, p. 163.

35 Ibid.; and *GBA*, XV, pp. 90–91.

36 See Lee Baxandall, 'Brecht in America, 1935', *The Drama Review* (Autumn 1967), pp. 69–87.

37 E.J.R. Isaacs in *Theatre Arts*, 20 (1936), p. 13; *Daily Mirror* (20 November 1935); and *Brooklyn Daily Eagle* (20 November 1935), respectively.

38 David Bathrick, 'Brecht's Marxism and America', in *Essays on Brecht: Theater and Politics*, ed. Siegfried Mews and Herbert Knust (Chapel Hill, NC, 1974), p. 212.

39 Bertolt Brecht, *The Private Life of the Master Race*, trans. and intro. by Eric Bentley (New York, 1944).

40 Eva Goldbeck, in *The New Masses* (31 December 1935), p. 27.

41 Lyon, *Bertolt Brecht in America*.

42 Mordecai Gorelik, 'Epic Realism: Brecht's Notes on *The Threepenny Opera*', *Theatre Workshop* (April–July 1937), pp. 29–40.

43 Mordecai Gorelik, *New Theatres for Old* (New York, 1940).

44 Bernhard Sobel, ed., *The New Theatre Handbook and Digest of Plays* (New York, 1959), p. 429.

45 Interview with Herbert Marcuse, paraphrased in Lyon, *Bertolt Brecht in America*, p. 258.

46 Journal, August 1941, *GBA*, XXVII, pp. 12–13.

47 *The Tui-Novel* (1931–54), *GBA*, XVII, p. 11.

48 Journal, 16 June 1942, *GBA*, XXVII, p. 105.

49 Journal, 12 May 1942, *GBA*, XXVII, p. 94.

50 See Ronald Taylor, ed., *Aesthetics and Politics: The Keys Texts of the Classic Debate within German Marxism* (London, 1980).

51 Letter to Willi Bredel, July/August 1938, *GBA*, XXIX, p. 107.

52 Title of an anonymous article in *Pravda*, cited in Knopf, *Brecht Handbuch*, iv, p. 233.

53 Ernst Bloch, 'Diskussionen über den Expressionismus', *Das Wort*, 6 (1938), reprinted in translation in Taylor, *Aesthetics and Politics*, p. 17.

54 Georg Lukács, 'Es geht um den Realismus', *Das Wort*, 6 (1938), reprinted in translation in Taylor, *Aesthetics and Politics*, p. 43.

55 Journal, 18 August 1938, *GBA*, xxvi, p. 321.

56 Walter Benjamin, Journal, 25 July 1938, *Gesammelte Schriften*, vi, p. 537.

57 Cited ibid., p. 539.

58 'Popularity and Realism' (1938), *GBA*, xxii, Part 1, pp. 408–9; Taylor, *Aesthetics and Politics*, pp. 81–2.

59 Jacques Rancière, *The Politics of Aesthetics* (London, 2004), pp. 12–13.

60 Theodor Adorno, letter to Walter Benjamin, 18 March 1936, reprinted in Taylor, *Aesthetics and Politics*, p. 121.

61 Walter Benjamin, 'Das Kunstwerk im Zeitalter seiner technischen Reproduzierbarkeit', *Zeitschrift für Sozialforschung* Jh. 5 (1936), reprinted in *Gesammelte Schriften*, 1/2, pp. 435–69.

62 Adorno, letter to Walter Benjamin, in Taylor, *Aesthetics and Politics*, p. 123.

63 Journal, 25 July 1938, *GBA*, xxvi, p. 315.

64 Journal, 9 August 1941, *GBA*, xxvii, pp. 12–13.

65 Jameson, *Brecht and Method*, p. 163, n. 26.

66 'Conversation about Classics' (1929), *GBA*, xxi, p. 310.

67 Journal, March, April, May 1943, *GBA*, xxvii, p. 150.

68 See Lyon, *Bertolt Brecht in America*, p. 278.

69 Letter to the American Guild for Cultural Freedom, 1 August 1940, *GBA*, xxix, p. 184.

70 *Refugee Dialogues* (1940–44), *GBA*, xviii, p. 197.

71 Journal, 12 February 1939, *GBA*, xxvi, p. 327.

72 Journal, 9 September 1938, *GBA*, xxvi, p. 324.

73 *Buying Brass* (1939–55), *GBA*, xxii, Part 2, pp. 695–6.

74 Ibid., p. 778.

75 Ibid., pp. 710–11.

76 'K-type and P-type in the Drama' (1938), *GBA*, xxii, p. 388, 'K-type and P-type and the Crisis of Empathy' (1938–9), *GBA*, xxii, p. 390.

77 *Buying Brass*, GBA, XXII, Part 2, p. 719.

78 The simplification of Brechtian aesthetics into a reproduction of modernist binaries has a long tradition; a recent example of attributing to Brecht a consideration of audience along an exclusive active–passive axis can be found in Jacques Rancière's 'The Emancipated Spectator', *Artforum* (March 2007), pp. 271–80.

79 *Buying Brass*, GBA, XXII, Part 2, p. 723.

80 Ibid., pp. 716–17.

81 Ibid., pp. 699, 753.

82 Lyon, *Bertolt Brecht in America*, p. 167.

83 'Laughton's Belly' (1944), GBA, XV, p. 108.

84 'Garden in Progress' (original title in English, 1944), GBA, XV, pp. 109–10.

85 Journal, 28 August 1944, GBA, XXVII, p. 202.

86 GBA, XXVII, pp. 224–5.

87 'Epistle to the Augsburgers' (1945), GBA, XXVII, p. 225.

88 Cited in Journal, 10 September 1945, GBA, XXVII, p. 232.

89 Journal, 20 September 1945, GBA, XXVII, p. 232.

90 GBA, V, p. 43.

91 Ibid., pp. 177, 179.

92 Jean-Paul Sartre, 'Episches Theater und dramatisches Theater', in Jean-Paul Sartre, *Mythos und Realität des Theaters* (Reinbek, 1979), pp. 74–107.

93 GBA, XXIX, p. 407.

94 Cited in Martin Esslin, *Brecht: The Man and His Work* (Garden City, NY, 1971), p. 83.

95 Cited in Lyon, *Bertolt Brecht in America*, pp. 330–31.

96 Cited in Esslin, *Brecht: The Man and His Work*, p. 82; 'Forward, We've Not Forgotten' (1931), GBA, XIV, pp. 116–18.

6 Realpolitik: Theatre of Socialism, 1947–56

1 GBA, XII, p. 125.

2 Letter to Gottfried von Einem, April 1949, GBA, XXIX, pp. 511–12.

3 Journal, 15 April 1948, GBA, XXVII, p. 268.

4 Journal, 6 January 1949, GBA, XXVII, p. 296.

5 *GBA*, XV, p. 205.

6 'Two Cities' (1948), *GBA*, XVIII, p. 451.

7 *GBA*, XXVII, p. 296.

8 Cited in Werner Hecht, *Brecht Chronik: 1898–1956* (Frankfurt, 1997), p. 915.

9 Cited ibid., p. 919.

10 'Notes about the Formalism Discussion' (1951), *GBA*, XXIII, p. 142.

11 Journal, 1 January 1948, *GBA*, XXVII, p. 259.

12 Andreas Klement, *Brechts neues Leben in der DDR: Die späte Lyrik* (Marburg, 2012), p. 104.

13 'Conversations with Young Intellectuals' (1948), *GBA*, XXIII, p. 101.

14 Journal, 24 December 1947, *GBA*, XXVII, p. 258.

15 Text for the back cover of the 1955 edition of the *War Primer*, *GBA*, XV, p. 290.

16 'Conversations with Young Intellectuals', *GBA*, XXIII, p. 101; Journal, 11 November 1943, *GBA*, XXVII, pp. 181–2.

17 'Construction Song' (1948), *GBA*, XV, p. 197.

18 'Regarding the Work of the Dramatists, Directors, Assistants and Students of the Berliner Ensemble' (1952), *GBA*, XXIII, p. 221.

19 See Klaus Schröder, *Der SED-Staat: Partei, Staat und Gesellschaft, 1949–1990* (Munich, 2000), pp. 119–24.

20 Cited in Martin Esslin, *Brecht: The Man and His Work* (Garden City, NY, 1971), p. 192.

21 Letter to Walter Ulbricht, 17 June 1953, *GBA*, XXX, p. 178.

22 'Urgency for a Great Dialogue', *Neues Deutschland* (23 June 1953), *GBA*, XXIII, p. 250.

23 See Esslin, *Brecht: The Man and His Work*, p. 194.

24 'Question' (1952), *GBA*, XV, p. 262.

25 'The Guys, before They Lay Their Girls' (1955), *GBA*, XV, p. 292.

26 'Great Time, Wasted' (1953), *GBA*, XII, p. 311; Klement, *Brechts neues Leben in der DDR*, pp. 66–8.

27 *GBA*, XXIV, p. 410.

28 Walter Benjamin, 'Diary Notes', August 1938, *Gesammelte Schriften*, VI, p. 539. Emphasis in original.

29 *GBA*, XXVII, p. 158.

30 Journal, 20 August 1953, *GBA*, XXVII, pp. 346–7.

31 *GBA*, XII, p. 310.

32 Slavoj Žižek, 'The Lesson of Rancière', in Jacques Rancière, *The Politics of Aesthetics* (London, 2006), pp. 74–5. It should be noted that Žižek's assessment of the revolutionary government's task is seated within a critique of Brecht's text, which he, along standard lines of interpretation, takes to be scornful 'of the arrogance of the Communist *nomenklatura* when faced with the workers' revolt'. Thus he criticizes the poem for being 'politically opportunistic' as well as 'simply *wrong* in the theoretico-political sense'.

33 Ibid., p. 74.

34 *GBA*, XXIV, p. 409.

35 Letter to Käthe Rülicke, June 1953, *GBA*, XXX, p. 180.

36 'Cultural Politics and Academy of the Arts' (1953), *GBA*, XXIII, p. 259.

37 'Foreword to *Turandot*' (1953), *GBA*, XXIV, p. 409.

38 Journal, 13 September 1953, *GBA*, XXVII, p. 348.

39 Journal, 20 August 1953, *GBA*, XXVII, p. 346.

40 'I Don't Need a Gravestone' (1933), *GBA*, XIV, pp. 191–2.

41 *GBA*, XII, p. 310.

Select Bibliography

Selected Works by Bertolt Brecht – English and original
German titles

All texts published in Bertolt Brecht, *Große kommentierte Berliner und
Frankfurter Ausgabe*, vols I–XXX, ed. Werner Hecht, Jan Knopf, Werner
Mittenzwei and Klaus-Detlef Müller (Berlin, 1989), hereafter *GBA*

'About §218' / 'Über den §218' (1930), *GBA*, XXI, p. 373
'About the Defeat' / 'Über die Niederlage' (1933), *GBA*, XXII, p. 19
'About: *The Rise and Fall of the City of Mahagonny*' / 'Zu: *Aufstieg und Fall der
    Stadt Mahagonny*' (1930), *GBA*, XXIV, pp. 78–9
'The Addiction for the New' / 'Die Sucht nach dem Neuen' (1926), *GBA*, XXI,
    p. 183
'Advice from an Older Whore to a Younger One' / 'Ratschläge einer älteren
    Fohse an eine Jüngere' (1926), *GBA*, XI, pp. 123–4
'After the Death of My Colleague M. S.' / 'Nach dem Tod meiner
    Mitarbeiterin M. S.' (1941), *GBA*, XV, p. 45
'Appeal to Karl Kraus' / 'Appell an Karl Kraus' (1934), *GBA*, XIV, pp. 560–61
'Argument against Hitler' / 'Argument gegen Hitler' (1933), *GBA*, XXII,
    p. 29
Augsburg War Letters / Augsburger Kriegsbriefe (1914), *GBA*, XXI, pp. 13–22
*The Baden-Baden Teaching Play on Agreement / Das Badener Lehrstück vom
    Einverständnis* (1929), *GBA*, III, p. 30
'The Ballad of François Villon' / 'Die Ballade vom François Villon' (1918),
    GBA, XIII, pp. 114–15
'The Ballad of Red Rosa' / 'Die Ballade der Roten Rosa' (lost; listed among
    the contents of the *Manual of Piety*'s 1922 draft)

The Horatians and the Curatians / Die Horatier and die Kuratier (1936), *GBA*, IV, pp. 279–303

In the Jungle of the Cities / Im Dickicht der Städte (1923/27), *GBA*, I, pp. 437–97

'Individual and Mass' / 'Individuum und Masse' (1929), *GBA*, XXI, p. 359

'July 1913' / 'Juli 1913' (1913), *GBA*, XIII, p. 32

'K-type and P-type in the Drama' / 'K-Typus und P-Typus in der Dramatik' (1938), *GBA*, XXII, pp. 387–9

'K-type and P-type and the Crisis of Empathy'/ 'K-Typus und P-Typus und die Krise der Einfühlung' (1938–9), *GBA*, XXII, pp. 390–92

'Laughton's Belly' / 'Der Bauch Laughtons' (1944), *GBA*, XV, pp. 108–9

'The Legend of the Dead Soldier' / 'Die Legende vom toten Soldaten' (1918), *GBA*, XI, pp. 112–15

'The Legend of the Harlot Evlyn Roe' / 'Die Legende der Dirne Evlyn Roe' (1918), *GBA*, XIII, pp. 102–4

'Let Us Return to the Crime Novel!' / 'Kehren wir zum Kriminalroman zurück!' (1926), *GBA*, XXI, pp. 128–30

'Liberation of Productive Resources' / 'Befreiung der Produktivkräfte' (1937), *GBA*, XXII, p. 302

'A Liturgy of Breath' / 'Liturgie vom Hauch' (1924), *GBA*, XI, pp. 49–53

'Looking through My First Plays' / 'Bei der Durchsicht meiner ersten Stücke' (1953), *GBA*, XXIII, pp. 239–45

Man Is Man / Mann ist Mann (1926), *GBA*, II, pp. 93–168

Manual of Piety / Hauspostille (1927), *GBA*, XI, pp. 37–120

The Measure Taken / Die Massnahme (1930), *GBA*, III, pp. 71–98

'Modern Legend' / 'Moderne Legende' (1914), *GBA*, XIII, pp. 73–4

'More Good Sport,' / 'Mehr guten Sport' (1926), *GBA*, XXI, pp. 119–22

The Mother / Die Mutter (1933), *GBA*, III, pp. 261–324

Mother Courage and Her Children / Mutter Courage und ihre Kinder (1939), *GBA*, VI, pp. 7–86

'My General Has Fallen' / 'Mein General ist gefallen' (1941), *GBA*, XV, p. 45

'A Necessary Observation regarding the Fight against Barbarism' / 'Eine notwendige Feststellung zum Kampf gegen die Barberei' (1935), *GBA*, XXII, pp. 141–6

'The Necessity of Propaganda' / 'Notwendigkeit der Propaganda' (1937), *GBA*, XII, pp. 65–7

'Notes about the Formalism Discussion' / 'Notizen über die Formalismusdiskussion' (1951), *GBA*, XXIII, pp. 141–2

'Regarding Rhetoric' / 'Über das Rhetorische' (1920), *GBA*, XXI, pp. 49–50

'Regarding the Declaration of the 26 United Nations' / 'Zur Erklärung der 26 Vereinten Nationen' (1942), *GBA*, XXIII, pp. 7–9

'Regarding the Programme of the Soviet Writers' / 'Über das Programm der Sowjetschriftsteller' (1935), *GBA*, XXII, pp. 134–6

'Regarding the Significance of the Ten-Line Poem in Number 888 of *Die Fackel* (October 1933)' / 'Über die Bedeutung des zehnteiligen Gedichtes in der 888. Nummer der Fackel (Oktober 1933)' (1934), *GBA*, XIV, pp. 195–7

'Regarding the State' / 'Über den Staat' (1937), *GBA*, XXII, p. 304

'Regarding the Suitability of a Viewer' / 'Über die Eignung zum Zuschauer' (1926), *GBA*, XXI, p. 127

'Regarding the Theory of the Learning Play' / 'Zur Theorie des Lehrstücks' (1937), *GBA*, XXII, pp. 351–2

'Regarding the Truth' / 'Über Wahrheit' (1934), *GBA*, XXII, pp. 96–7

'Regarding Unrhymed Poetry with Irregular Rhythms' / 'Über reimlose Lyrik mit unregelmässigen Rhythmen' (1939), *GBA*, XXII, pp. 357–64

'Regarding the Work of the Dramatists, Directors, Assistants and Students of the Berliner Ensemble' / 'Über die Arbeit der Dramaturgen, Regisseure, Assistenten und Schüler des Berliner Ensemble' (1952), *GBA*, XXIII, pp. 221–2

'The Relationship of the Augsburger to Piscator' / 'Verhältnis des Augsburgers zum Piscator' (1939), *GBA*, XXII, p. 763

'Remarks Regarding *Arturo Ui*' / 'Bemerkungen zu *Der aufhaltsame Aufstieg des Arturo Ui*' (1953), *GBA*, XXIV, pp. 315–19

'Reply to the Open Letter by the Personnel of the Stadttheater' / 'Erwiderung auf den offenen Brief des Personals des Stadttheaters' (1920), *GBA*, XXI, pp. 85–8

'The Return' / 'Die Rückkehr' (1943), *GBA*, XII, p. 125

The Rise and Fall of the City of Mahagonny / Aufstieg und Fall der Stadt Mahagonny (1929), *GBA*, II, pp. 333–92

The Round Heads and the Pointed Heads / Die Rundköpfe und die Spitzköpfe (1933), *GBA*, IV, pp. 147–263

'Rowing, Conversations' / 'Rudern, Gespräche' (1953), *GBA*, XII, p. 307

'Sacrifice!' / 'Opfere!' (1913), *GBA*, XIII, pp. 16–17

'Schiller's "Robbers" at the Stadttheater' / 'Schillers "Räuber" im Stadttheater' (1920), *GBA*, XXI, pp. 78–9

Threepenny Novel / Dreigroschenroman (1934), *GBA*, XVI, pp. 8–391

Threepenny Opera / Dreigroschenoper (1928), *GBA*, II, pp. 229–323

'The *Threepenny* Process: A Sociological Experiment' / 'Der
    Dreigroschenprozeß: Ein soziologisches Experiment' (1931), *GBA*, XXI,
    pp. 448–514

The Trial of Lukullus / Das Verhör des Lukullus (1940), *GBA*, VI, pp. 87–113

'The Tsar Spoke to Them' / 'Der Zar hat mit ihnen gesprochen' (1956), *GBA*,
    XV, pp. 300–1

The Tui-Novel / Der Tuiroman (1931–54), *GBA*, XVII, pp. 9–161

The Tui-Novel / Der Tuiroman (notes, 1935–7), *GBA*, XVII, p. 153

*Turandot or The Congress of the Whitewashers / Turandot oder Der Kongress
    der Weisswäscher* (1954), *GBA*, IX, pp. 127–98

The Tutor / Der Hofmeister (1949), *GBA*, VIII, pp. 319–71

'Two Cities' / 'Zwei Städte' (1948), *GBA*, XVIII, p. 451

'Upon the Nobel Prize Winner Thomas Mann's Authorizing the Americans
    and the English to Punish the German People Ten Years for the Crimes
    of the Hitler Regime' / 'Als der Nobelpreisträger Thomas Mann den
    Amerikanern und Engländern das Recht zusprach, das deutsche Volk
    für die Verbrechen des Hitlerregimes zehn Jahre lang zu züchtigen'
    (1943), *GBA*, XV, pp. 90–91

'The Uppercut' / 'Der Kinnhaken' (1925), *GBA*, XIX, pp. 205–9

'Urgency for a Great Dialogue' / 'Dringlichkeit einer grossen Aussprache'
    (1953), *GBA*, XXIII, p. 250

*The Vita of the Boxer Samson-Körner / Der Lebenslauf des Boxers Samson-
    Körners* (1926/7), *GBA*, XIX, pp. 216–35

'Vulture Tree' / 'Geierbaum' (1917), *GBA*, XIII, pp. 95–6

War Primer / Kriegsfibel (1940–55), *GBA*, XII, pp. 127–283

'The Weights on the Scale' / 'Die Gewichte auf der Waage' (1956), *GBA*, XV,
    pp. 301–2

What Does the Iron Cost / Was kostet das Eisen (1939), *GBA*, V, pp. 309–27

'When It Was Time' / 'Als es soweit war' (1941), *GBA*, XV, p. 41

'When the Father with the Son with the Owl . . .' / 'Wenn der Vater mit
    dem Sohne mit dem Uhu . . .' (1926), *GBA*, XXI, pp. 158–60

'Why the Threat of Petty Bourgeois and Even Proletarian Strata Changing
    Over to Fascism?' / 'Warum droht die Abwanderung kleinbügerlicher
    und sogar proletarischer Schichten zum Faschismus?' (1939), *GBA*, XXII,
    pp. 587–8

'Word to Old Age' / 'Worte an das Alter' (1926), *GBA*, XXI, pp. 167–8
'Workers' / 'Arbeiter' (1913), *GBA*, XXVI, pp. 15–17
'Young Stage – Social Revolutionaries' / 'Junge Bühne –
    Sozialrevolutionäre' (1929), *GBA*, XXI, pp. 286–7

Selected Writings in English

Willett, John, trans. and ed., *Brecht on Theatre* (New York, 1964)
—, and Ralph Manheim with Erich Fried, eds and trans., *Bertolt Brecht:
    Poems, 1913–1956* (New York, 1976)

Selected Writings on Brecht

Arendt, Hannah, *Men in Dark Times* (New York, 1955)
Arnold, Heinz Ludwig, ed., *Bertolt Brecht – Text und Kritik*, vols I and II
    (Munich, 1972 and 1973)
Barthes, Roland, 'Brecht and Discourse: A Contribution to the Study of
    Discursivity' (1975), reprinted in *The Rustle of Language* (New York,
    1986), pp. 212–22
—, 'The Task of Brechtian Criticism', in *Critical Essays*, ed. Roland Barthes
    (Evanston, IL, 1972), pp. 71–6
Bathrick, David, 'Brecht's Marxism and America', in *Essays on Brecht:
    Theater and Politics*, ed. Siegfried Mews and Herbert Knust (Chapel
    Hill, NC, 1974), pp. 209–25
Baxandall, Lee, 'Brecht in America, 1935', *The Drama Review* (Autumn
    1967), pp. 69–87
Benjamin, Walter, *Versuche über Brecht* (Frankfurt, 1971)
Die Bibliothek Bertolt Brechts, published by the Bertolt-Brecht-Archiv
    (Frankfurt, 2007)
Dyck, J., et al., eds, *Brechtdiskussion* (Kronberg/Taunus, 1974)
Esslin, Martin, *Brecht: The Man and His Work* (Garden City, NY, 1971)
Frisch, Werner, and K. W. Obermeyer, eds, *Brecht in Augsburg* (Frankfurt, 1976)
Gersch, Wolfgang, *Film bei Brecht* (Berlin, 1975)
Gorelik, Mordecai, 'Epic Realism: Brecht's Notes on *The Threepenny Opera*',
    Theatre Workshop (April–July 1937), pp. 29–40

Grimm, Reinhold, *Brecht und Nietzsche, oder Geständnisse eines Dichters* (Frankfurt, 1979)

Harvey, Sylvia, 'Whose Brecht? Memories for the Eighties: A Critical Recovery', *Screen*, 23 (1982), pp. 45–59

Hecht, Werner, *Brecht Chronik: 1898–1956* (Frankfurt, 1997)

—, 'Der Augsburger Theaterkritiker', in Werner Hecht, *Sieben Studien über Brecht* (Frankfurt, 1972), pp. 7–24

Hecht, Werner, et al., eds, *Bertolt Brecht. Sein Leben und Werk* (Berlin, 1969)

Jameson, Fredric, *Brecht and Method* (London and New York, 1998)

Klement, Andreas, *Brechts neues Leben in der DDR: Die späte Lyrik* (Marburg, 2012)

Knopf, Jan, ed., *Brecht Handbuch in fünf Bänden* (Stuttgart, 2001)

Kracauer, Siegfried, 'Ein soziologisches Experiment? Zu Bert Brechts Versuch: "Der Dreigroschenprozeß"' (1932), reprinted in *100 Texte zu Brecht*, ed. Manfred Voigts (Munich, 1980), pp. 138–45

Lennox, Sara, 'Women in Brecht's Works', *New German Critique*, 14 (Spring 1978), pp. 83–96

Long, J. J., 'Paratextual Profusion: Photography and Text in Bertolt Brecht's *War Primer*', *Poetics Today*, XXIX/1 (Spring 2008), pp. 197–224

Lunn, Eugene, *Marxism and Modernism: A Historical Study of Lukács, Brecht, Benjamin, and Adorno* (Berkeley and Los Angeles, CA, 1984)

Lyon, James K., *Bertolt Brecht in America* (Princeton, NJ, 1980)

Mayer, Hans, *Brecht in der Geschichte* (Frankfurt, 1976)

Parmalee, Lee, *Brecht's America* (Miami, FL, and Columbus, OH, 1981)

Steinweg, Reiner, ed., *Brechts Modell der Lehrstücke: Zeugnisse, Diskussion, Erfahrungen* (Frankfurt, 1976)

Sternberg, Fritz, *Der Dichter und die Ratio: Erinnerungen an Bertolt Brecht* (Göttingen, 1963)

Tucholsky, Kurt, 'Bert Brechts Hauspostille', *Weltbühne* (28 February 1928), reprinted in *Gesamtausgabe*, vol. X: *Texte und Briefe* (Reinbek, 1999), pp. 84–8

Unseld, Siegfried, ed., *Bertolt Brechts Dreigroschenbuch* (Frankfurt, 1960)

Voigts, Manfred, *Brechts Theaterkonzeptionen: Entstehung und Entfaltung bis 1931* (Munich, 1977)

Wyss, Monika, ed., *Brecht in der Kritik* (Munich, 1977)

Acknowledgements

Any rigorous study of Brecht would be impossible without the fundaments of Brecht scholarship – the collected works, commentaries and in-depth examinations of the histories of specific works and their contexts of production. This book owes a great debt to the Bertolt Brecht Archives in Berlin, the *Berliner und Frankfurter Ausgabe* of Brecht's *Gesammelte Werke*, and the five-volume *Brecht Handbuch* edited by Jan Knopf, as well as meticulous enquiries into Brecht's life, methods and ongoing relevance including Klaus Völker's *Bertolt Brecht* (1976), James Lyon's *Brecht in America* (1980) and Fredric Jameson's *Brecht and Method* (1998).

I would like to express my deepest gratitude to all those who have generously and patiently supported and encouraged my interest in Brecht's work and its influence: Alexander Alberro, Nora Alter, Geoffrey Batchen, Benjamin Buchloh, Ron Clark, Vivian Constantinopoulos, Fabien Danesi, Christa and Michael Glahn, Iris Glahn, Romy Golan, Martha Jay, Branden Joseph, Jordan Kantor, Cary Levine, Stuart Liebman, Nell McClister, Matthias Oehme, Grischka Petri and Doris Lehmann, Silka Quintero, Judith Rodenbeck, Norm Roessler, Katia Schneller, Anett Schubotz, Gregory Sholette, Katy Siegel, Robert Storr, Hélène Trespeuch, Karen Van Meenen, Greg Williams, Richard Wolin, Lisa Young and my colleagues and students at the Tyler School of Art, Temple University, Philadelphia, especially Richard Hricko, Margo Margolis, Mark Shetabi and Robert Stroker. This project was supported by Tyler and Temple through a Dean's Research Grant, a Summer Research Grant and a Sabbatical Award.

Photo Acknowledgements

The author and publishers wish to thank the below sources of illustrative material and/or permission to reproduce it:

Photo courtesy Bertolt Brecht Archiv, Akademie der Künste, Berlin: pp. 11 (Photo: Roger Pic/Sign. FA 09/184 ÜG), 23 (Sign. FA 06/033), 101 (Sign. FA 06/099), 175 (Sign. FA 02/104), 191 (Sign. FA 09/061); © Eulenspiegel Verlag: pp. 159, 161; The Granger Collection, New York: pp. 6 (Zander and Labisch/ullstein bild), 41, 76 (Alice Domker/ullstein bild), 78, 81 (ullstein bild), 89 (ullstein bild), 115 (Kluger & Szogethy/ullstein bild), 117 (Otto Storch/ ullstein bild), 119 (ullstein bild), 124, 127 (ullstein bild), 145, 149, 199 (Heinrich von der Becke/ullstein bild); photo courtesy Kunstsammlung, Akademie der Künste, Berlin: p. 194 (© 2013 Artists Rights Society (ARS), New York/VG Bild-Kunst, Bonn).